# ROUSSEAU'S ECONOMIC PHILOSOPHY

ARCHIVES INTERNATIONALES D'HISTOIRE DES IDÉES

INTERNATIONAL ARCHIVES OF THE HISTORY OF IDEAS

159

# ROUSSEAU'S ECONOMIC PHILOSOPHY

## Beyond the Market of Innocents

by

BERTIL FRIDÉN

# ROUSSEAU'S ECONOMIC PHILOSOPHY

## Beyond the Market of Innocents

*by*

BERTIL FRIDÉN

*Institute of Conservation,*
*Göteborg University, Sweden*

SPRINGER SCIENCE+BUSINESS MEDIA, B.V.

A C.I.P. Catalogue record for this book is available from the Library of Congress.

ISBN 978-94-010-6228-2 ISBN 978-94-011-5294-5 (eBook)
DOI 10.1007/978-94-011-5294-5

*Printed on acid-free paper*

*Votre tein est vermeil comme la fleur de Grenade*
*votre parler un parfum dont je suis inséparable ami.*
*Le monde n'a rien de stable, tout y passe.*
Persian song. DICTIONNAIRE DE LA MUSIQUE

*To Homa*

# Contents

PREFACE . . . . . . . . . . 11

1. INTRODUCTION
*Jean-Jaques Rousseau and Political Economy* . . . . . . . . . . 13

2. READING ROUSSEAU
*From Heart to Heart* . . . . . . . . . . 19

3. THE MARKET AS A BROTHEL
*Information Costs and the Dual Economy of Bread and Lapri* . . . . . . . . . . 33

4. EVERYONE MUST LIVE
*Blueprint for an Autarchic Economy* . . . . . . . . . . 51

5. STARVING FOR CANDY
*The Futility of Mercantilism* . . . . . . . . . . 63

6. THE IRON LAW OF PEASANT MISERY
*The Maladie of the Corn Market* . . . . . . . . . . 81

7. THE SELF COMMON TO THE WHOLE
*Democracy Necessary and Impossible* . . . . . . . . . . 95

8. CHAINS OF DEPENDENCE
*From Abuse to Use* . . . . . . . . . . 105

9. THE JEWS ARE CITIZENS
*The Realism of the Republic of Hearts* . . . . . . . . . . 123

10. NOTHING SOLID FOR THE HEART
*An Economy for the Quality of Life* . . . . . . . . . . 137

BIBLIOGRAPHY . . . . . . . . . . 157

INDEX . . . . . . . . . . 165

# *Preface*

THE PRESENT WORK has been generously supported by grants from the Swedish Council for Research in the Humanities and Social Sciences. The Institute of Economic History, and the Institute of Conservation both at the University of Göteborg have in different ways housed the project. An anonymous reader at Kluwer Academic Publishers provided a very wise, constructive and concerned critique. This and the carefulness of the editors have been stimulating. Jan Bohlin, Eva-Lena Dahl, Örjan Emanuelsson, Lars Herlitz, Urban Herlitz and Martti Rantanen have given important information as well as encouragement. Unfortunately I have not been able to use their advice to the extent I would have liked. Kyra and Michael Landzelius have been of help concerning the format of the essay. Kyra has kindly processed my English. Gus Kaage gave the text its final touch in spite of a lot of nuisances like my unreadable corrections, and having to do the job on the most wonderful summer days in years. The photographer Bert Leandersson responded in a very sensitive way to my vague requests. I feel privileged to be able to include one of his photos. And Nils Fridén helped in several ways with the design of the book.

I wish to express my deep gratitude to them all.

Göteborg in July 1997

*Bertil Fridén*

## I. INTRODUCTION

# *Jean-Jacques Rousseau and Political Economy*

ONE OF THE MOST beautiful spots in our inherited intellectual landscape has long lain peculiarly untrodden. It belongs to that multicoloured garden of concepts, ideas, observations and reflections created by Jean-Jacques Rousseau. It has usually been excluded from our reading routes while other corners have not. His work in drama, fiction, music, politics, social and moral philosophy, linguistics, botanics, education, like his autobiographies and his immense correspondence, keep appearing again and again within our most vital strains of thought, always concerning us, convincing and confusing, causing comfort and contempt. But this ignored spot merits our presence. It could shed new light on some important social dilemmas, discussed with far too little historical depth in modern literature. The spot is Rousseau's economic philosophy, and that interval in the spectrum of economic reflection which deals with values and goods badly handled by the market mechanism.

The spot was not always marginal. In the enlightened salons of Paris during the decades just before the fall of the Ancien Régime, Rousseau's economic philosophy was evidently a hot topic. The editors of the great ENCYCLOPÉDIE selected Rousseau to write the article on "political economy" in tome V. They selected him, not Quesnay, Mirabeau, Turgot, Forbonnais, Condorcet or Diderot himself. All of these great thinkers were well-established writers on economic matters.

But the attention of the reading audiences soon vanished and was directed elsewhere. If they were ever noticed, Rousseau's economic ideas were delegated to some curiosa cabinet of obsolete and eccentric fairy-tales, disclosing little economic insight. Some commentators noticed his reluctance to market exchange. But most of them found his views of little use besides that of serving as exemplary or warning instances of political ideas they preferred or despised. Only a handful of commentators found it worthwhile to try to penetrate his conceptualisations further.

One such commentator is Jean Starobinski. In his famous book: JEAN JACQUES ROUSSEAU: LA TRANSPARENCE ET L'OBSTACLE, Starobinski approaches Rousseau's anti-market views from an extra-economic perspective and exposes them as an "autarchy myth", an "imaginative flight" dictated by Rousseau's *psychological* constitution. This argument may seem to legitimise the conclusion that an analysis of the intrinsic contents of Rousseau's economic philosophy is redundant since it can be explained away.

However, such a conclusion would be deeply unjustified. Starobinski's argument is overwhelmingly elegant and delightful. But it is, nevertheless, misleading; at least if it is to be taken as the exhaustive truth. Indeed, those very formulations (by Rousseau) on which Starobinski bases his argument, reveal a strikingly consistent and well-informed position that per se is worth a serious analysis. Starobinski may be right or wrong on the character of Rousseau's personality and even about its impact on his economic views; but the passages he discusses have intrinsic qualities that justify a profound analysis of the larger issue. It is, in other words, not necessary to explain Rousseau's statements as "imaginative flights". They can be read as expressions of a carefully elaborated economic philosophy which should concern us for several reasons.

Firstly, Rousseau's economic philosophy appears, in certain ways, as an attractive alternative to competing positions by contemporaries such as Adam Smith, David Hume, Ferdinando Galiani, François Quesnay, Sir James Steuart and others; and it relates to those of theorists such as Bernard Mandeville, John Locke and Richard Cantillon. To study and evaluate Rousseau's economic philosophy from a comparative perspective alone would be an interesting task in and of itself.

But an even more useful way to configure the impact of Rousseau's economic theories in this fertile intellectual climate would be to contemplate them according to the way in which their specific *premises* differ from those of other significant analyses. If the premises differ, the space within which the theories are valid also differs. The respective premises ascribe to each theory a specific domain within which it is applicable. The tensions between different analyses can then be rewritten as competing claims concerning how far-reaching the validities of the various domains are, rather than taken as a question only of their mere inherent consistencies. We would then have to clarify not mainly to what extent Smith or Rousseau were right or wrong in their economic-political descriptions, but rather, when their prescriptions could be validly applied and when not. This opens the possibility for several kinds of possible criticisms against an argument. It could be accused of inconsistencies, but also of claiming too extended a validity for a particular doctrine, or of treating esoteric problems of little interest. But the various authors and their texts could also be treated as representatives of *complementary domains*.

Three typical domains could then be suitably represented by Smith, Hume and Rousseau. Smith's doctrine is elaborated within a domain wherein people's "regard to their own interest" generates a socially optimal resource allocation. It includes cases when, metaphorically speaking, it is not "the benevolence of the butcher, the brewer or the baker" that causes the product to be supplied and offered to the customer; it is an "accidental concurrence" of "passions" that directs, like an "invisible hand", everything to a state which is the best for all. Rousseau's strategy, on the other hand, operates within the complementary domain wherein people's regard for their own interest counteracts and even impedes a socially optimal resource allocation.

Hume's writings, in comparison, sometimes concern situations occurring within a third, intermediate domain. Here rational, self-interested agents fail to produce a Smithian result merely because they lack a specific asset: information about the choices of others. Like two men rowing in a boat or two drivers encountering one another on a road, they are in need of coordination (determining the rhythm of rowing or on which side of the road to drive). It is not too difficult for rational agents to meet this need by creating or conceding to a *convention* – formal or informal. When a convention has been established it will easily remain intact because every agent has an interest in its persistence.[1]

It is, of course, no innovation to look at economics in terms of domains. At least since the 1870s,[2] formulations of economic theory have separated different "special sectors"[3] for situations where individual and collective rationality conform and when they do not, but usually all effort has been devoted to the former, Smithian, kind of analysis. Neither is it an innovation to bring in significant old philosophers to get an interesting perspective on specific modern "non-Smithian" theories of collective choice (without reducing them to mere predecessors). But such an approach has not been undertaken very systematically. Arguably, the history of economic doctrine could be penetrated more deeply from a domain perspective.[4] Perhaps the disappearance of Rousseau the economist from the agendas of economic discourse can be explained precisely by the fact that economic theory for so long focused on Smithian rather than on Rousseauan or Humean premises. Conversely, it may now be time: with pollution, waste and other environmental problems as well as the economic dilemmas of health care, education and art, the attention of economic theory is shifting towards more Rousseauan premises.

The second reason for paying attention to Rousseau's economic philosophy is connected with the first. Traditional economic doctrine during Rousseau's time focused on somewhat marginal aspects of human welfare. At best, its declared topic was to show how to maximise the "national wealth". That was often no more than a rhetorical ornamentation of self-interested, rent-seeking activities. But even if taken at its word, this doctrine was reductionist. And it concerned only a marginal part of human wellbeing. These two aspects were pointed out both by Rousseau and by Adam Smith (at about the same time). Smith argued that the doctrine of mercantilism was little more than a disguise for the interests of the merchant classes. Its arguments were formulated by "merchants to

1. There is a unique paretooptimal equilibrium, a situation where no one can become better off, but at the cost of someone else.
2. Walras (1874) 1954, lesson 22:223.
3. Samuelson 1954, p.387ff.
4. Locke, Hobbes, Rousseau, Hume and others have, of course, appeared in recent studies of collective rationality. See for example Cohen 1986, Cohen 1986a, Grofman and Feld 1988, Hampton 1986, R. Hardin 1982, de Jasay 1989, Lewis 1969, Runciman and Sen 1965 and Sugden 1986.

parliaments, and to the councils of princes, to nobles and to country gentlemen; by those who were supposed to understand trade, to those who were conscious to themselves that they knew nothing about the matter." And they in fact never had reason to find out whether it would benefit the country or not. Smith describes the transition to a commercialised economy (of which mercantilist doctrine was part) and claims that it was brought forward by classes (the great proprietors of land and merchants) "who had not the least intention to serve the publick". The merchants acted only "from a view to their own interest and in pursuit of their own pedlar principle of turning a penny wherever a penny was to be got." And the economic possibilities that tempted the landlords were marginal, "childish":

> To gratify the most childish vanity was the sole motive of the great proprietors.[1]

Rousseau, likewise, (prior to Smith, but in similar words) accuses traditional doctrine of ignoring the really important concerns of mature people, of merely caring for "childish" fickleness. In the CONSIDÉRATIONS SUR LE GOUVERNEMENT DE POLOGNE, he writes about a doctrine which he compares to the propensity of children to cry for ever more candy. In contrast, he calls for an economic philosophy relevant to the essential human concerns, concerns that matter for those who had grown up from the innocence of infancy.[2] And he claims to attempt such an economic philosophy, consistent with the moral responsibility one would expect from an adult, basing her preferences on deliberated choices.[3] And from his other texts we can learn that, in his view, such concerns could not easily be expressed and managed within a Smithian domain. In fact, his project in economic philosophy is largely about the consequences of the fact that such needs often demand a different domain:

> If what you wish is merely to make a great splash, to be impressive and formidable, to influence the other peoples of Europe, you have before you their example: get busy and imitate it! ... and then, like Pyrrhus, like the Russians, which is to say like little children – you will be able to say: 'When the world is mine, I am going to eat lots and lots of candy.'[4]

1. From AN INQUIRY INTO THE NATURE AND CAUSES OF THE WEALTH OF NATIONS. Smith (1776) 1976, III:IV:17 and IV:I:10. See also Herlitz 1964, pp. 102f.
2. This was written prior to April 1772, at the latest, although it was not printed until in 1782. It is known that the manuscript was circulated already in the early 1770s. Several versions are preserved. With regard to the relation between Rousseau and Smith, it is known that Smith knew Rousseau's writings. Cf., Raphael and Macfie 1976, p.10.
3. My expression is an attempt to translate the Greek word bouleuontai which is crucial in Aristotle's moral system, NICHOMACHEAN ETHICS. See pp.132-133. Although Rousseau never used the expression its spirit is present throughout his philosophy.
4. OC III p.1003, [Rousseau 1985, p.67]. Here and throughout this essay, italics within a quotation are present in the quoted text unless explicitly stated otherwise. Words within brackets ([ ]) are added by me. When a reference is given to an English edition of Rousseau's works I have used its translation. Otherwise, the translations are my own.

He very clearly, in the CONSIDÉRATIONS, emphasises that it is not for people with such childish vanity that his text is developed. It is for those, only, who, "perchance" wish to constitute "a free nation". Others should stop reading.

What would an economy for adults be like? What qualities would such an economy strive for? It is not obvious that we should expect an answer in Rousseau's writings. Since, as I shall show, Rousseau tried to develop a philosophy for a truly democratic economy, it is logical that he leaves the choices to the citizens, not to be prescribed by philosophy. Nevertheless, for reasons spelled out below, we may get a glimpse of what Rousseau personally would have chosen.

One instance can be found in JULIE OU LA NOUVELLE HÉLOÏSE. Here we encounter a metaphor of the good life. It portrays a growing garden, tended by Julie: her Elysium. The Elysium is an alloy of culture and wilderness, of artefact and natural growth. Julie's richness consists of a diverse endowment of goods, some of which are produced by means of a subsistence economy, others are bought commodities, and still others are wild plants and animals. Not only the animals and plants but also the artefacts are, in a sense, left to live their own lives, also when they are in Julie's hands. Wellbeing is achieved, but not simply by attaining a basket of goods with a maximum amount of utility and pleasure. In order to live a good life, one's basket of goods must be tended and given a continuing vitality. If richness is such, then the key to true happiness is not only the size of the bundle of goods, but one's (here, Julie's) own capability to tend one's endowments and to find pleasure in them. It is also the soil, the context wherein the good is placed and tended. In Rousseau's economic philosophy this endowed capability to deliver a good life should constitute the prime concern for economic activities. *Economizing for the optimal endowed capability of adult women and men to partake and find pleasure in a living natural and social environment is its fundamental concern.*

A third reason to reflect on Rousseau's economic philosophy is that it may facilitate an understanding of Rousseau's general philosophical position. As I shall try to show, certain of his most debated statements – on the projected theatre in Geneva, on women, on music, on the dictatorship of Sparta, etc. – can be enlightened in the context of his economic philosophy. The understanding of welfare as an endowed capability is an expression of the enormous importance Rousseau, in all his philosophy, gives to freedom. It is decisive for the quality of life. And this emphasis on freedom is, in its turn, closely related to that particular quality which, in Rousseau's ideology, distinguishes man from other species: his striving for perfectibility.

Rousseau's economic philosophy contains a unique legacy: the ideas and reflections by one of the keenest observers of "modern" society at the time of its birth. He discusses such urgent matters as how to organize economic life, the nature of welfare, resource allocation and the management of the environment. In this essay I want to focus on this legacy and discuss Rousseau's views primarily as expressions of a philosophy of political economy. This means that the reader cannot expect to encounter a formulation of purely instrumental economic theory in the spirit of neoclassical economic theory. Rousseau himself would have judged it a waste of time to try to formulate theories about reaching an optimal resource allocation or a maximal economic growth without any concern for the fairness, and wisdom of the solution. His conceptualisations contain both theoretical and normative components and claim to demand realistic premises.

* * *

This essay consists of ten chapters. In the second chapter I shall describe my reading approach to Rousseau's writings. The third chapter will discuss Starobinski's interpretation of Rousseau's scepticism versus market exchange. The outlines of an autarchic economy proposed by Rousseau and the reasons for it, are drawn in Chapters 4 and 5. Chapter 6 discusses Rousseau's view on corn trade and the market price. The democratic foundation of the political economy is treated in chapter 7. Then follow two chapters that present Rousseau's emphasis on the social morale and his strategies to reach it. Finally, in Chapter 10, Rousseau's concepts of richness and abundance are penetrated.

In summary, this essay is an attempt to present an unusual conceptualisation of a true welfare economy, a conceptualisation which continues to challenge. It demands an economic philosophy beyond that of innocent children's naïve cries for ever more candy, and an economic strategy relevant to what is really important in life for free and adult women and men. It is about creating and stewarding an endowed capability to give life to and sustain artefacts and natural life: As the crooked stem of the planted and tended tree in Julie's Elysium.

## 2. READING ROUSSEAU

# *From heart to heart*

HOW DOES ONE GO about trying to learn something useful about the modern economic predicament from Rousseau? How can he be made instrumental in one's struggle to understand the options for a sustainable high quality of life? How does one capture the way he configures his domain? How should one approach the relationship between his economic philosophy and other areas of his thought? A crucial task in such a work is to thresh out those core conceptions in this arena that are most fertile for the particular purpose of this essay. For, how one should read and portray the writings of such a complicated and cunning author as Jean-Jacques Rousseau depends, of course, on the specific motives for one's reading.

The purpose of the essay is to chisel out some contours of a consistent view on political economy, if there is one. The resulting conceptual body is to be valuable in a still ongoing intellectual attempt to understand and humanize society. The essay, then, is an interpretative exercise, primarily limited to the philosophy of political economy. For this purpose, neither original philological scholarship nor a systematic treatment of the history or origin of Rousseau's ideas are the most urgent tasks – at least not at this stage of the study. The purpose is not to present a biography of Rousseau, not even one of him as a philosopher of political economy. Further, the main objective is not to try to determine, with great precision, his due place, his importance or lack of importance, in the discourse of descriptive or analytical economics. The essay is simply an attempt to make a consistent interpretation of a possible economic philosophy, an attempt for others to evaluate. This chapter will spell out how I attempt to go about this task.

In my attempt to interpret the texts I shall try to use an attitude of which Rousseau himself approved. The attitude is revealed by his reply to an enthusiastic reader who had written to him about the DISCOURS SUR L'ÉCONOMIE POLITIQUE (the Encyclopédie article). In his response, Rousseau noted that: "my heart dictated it and yours read it".[1] This attitude was far from unique. Contemporaries talked about writing in "sympathetic ink",[2] needing the receiver's friendly heart to appear. To spell out how this ink is to be made visible in my errand, comprises the task of this chapter. *Simulating* the presence of old concepts and ideas in modern contexts, ***using a rich text material*** and ***a positional reading*** are the three main pillars in my strategy.

## *A Simulated Presence*

Firstly, most texts are parts of more or less "sympractical" discourses. They refer to nonverbal or implicitly assumed components in their environment, and are created by subjects undergoing constant change. Their signs are developed and modified within a continuous communicative exchange. Any serious attempt at interpretation should acknowledge this complexity of the verbal message, as well as its polysemic character. Real or apparent logical inconsistencies or lacunae in the texts, as well as the diffuseness and manifoldness of expressions, must be acknowledged and treated in one way or another. The reader is thereby forced to choose between different reading options. Such choices involve complexities which cannot be handled in a penetrating way here. Roughly speaking, two fundamental and contrary attitudes in handling fissures or vagueness in a text are the "principle of charity" and the "hermeneutics of suspicion".[3] The reader is, according to the former, to choose the interpretation option best suited for reconstructing an internally consistent position. According to the second attitude, she should rather try to deconstruct the text by highlighting its fissures, lacunae and inconsistencies.

My choice is to try the former option as a start. At best, the resulting outline could indicate an initial path to the neglected spot in Rousseau's garden. Rousseau's position on economic issues is so unknown and poorly represented in the literature that it seems necessary to try to make the reader aware of the possibility that a consistent, well-informed and urgent message on economics exists in his writings. The deconstruction of his thought is perhaps also a relevant task, but it is nevertheless postponed and not attempted here.

One consequence of my choice of strategy is, therefore, that I put limited effort into tracing developments or changes in Rousseau's thinking, although I am aware that such changes are reflected in the texts. Here, his texts are, in that sense, rather looked at as one single entity, one text. In other words, an attempt will be made in this essay to read Rousseau's reconstructed "text" with an "unpolemical", "friendly" attitude, as the Danish philosopher Lars-Henrik Schmidt expresses it. In order to integrate the "text" a specific perspective is employed: putting Rousseau's words into a modern context. The work done by the reader when reading a text in a "friendly way", consists (again in Schmidt's words) of

1 CG tom II, p. 273, commented by Derathé in OC III p. LXXII. "Vous êtes contents de l'article Economie je le crois bien, mon cœur l'a dicté et le vôtre l'a lu."
2. Cf., Marshall 1988.
3. Gilje and Grimen 1992.

establishing a "simulated presence", lifting out old formulations of fundamental problems from one context into a new and different one:

> ...*the simulated presence is the work of the treatise or the reading. Our contribution* [as readers] is the work of reading as an art of simulation . . .

Schmidt characterizes his treatment of Rousseau and Nietzsche in the following way:

> We replace the question about what and how they [Rousseau and Nietzsche] thought, by another: what and how we can think by their help; what of relevance we can have them express...[1]

By such work, and perhaps by such work only, is it possible to make the text "live up to a new time playing through the old problems." As in all knowledge formation, it matters both that the input is in some sense true, and that the message is in some sense found significant by the receiver. Otherwise the meaningfulness is endangered by the Scilla of the psychotic who diffuses reality and fantasy and the Charybdis of the game addict who keeps playing an entertaining glass bead game without caring whatever happens around her– even when, as in Rousseau's example, someone is about to be murdered beneath her window. In order to preclude a potential misunderstanding I do firmly claim that my reading is compatible with what Rousseau really intended. The reader of the following essay should not expect to be cheated by an, at best, interesting piece of pure fantasy, describing something that is not really there. Rather, an attempt is made to enlighten something which certainly exists, admittedly from an angle of my own choice. The method attempted will be somewhat like studying rock engravings with a torch, pointing the light-beam at awkward angles towards the cliffs hoping to discover new rock carvings or see hitherto unseen connections in their composition. It is for this purpose irrelevant whether or not such a light was ever used by the carvers themselves.

## *A Rich Body of Text*

Secondly, it seems natural that the information on which the friendly interpretation is to be based is as rich as possible. Most judgments about Rousseau's economics have, so far, been based on the three loci (except for singular passages) most often referred to by those few who have commented upon his economic philosophy or "public finance"[2]: the DISCOURS SUR L'ÉCONOMIE POLITIQUE, originally written for the Encyclopédie, the PROJET DE

1. Schmidt 1987, p.18: "Vi skal gennem to afhandlinger vise, hvorledes disse aktuelle problemer ikke er fraværende – hvilket ikke er helt det samme som at sige, at de er nærværende. Det er rettere en verden til forskel mellem et naervær og et fraværende fravær, *og det simulerede nærvær er afhandlingens eller læsningens arbejde.* Vores indsats er læsearbejdet som en simulationskonst, der forhåbentlig formår at få teksterne til at leve op til en ny tids gennemspilning af de gamle problemer..."
"Vi erstatter spørgsmålet om hvad og hvordan de tænkte med et andet, nemlig hvad og hvordan vi kan tænke ved hjælp af dem; hvad kan vi få dem til at udtrykke af relevans?"
2. Villers 1964, p. 335.

CONSTITUTION POUR LA CORSE, and CONSIDÉRATIONS SUR LE GOUVERNMENT DE POLOGNE. Rousseau also treated economic questions in several other works, however. This is evident from a look at Michel Launay's systematic inventory of Rousseau's political vocabulary.[1] My interpretative attempt must use as much as possible of all relevant information. It means among other things that I shall have to treat literary pieces such as EMILE and JULIE OU LA NOUVELLE HÉLOÏSE.

Another important source that must be included in the "rich" text is Rousseau's own life. To an unusually high degree Rousseau's own life is interwoven with his writings.[2] In order to read the "text" with as much of its full richness as possible the reader has to take account of Rousseau's biography. As Starobinski emphasized, Rousseau: "conforms his life to the demands of his theoretical thought" (although one may wonder about some of his actions; for instance, his sending of the children to an orphanage). But the dependence of life on thought is reciprocal:

> inversely he adapts his system to the demands of his 'sensibility', that is, so to speak, to his needs of affective satisfaction.[3]

Although one may contest Starobinski's understanding of how this dependence should be conceived (which I do in the next chapter), the existence of an unusually strong interdependence stands without question. It is obvious that Rousseau used his own life as a source for his writings. This is most clearly indicated in his autobiographic writings, but also elsewhere. For the reader not familiar with Rousseau's biography I have outlined below a few basics of his life-"text".

Jean-Jacques was born in 1712 and became motherless at one week of age. He lived first with his father for a time, and later, as an adolescent, with Madame Warens at Annecy and Chambéry. During this period he traveled extensively. He became the tutor of the children of Jean de Mably[4] at Lyon, and settled in Paris during the period 1742-1756. In Paris, he worked with his friend and patroness, Madame Dupin, on a treatise on women, composed an opera and other pieces of music, published an essay on a new sign system for music, authored articles on music for the Encyclopédie, wrote the two discourses, etc. On April 20, 1751 he wrote a letter to Madame Dupin, telling her that he had gone through a radical reform of his private life - which he later found decisive: he decided to disrupt his adaptation to high society, his "undignified" appearances in the fashionable salons of Paris.[5]

Rousseau moved to the Hermitage, in Madame d'Epinay's park at Montmorency in April 1756. During the following seven years he mostly stayed at the Hermitage or (when finally thrown out the door by Mme. d'Epinay)

1. Launay 1977. The inventory includes his main works but not the immense correspondence. Economic matters are treated in more or less detail in at least 17 different works including the three mentioned in the text.
2. As is the case with other authors. See, e.g., Lagercrantz 1979 on August Strindberg.
3. Starobinski 1971, p. 55.
4. Jean de Mably was the brother of the more well-known writer and social critic, Gabriel Bonnot de Mably. Cf., Drivier 1930, p. 228.
5. Cf., Launay 1989.

elsewhere in Montmorency. During that time he wrote some of his most well-known works: JULIE OU LA NOUVELLE HÉLOÏSE, EMILE, DU CONTRAT SOCIAL, and LETTRE À D'ALEMBERT SUR LES SPECTACLES.

For the following six years, Rousseau lived an ambulant life with many hardships. He visited David Hume in England but parted from him after a total break. Further, he was involved in a bitter conflict with Madame d'Epinay, who at this time attempted to get the police to prevent his public readings of the CONFESSIONS.

In 1770, he moved to Paris and in 1772-78 he wrote some self-reflective and apologetic texts, such as RÊVERIES DU PROMENEUR SOLITAIRE (1776-7). In 1772, he worked on the CONSIDÉRATIONS SUR LE GOUVERNEMENT DE POLOGNE at the request of some of the modernists in Poland. He died on June 2, 1778 at Ermenonville, 50 km. from Paris.

## *A Positional Reading*

Thirdly, the interpretation should handle some obviously conflicting positions which seem difficult to reconcile with Rousseau's basic philosophy. For example, Rousseau is himself an accomplished writer of opera but condemns the building of a theatre in Geneva. Uncompromisingly, like none before him, he demands the emancipation of the unfree, but praises Lycurgos the dictator in classical Sparta. Describing women as superior to men, he suggests that they should be excluded from public politics. Regarding private property as one of the symptoms of degeneration in the state of society, he claims that private property is the most important human right. The list could be much longer. Here I shall try to display my approach by means of another example: his relation to the nobility. In the unpublished treatise on the government of feudal Poland (with its still-existent serfdom), he gives us a lot of puzzling passages. The discussion of this example must be somewhat lengthy.

The example can be found in the CONSIDÉRATIONS SUR LE GOUVERNEMENT DE POLOGNE. In an extensive study, from 1934, JEAN-JACQUES ROUSSEAU, MORALIST, Charles Hendel[1] finds this text a logically consistent application of ideas which Rousseau had earlier developed in the CONTRAT SOCIAL. The text is, according to Hendel, concerned with the freedom of the Polish people, and thereby, like the CONTRAT SOCIAL, with "the cause of liberty".[2]

It is, of course, not surprising that this interpretation was challenged. In an essay appearing in 1966, Willmoore Kendall confronts Hendel's view with several features of the text. If Hendel were right, how would we explain the absence of any demand for the surrender of noble privileges and the abolition of serfdom? Why the presence of uncritical references to natural law? And what about the silence concerning the lack of religious freedom – in a multi-religious country with a dark record on religious persecution? Kendall asks these questions and argues that all this is brutally contradictory to the spirit of the CONTRAT SOCIAL. And, he adds, what is also remarkable is that Rousseau does not with one word mention the basic requirement of any government – according to the CONTRAT

1. Hendel 1962. The book was initially published in 1934.
2. Kendall 1985 p. XII

SOCIAL, and, as I shall show, the DISCOURS SUR L'ÉCONOMIE POLITIQUE – that government be democratic; that is, performed according to the general will, "from whose formation no individual is flatly excluded".

> Thus the first thing we should expect him to say to Poland, which concentrates all political power in the hands of an aristocracy and keeps most of its population in perpetual serfdom, is that it is illegitimate, a tyranny. But THE GOVERNMENT OF POLAND does not, even by the remotest implication strike any such note.[1]

This is all the more remarkable since Rousseau in the same CONSIDERATIONS argues for the limited size of nations, for just this reason: that it increases the possibility of democracy. Kendall's objection also carries implications for Rousseau's other texts: the reader has to confront what appears as inconsistencies between the texts. Likewise, the present essay, which is to be an exercise in a "friendly reading", cannot leave them untouched, as unbridged lacunae. The relevant "inconsistencies" must be interpreted.

Kendall suggests, as one possibility, that Rousseau simply changed his mind when getting older and took a more conservative position. In a sense this mode of reading, like Hendel's, is *rhetorically naïve*. It does not account for the possibility that the writer's strategy of writing was dependent on the expected audience or the particular context of the text. Kendall presents, however, several alternative interpretations which offer a number of alternative rhetorical readings,[2] without expressing any clear preference of his own.

Kendall's second suggestion focuses precisely on the idea that Rousseau's text reflected that he badly wanted to get certain crucial messages across to his readers. Rousseau found it necessary to sacrifice principles and messages of secondary importance, the communication of which might seem futile, in order not to impede the communication of the crucial main point. For that reason he sometimes pretended a conservative position (which was never his) on some, for the moment, secondary issues, in order not to alienate the reader. Sometimes he found that certain messages would be ridiculed by contemporary readers (like Voltaire); for that reason he tried to express them in a kind of hidden language intended for future readers. As Rousseau was convinced that the messages were essentially correct, he hoped that future, more open-minded generations would understand them more readily. Such an intention would have been a peculiar expression of the "encre sympathique".

The third choice in Kendall's menu is a variant of Hendel's suggestion. It is inspired by Leo Strauss' notion that the text is to be regarded as a general and practical application of some very abstract and unrealistic principles in the CONTRAT SOCIAL. In this case, the reason why the two texts seem inconsistent is that the concrete preconditions faced in the Polish case are different compared to the sterile ones in the earlier text. Some texts, like the CONTRAT SOCIAL, can, according to this view, be understood as abstractions. We could perhaps think of

1. Ibid., and ibid. p. XIV.
2. The expression is mine.

them as something like, for example, economic theorems. Never intended to be realistic, they are sterile, distilled principles, necessarily compromised in real life, while other texts are attempts to apply the general principles to a realistic setting which necessitates accommodation and compromise.

A full discussion of each of these selected kinds of readings is hardly possible in the present context. I shall merely suggest a way of reading which is slightly different from the previous interpretations. But first I shall discuss Rousseau's relation to the nobility in more general terms.

## *An "ideologie nobiliaire"?*

If there is a class bias in Rousseau's political philosophy one would perhaps not expect the great apostle of freedom to support the case of the seigneurs. It would be more natural for him to be in favour of the artisan classes to which his father belonged and with which he was so familiar during his youth in Geneva. He often referred to a kind of fictional and idealized Geneva as his New Jerusalem or "antique city" (which are two key concepts presenting some of his ideals of society).[1] These references indicate that, by applying a "meta-ideology", he carried the interests of the lesser or middle bourgeoisie. This meta-ideology was not directly readable in his writing but rather a kind of undercurrent reflected in many and divergent political judgments. It would be possible to argue that his writings express the interests of the petty artisans and farmers versus the competing interests of a progressing merchant class and those of the seigneurs. For that reason he opposed a commercialization of the economy, since commercialization would strengthen the position of the merchant classes and thereby the privileges of the seigneurs, causing the general productivity to decline and the economy to become perverted. This process would progress at the cost of the humbler classes. Such an interpretation was argued by Eva-Lena Dahl.[2]

In 1989, however, a provocative study by Renato Galliani appeared which also used a "socio-historical" class perspective on Rousseau's ideas, but with a very different result. Galliani argued forcefully that Rousseau's texts could be associated with doctrines in favour of the nobility rather than the humbler classes. These doctrines made up an "ideologie nobiliaire". Rousseau's references to ideals such as the "antique city", and his discussions on agriculture, money, luxury, sumptuary laws, commerce, equality, feasts, frugality, and property conformed beautifully with such a prevalent conventional "ideologie nobiliaire".

In this context the praise of "the antique city" became a means in the aristocratic propaganda against the threatening bourgeoisie. It glorified the golden age before modern ideas challenged the feudal state of society.[3] And Rousseau's description of the civilisation process as a degradation from a wonderful golden age (the state of nature) was also fully in line with this propaganda. It fitted this ideology perfectly well to picture, as Rousseau did, urbanization, the city life, the ever-more competitive moneyed non-aristocratic land-owners, the

1. Ellis 1977.
2. Dahl 1977 p. 223
3. Madeleine Ellis presented a very different interpretation (Ellis 1987) wherein "the antique city" was seen as a utopian device for organizing the chaotic mental universe of the perceptive reader.

growing international economic dependence and other features of modern society, as steps in a process of decay. It was precisely these developments that penetrated and undermined the feudal power structure. And Rousseau's condemnation of luxury was consistent with the traditional sumptuary laws supporting an old feudal principle claiming that no one should consume more than was proper according to one's social status. Thus it is far too simple to regard Rousseau as a revolutionising carrier of the interests of the "humbler classes".[1] Those many modern interpreters of Rousseau who regard his writing as utopian and democratically idealistic are badly mistaken, declared Galliani.

Galliani claims that his interpretation dissolves several of the most disturbing paradoxes in Rousseau's writings. Being part of an "ideologie nobiliaire" the texts were not always literally intended. The talk by various participants in the contemporaneous debates about the use of arts and science, was usually not intended to imply that *everybody* was entitled to them. In a similar way, Rousseau's words (on freedom, democracy, equality, etc.) were likewise not always literally intended. The fact that Rousseau, a declared liberal, in some contexts advocated aristocratic totalitarian government can be explained by the fact that he regarded liberty with aristocratic eyes. Words such as virtue, liberty and enlightenment were never really intended to concern the people.[2] They were rather symbolic figures of persuasive rhetorics, an ornamental part of a broad propaganda-like semantic style. This ideology was not in every sense reactionary, but it was something other than what 19th century radicals believed it to be. They used Rousseau's essentially conservative message to legitimise radical political ideology. Such concepts as "equality", "liberty" and "community" had in their philosophy absorbed entirely different connotations than in the "ideologie nobiliaire".

Suppose that Galliani is right in his assertion that Rousseau uses concepts and rhetorical figures typical for an "ideologie nobiliaire". Does that make them uninteresting in the present perspective? More generally, does the fact that an author expresses his position in words closely connected with the interests of a social class or even uses some rhetorics of a certain class-based social ideology, really disqualify his texts from possessing properties that may be interesting in themselves, regardless of their class basis? I suggest that the answer is no.

And indeed: Galliani definitely does not succeed in showing that Rousseau was a supporter of an "ideologie nobiliaire". He may be right that many concepts and figures of thought which Rousseau used were suitable for, and even used by others as, an apology for the case of certain aristocratic groups in contemporary France. But to verify that these elements really add up to a distinctive "ideologie nobiliaire" which Rousseau shared is a logically far more demanding procedure. Here Galliani's argument is less convincing. It is evident that some of the alarm about and objections to monetary economy, urban life, inequality and individualism partly had other connotations and associations for the reader in the 18th century than they do for readers today. Some of these concepts may well have been agreeable to certain groups within the nobility (some of whom

1. Galliani 1989, p. 358ff.
2. Ibid., p.372f.

obviously appreciated Rousseau's work for one reason or another). They may even have been exploited to legitimate the "ancien regime".

But how do we, by such a semantic "guilt by association" argument as Galliani's, know that it wasn't also the other way around, compared to what he claims: That Rousseau, by using well-known ideas and concepts, wanted to catch the attention of the reader? That he not only wanted to pass the public censor, but moreover tried to touch the reader? Perhaps he had tried a perspective-changing technique such as that used by William Shakespeare and more recently Ettore Scola, for example in his film LE VOYAGE DU CAPITAINE FRACUNE FRACASSE of 1990. Scola makes the audience believe that it is viewing a real-life story about an ambulatory theatre in 17th century France until at the end of the film the camera perspective widens and it becomes apparent that everything has been a theatrical performance in contemporary Paris, a play within a play. Likewise, in many of Shakespeare's plays the players sometimes shift roles by participating in the performance of a play within the play. In a similar manner, Rousseau may have used a conventional rhetorical technique to introduce his audience to a certain problem in order to lift the curtain for further discussions. This is in fact the case in the counterfactual argument in the second DISCOURSE.[1] He may have wanted to show the consequences of the, perhaps merely ornamentally intended, concepts that were used within an *"ideologie nobiliaire"*.

Galliani, of course, never confronts this possibility. Neither does he take into consideration the *fact* that when Rousseau really could choose, when he wrote from a position where we know that it was meaningful for him to choose freely – like in the PROJET DE CONSTITUTION POUR LA CORSE – he clearly rejected even modest aristocratic claims. In the case of Corsica, it was suggested to him in a very honourable way[2] that he should support an aristophilic constitution; yet he not only rejected the proposal, but also spent considerable space justifying his resistance to noble privileges.

So why, to return to the problem of the CONSIDÉRATIONS, did he not do the same in the case of Poland? We now have a number of interpretations: (1) that the text is logically consistent with Rousseau's general philosophy "in the cause of liberty"; (2) that he changed his mind and became conservative when older; (3) that he pretended certain views in order to be more attractive to readers; (4) that the text is an accommodated application of general principles, like applied economics; and, (5) that it is part of a consistent philosophy within an "idéologie nobiliaire". My objection to all of these interpretations is that they fail to take due account of the *position* of the author.

The CONSIDÉRATIONS were written at the request of groups within the Polish nobility and were unlikely to be read by anyone in Poland outside of this privileged group.[3] In fact, Rousseau never published any of the several manuscripts that were available, and was very upset when it became known to him that they were being circulated in public. Given that few people outside the nobility were even literate, by denouncing the seigneurial privileges he would have

1. See below p. 108f
2. This is in itself an example of the fact that his ideas were also feasible in some noble circles.
3. See below p. 70.

condemned and alienated the very basis of probably his entire readership in Poland. This he might have found somewhat pointless. In this sense, the situation was very different from the case of Corsica where his prospective recipients constituted a much larger segment of the people. Moreover, it is quite reasonable that he, on the contrary, found it meaningful to advise the Polish enlightened nobility on the issue of Poland's survival as a nation. In Rousseau's eyes this may have been important for the welfare (and freedom) of the people in the long run. The rhetorically-conscious Rousseau had, at this time, 40 years of first-hand experience of aristocratic ideology. That he was extremely aware of the futility of disputing claims, close to the heart of the seigneurial class, is abundantly clear from his LA NOUVELLE HÉLOÏSE, where in numerous pages and in great detail he describes how Julie's father is prepared to devastate the life of his wife, his daughter Julie, and her lover Saint Preux, only in order to get Julie married to a man of acceptable, noble blood.

From a critical perspective there is a fundamental assumption underlying all five interpretations that seems somewhat naïve. Some recognize that Rousseau probably accommodated his rhetoric to the rhetorical context, i.e., to the prospective reader. But still they all seem to assume that his passages can be understood as partial manifestations (perhaps with different rhetorical techniques) of an attempted *complete and plain* ideology. They seem to assume in a sense that all statements at least can be deduced from premises at one and the same level of basicness[1] – making up a complete social theory. And other authors do the same. When Fetscher, on the basis of the PROJET DE CONSTITUTION POUR LA CORSE, claims that there is a general étatist propensity in Rousseau's economic statements,[2] his argument is based on a similar assumption.[3] But is such an assumption really reasonable or necessary?

I am not here raising the much debated issue in post-structuralism of a metaphysics of presence as related to the credibility of assuming a centred, coherent authorizing subject behind the text, but rather that of a possible main orientation of the intellectual and political itineraries of the projects Rousseau in fact attempted. Did he ever claim to have a full social theory on class relations? Should we not, instead, regard his theories and proposals as something rather like the engaged and enlightened spectator's advice and instructions to the player in a certain position on a sporting team, for example the forward in a soccer team? To the spectator, the strategy and tactics applied by the team are given, and beyond his influence. His position is different from the "modernist" coach who, with his commands, training, recruitment and formation of the team, possesses (or at least believes he does) fuller control of the strategy and tactics of the game. Might not Rousseau, asked by a handful of noblemen, in view of their positions and with a rhetorical apparatus ruthlessly applied to that purpose, have straight-

1. See below p. 30.
2. Fetscher 1960, p. 236 ff.
3. Another case of such a homogenic reading is Fetcher's interpretation that the artisan in EMILE and the peasant in the PROJET for Corsica represent different stages in a process of history. Fetscher does not discuss the possibility that they represent different perspectives, such as that of the private economy of a young man in a given political economy, versus the political economy of society at large. Fetscher 1960, p. 223f.

forwardly attempted a realistic strategy to get them to the best move he found possible? This would not exclude the possibility that Rousseau had a fully *consistent* moral philosophy – complete or not.

We may look, I suggest, for a bystander's perspective, look for a *positional rhetoric* where the perspective is conditioned by *the choice situation* to be faced. Rousseau himself, in a way, testifies that we should understand him in that manner. The CONSIDÉRATIONS were addressed to a highly selective audience and during a critical international situation for the country. Poland was extremely dependent on this specific audience, its seigneurial élite. In introducing the CONSIDÉRATIONS Rousseau pronounced some highly restrictive preconditions for the text. He saw his task as a most limited one concerning the inner government:

> I shall describe below a system of administration that, *leaving the deeper levels of your laws virtually untouched,* seems to me what you need in order to raise the patriotism of the Poles.[1]

Could it not be that his CONSIDÉRATIONS were intended to be precisely what Rousseau said they were to be, and nothing more: a reply to the Polish nobility about what he thought it feasible and wise to try to persuade them to do at that very precarious or fatal moment without altering Poland's basic constitution? Nowhere does he in any sense concede that the CONSIDÉRATIONS were to express a general blueprint for a society of his own liking. Such had been his intentions in the DISCOURS SUR L'ÉCONOMIE POLITIQUE, when he restricted the topic for the article to the "*popular* political economy".[2] But nothing at all of that sort appears here. For one reason or another, his proposals are far from unconditional.

Rousseau sometimes even chooses to analyse society from the perspective of a single person. EMILE is an example of Rousseau's use of such a radically different perspective. Society is portrayed from the perspective of an individual: what society and the economy are like for a boy who tries to figure out how to live an authentically human life and who can vote with his feet, possessing the option to exit by vagabondage but certainly not change it all by himself.

That Rousseau is very well aware of the fact that the position of the writer matters is obvious from a formulation in JULIE OU LA NOUVELLE HÉLOÏSE. In a letter to his Julie, Saint-Preux, her lover, writes from his involuntary stay in Paris about "studying the world" in words that may well reflect Rousseau's views on his own work. Here it seems that Saint-Preux (Rousseau) recognizes that it is impossible – or at least infinitely difficult – to get a full and objective picture of social reality. The viewer has to choose his perspective:

> ...I begin to see the difficulties in studying the world, and I don't even know from which perspective one should choose to get to know it. The philosopher is too far from it, the man of the world too close. The one sees too much to be able to reflect

1. OC III, p. 961, italics added.
2. On that concept, see p. 96ff. below.

> about what he sees, the other too little to be able to evaluate the total picture. All that strikes the philosopher is what he watches by himself and he cannot discern the relations to other phenomena lying outside of his perspective. He never watches a thing in its context and neither understands its origin nor the effects of it. The man of the world watches it all but has no time to think about anything. The changeability of the things only allows him to catch a glimpse of them, not to observe them. They extinguish one another quickly and for him only vague impressions similar to chaos remain.[1]

The positional character of the judgment implies that both the informational contents of the judgment and the value contents are relative to the position from which they are uttered. Sometimes they are based on a thorough analysis; while in other cases, a mere glimpse is the sole informational basis for the judgment.

### *Basic and non-basic judgments*

In looking for a consistent position of Rousseau's, one would be wise to factor out what is *basic* and what is instrumental and conditional in his work. Certain judgments can surely be shown to be instrumental to more basic values. In this regard, I shall use the concepts "basic" and "non-basic" judgments in the sense of the following useful formulation by Amartya Sen:

> A value judgment can be called 'basic' to a person if no conceivable revision of factual assumptions can make him revise the judgment…[2]

It seems that in order to read Rousseau's economic philosophy positionally one should also try to determine the "basic-ness" or "nonbasic-ness" of different judgments. Such a strategy of reading is far from trivial within contemporary economic discourse. Modern welfare economics, of course, generally regards the agent's value system as none of its business (as long as it is full, consistent, etc.). Rather, the theory treats all preferences and values held by a person as of exactly equal importance, and as given. The exogenously given value constraint – the preferences the agents reveal by their choices on the market – is painted flatly, with no shades or depth.

But it seems inevitable that most people have a value structure wherein some judgments are more basic than others. The economic consequences of that (for example, on the structure of demand) has been explored in an interesting way by Gary Becker.[3] And truly, it is hard even to imagine what the alternative would be like. The assertion that there is a depth dimension to most people's (at least) value system does not by any means imply that these systems are, in any sense, complete. Be that as it may; I intend to try to factor out at least some basic judgments in Rousseau's economic philosophy, without any intention to picture the entire system (if there is one).

1. OC II, pp. 245f.
2. Sen 1967, p. 50.
3. Becker finds that people demand "commodities" which in their turn can be acquired by market exchange as "goods" or as production within the household or through a combination. The commodity demanded is, then, more basic than the good. Becker 1981.

* * *

Rousseau lived and traveled all over Europe (from old-fashioned subsistence peasantry districts to modern rural industry and commercial centres) and could see, hear, smell and even taste the dawn of the industrial revolution. His richness of experience and perception makes him worth attending to, even today, in spite of his ignorance of our predicament and ways of thinking.

In this essay, I shall try a friendly (i.e., simulating, rich and positional) reading of his work. In so doing, I shall attempt to establish some basic judgments and the informational-normative character of some non-basic ones. I shall conclude the essay by discussing what I take to be some basic value judgments concerning richness and economy.

## 3. THE MARKET AS A BROTHEL

# *Information Costs and the Dual Economy of Bread and Lapri*

ROUSSEAU OFTEN rejects market exchange. He again and again expresses his preference for autarchic modes of provision and the immediacy between production and consumption. Similarly, when writing autobiographically he testifies to a desire to live independently and transparently. Jean Starobinski has argued forcefully that the former, Rousseau's rejection of market exchange, is generated by the latter. His personal emotional disposition has been redressed to a general ideological aversion against market exchange. Others have taken this as evidence that his rejection is not based on rational argument. They have treated it as a basic judgment (that is to say, as an emotionally-founded one). A closer look shows, however, that a consistent and careful economic analysis is hidden underneath the various formulations and that the market rejection is a nonbasic part of his philosophy.

### *The Autarchy Myth*

Starobinski's interpretation can be found in the famous work: JEAN-JACQUES ROUSSEAU: LA TRANSPARENCE ET L'OBSTACLE, from 1971. It claims that Rousseau transforms his own personal fear of nontransparent relations into a myth of "collective autarchy". Rousseau projects his personal emotional constitution onto society at large and applies his individual behavioural choices to economic policy.[1] Being enchanted by the attractive stoic vision of being a self-sufficient solitary, he makes himself believe the autarchic subsistence economy to be a realistic option for a community, in this way creating an autarchy myth. In Starobinski's own words:

> In an imaginative flight he [Rousseau] transposes the ideal of the self-sufficient ego into a myth of the self-sufficient community.

1. Jean Fabre, likewise, in his annotations to the Pleiade edition of the CONSIDÉRATIONS argues that Rousseau's contempt for money was based mainly on emotional reasons. Fabre OC III, p. 1785.

The sage's solitary self-sufficiency is proliferated into "a consoling dream of 'collective autarchy'".[1]

In these, Rousseau's visionary paintings of an ideal economy, Starobinski finds a universe of idyllic or mythical social constructions where there is "neither the alienation of unsatisfied desire nor that of superfluous wealth" and where,

> the moral ideal of autarchy, transposed to the economic plane, took the form of a hermetic society capable of providing for its own material needs.[2]

In this ideal society, no accumulation of capital or money takes place and the possessions of the citizens are "frugal". There is, however, an accumulation of "abundance" and "joy":

> but the accumulation rests proportionate to the needs of a community whose only economic goal is to suffice to itself. One does not work in order to get rich, but only to make oneself *independent*.[3]

All work has as its purpose to fulfill "natural needs", it is performed for its use value. And, as it does not have a commodity character, alienation is absent. Consumption and production are dictated by genuine needs rather than by anyone's drive to be well considered. Rousseau paints an idyllic state which is to end the "tyranny of opinion and root out the evils of civilization without eliminating its advantages,"[4] writes Starobinski. Autarchy, in Starobinski's reading, protects the independence of the individual, and maximises the transparency of her life, making her free to choose how to use it and her endowments. In summary:

> economic success consists in meeting all local needs without producing a surplus that might necessitate recourse to sale and exchange, those twin clouds hovering on the horizons of transparency.[5]

In the Rousseauan utopic economy, money is redundant because people "consume *immediately* what they produce".[6] By these formulations Starobinski ties Rousseau's economic philosophy and the "autarchy myth" to the transparency theme in Rousseau's writing. He makes the preference for economic autarchy a necessary moral choice (in order to secure the clear horizon of transparency and immediacy in consumption) at a rather basic level in Rousseau's thought. Starobinski, in this way, reads these passages as if Rousseau preferred autarchy because of its own intrinsic properties (like the beauty of the clear sky).

1. Starobinski 1971, p. 135, [1988, p. 109].
2. Starobinski 1971, p. 131, [1988, p. 105.
3. Starobinski 1971, p. 130.
4. Starobinski 1971 p. 133, [1988, p. 107].
5. Starobinski 1971, p. 134, [1988, p. 108], italics added.
6. Starobinski 1971, p. 131.

Rousseau wrote self-reflective texts throughout his life. Naturally he had reason then, to reflect about his behaviour in relation to the market. And he found himself appalled by it. Several times he expressed that his personality caused him to avoid market transactions. Here, for example, in the CONFESSIONS:

> None of my predominant tastes involves things that can be bought. I require none but good pleasures, and money poisons everything...[1]

So far it is a personal thing, a question of his individual taste. But Starobinski shows that there is a well-articulated defense of transparency in Rousseau's writings, a kind of personal ideology. Rousseau's preference for non-mediatedness or im-mediacy (in all senses of the word) in subsistence production could be seen in that context. Already in the first DISCOURSE, Rousseau expresses how sweet it would be to live where the exterior appearance of people corresponded to the true state of their hearts.[2] It is the fact that people put up delusory surfaces towards others that causes the vicissitudes of the state of society in Rousseau's thinking, claims Starobinski. It is not its collective nature *per se*. The problem arises because transparency is impeded.[3] The evils of the world begin with the shaft that separates the heart and the appearance.[4] A veil is then raised between people, a veil that impedes confidence.[5] Instead of simply being, people appear; and by appearing they loose the innocent immediacy of mere being and become vicious.[6] The discrepancy is further strengthened by culture and science as "flower garlands hanging on and concealing the iron chains to which humans are fettered."[7] The traditional praise of immediacy of the classical poets (e.g., Hafez) reappears here with Starobinski's Rousseau. It is brought forward every time he moarns the loss of transparency. People have become cunning calculators, unable to become friends, perhaps because the delusory veils between them prevent efficient communication.[8]

> The souls are not visible, friendship is not possible, confidence can never last, no certain sign permits us to get to know the disposition of the hearts.

The economy in this situation is steered, not to the true needs of people, but to false desires in the service of one's wish to be well-considered.[9] To counter these problems, a good society requires a policy for the return to transparency.[10] And

1. Starobinski 1971, p. 132, [1988, p. 106]. OC I pp. 36f. "Ajoutez qu'aucun de mes gouts dominans ne consiste en choses qui s'achettent. Il ne me faut que des plaisirs purs, et l'argent les empoisonne tous."
2. OC III, p. 7.
3. Starobinski 1971, p. 62.
4. Ibid., p. 13.
5. Ibid., p. 19
6. Ibid., p. 19
7. OC III, p. 7.
8. Starobinski 1971, p. 15.
9. Ibid., p. 43.
10. Ibid., p. 25.

that is precisely what Starobinski's Rousseau attempts. In his writings, a direct and close relation is established between economic and moral matters. "Rousseau connects profoundly the moral problem and the economic problem."[1] And again:

> Rousseau has constantly aligned the problem of conscience to the economic problems: according to him it is only possible to possess an independence of conscience if it is supported and secured by an economic independence. It is a moral demand, most certainly with a stoic origin, that wants that the I searches her satisfaction uniquely in herself and in goods that are her *own,* with no external assistance.[2]

To Starobinski there is, in Rousseau's 'text', a rather basic moral principle demanding market avoidance. The market should be avoided because it impedes transparency.

Starobinski also emphasizes another disadvantage of market provision which is present in JULIE OU LA NOUVELLE HÉLOÏSE. It creates distributional conflicts in society and thereby threatens its harmony and persistence. Zero sum games about the distribution of production results are allowed to cause serious social conflict; for example concerning how to allocate productive resources or how to distribute goods. In Rousseau's mythical economy everyone is content with his "estate". Starobinski quotes an astonishing passage from the novel, where it seems clear that the absence of such games is an important property of the "myth":

> No man thinks that he can increase his own fortune in any way other than by improving the welfare of all.[3]

The quote has a flavour of the Pareto optimum: the situation where there is no alternative resource allocation in society that would give anyone more utility except at the cost of others. Rousseau had an untenable idea of the self-sufficient economy, Starobinski finds: "It is a sentimental chimera".[4]

But contrary to what Starobinski thinks, there are several substantive arguments by which Rousseau supports his advocacy of autarchy. These arguments are not at all considered in Starobinski's myth interpretation. So let us take a look at the evidence Starobinski presents. The intention is neither to try to simply retell Starobinski's fascinating story, nor, of course, to try to refute it completely. But there are, obviously, some components in Rousseau's dreams of non-commercial domestic economies that are of marginal interest, perhaps, in Starobinski's story, but that deserve closer attention in the present discussion.

1 Ibid., p.43.
2 Starobinski 1971, p.130.
3 Starobinski 1971, p.13, [1988, p. 107]. OC II, p. 548. "nul ne croit pouvoir augmenter sa fortune que par l'augmentation du bien commun."
4 Starobinski 1971, p. 135.

## *Starobinski's Evidence*

It is not hard to find support for Starobinski's thesis that transparency carries a value of its own. One may, for example, refer to a passage in the CONFESSIONS, where Rousseau tries to explain small thefts he had committed in his youth.

> I am less tempted by money than by things, because *there is always an intermediary* between money and the desired possession, whereas between a thing and the enjoyment of that thing there is none. I see the thing and it tempts me; if I see only the means of acquiring it, it does not tempt me.[1]

Starobinski can also refer to JULIE OU LA NOUVELLE HÉLOÏSE where Rousseau describes a persona that is ideally virtuous – De Wolmar, Julie's husband, and St. Preux's rival. He is, in a sense, the moral opposite of Jean-Jacques, the thief of the CONFESSIONS. But still, Starobinski shows, the virtuous De Wolmar expresses an attitude strikingly similar to that expressed by the vicious but apologetic kleptomaniac. He reveals a strong preference for consuming the produce of his own estate. Self-sufficiency is the key to the richness of his household:

> Our great secret for being rich ... is to have little money, and in using our wealth, to avoid as much as possible intermediate exchanges between production and use...[2]

Consumption without exchange can be enjoyed in "pure pleasure", as Rousseau words it in the CONFESSIONS.[3] Starobinski's interpretation is that, to Rousseau, buying the good diminishes the pleasure because it makes the utility, the consumption, non-transparent. This added negative value can also be seen when Rousseau, in the first book of the CONFESSIONS, describes his own personality.

> None of my predominant tastes involves things that can be bought. I require none but good pleasures, and money poisons everything... By itself it is good for nothing; it must be *transformed in order to be enjoyed*.[4]

Starobinski interprets this passage:

> Money is in effect something that cannot be enjoyed immediately: all the pleasures it can buy are necessarily mediated pleasures. A pleasure acquired by means of money no longer has the purity of immediacy: it is poisoned.[5]

1. OC I, pp.36f. Starobinski 1971, p.132, italics in the original.
2. OC II, 548, part 5 letter 2. Starobinski 1971, p.132, [1988, p. 106].
3. OC I, pp.36f.
4. Starobinski 1971, p.132, [1988, p. 106]. "Ajoutez qu'aucun de mes gouts dominans ne consiste en choses qui s'achettent. Il ne me faut que des plaisirs purs, et l'argent les empoisonne tous... ... il n'est bon à rien par lui même; il faut le transformer pour en jouir."
5 Ibid.

I see no reason to dispute Starobinski's reading of these lines. What he finds certainly seems to be there. It appears clearer still in parts of Rousseau's ornamentation to which Starobinski does not refer. Still, Starobinski misses the edge of the poison metaphor. The accomplished master of rhetoric, Rousseau, tries to win his point by a very efficient and revealing metaphor. He compares his feelings for a good he has bought on the market with exploiting a whore. In the dichotomy of Aristotle, Rousseau cannot enjoy goods produced for their exchange values, only those produced for their use values. Emotionally, to Rousseau, all market exchange is like prostitution. And he expects as little satisfaction in using a bought good as if he had hired a whore:

> If the fire in my blood demands women, the emotion in my heart cries more loudly for love. Women who can be bought, lose all their charm for me. I doubt whether I could even take advantage of the situation. It is the same with all the pleasures within my reach. If they are not to be had for nothing, they have no attraction for me. The only things I like are things that belong to no one but the first person who knows how to enjoy them.[1]

Does this not suffice to verify Starobinski's point? What more would be needed? What would be the use of an always ever-larger accumulation of goods when the buyer cannot consume them – as Rousseau fears he cannot in being unable to "take advantage" of the whore? And a few lines further on he describes his emotions as some kind of phobia:

> Countless times, during my apprenticeship and since, I have gone out with the idea of buying some dainty. As I come to the pastry-cook's I catch sight of the women behind the counter and can already imagine them laughing among themselves and making fun of the greedy youngster... ...But in the end I go home like an idiot... ...not having dared to buy anything.[2]

If this is not an emotionally-based distaste for "intermediate exchanges" or the presence of money – then what is?

1 OC I, p. 36f. [Rousseau 1984, p. 44.]: "Si mon sang allumé me demande des femmes, mon coeur ému me demand encore plus de l'amour. Des femmes à prix d'argent perdroient pour moi tous leurs charmes; je doute même s'il seroit en moi d'en profiter. Il en est ainsi de tous les plaisirs à ma porté: s'ils ne sont gratuits je les trouve insipides. J'aime les seuls biens qui ne sont à personne qu'au prémier qui sait les gouter."
2 OC I, p. 37. [Rousseau 1984 p. 45.]: "Mille fois, durant mon apprentissage et depuis, je suis sorti dans le dessin d'acheter quelque friandise. J'approche le butique d'un pâtissier: j'apperçois des femmes au comptoir; je crois déja les voir rire et se moquer entre elle du petit gourmand."

### *Starobinski's Three Cases*

Several readers accept Starobinski's reading of these paragraphs not only as a partial perspective but as the *full* explanation of Rousseau's taste for autarchy.[1] To them, these lines signify Rousseau's general aversion to money. Rousseau *acknowledges*, in an economic-theoretical context, the "utility and significance" of money, they claim, but rejects it for emotional reasons. They refer to Rousseau's personal distaste for money. "Rousseau's malaise before all sorts of mediation" was reflected also in his personal life and correspondence. His suspicions against the royal pension once offered him by the British king, his criticism of Sofie d'Houdetot, "the only real love in his life", for holding money as her most important concern, his correspondence with his publishers, etc., all can be offered as examples of his "malaise". This has been pointed out by proponents of Starobinski's thesis. Along these lines, Gagnebin and Raymond claim that Rousseau even disliked monetary mediation in philanthropy because, like any other use of money, it corrupted both the giver and the receiver.[2]

The Gagnebin and Raymond interpretation can be characterised as a "value-added" theory. Acquiring the good by market exchange contaminates the use of the good. Because it diminishes the pleasure of using it, it reduces its value. When buying a good, one receives its utility (x) minus something (y). This *y* is treated as a negative value *added* by the act of buying in itself. Something negative is added not to the utility of the good *per se*, but to the emotional experience of the buyer. This negative value-added is caused by the lack of transparence and consists in a sense of charmlessness or even emotional poison.

But the value-added interpretation is simply not correct. Neither are the claims of Gagnebin and Raymond that Rousseau acknowledges the "utility and significance" of money and market exchange, and rejects it on an emotional basis. On the contrary, Rousseau explicitly questions the utility and significance of money. He describes how market provisioning may add a negative quality (an emotional experience) to the value of the good, but this is certainly not his main errand. For, emphatically and systematically, he describes how the utility and cost *per se* of the good are dependent on the mode of provision (market or subsistence). The point is not, then, that market exchange imposes a (negative) value-added (in the sale transaction), but that it diminishes the probability that the primary value of the good (net of all costs) in itself will be reasonable. Rousseau claims that provision by market exchange implies several circumstances that diminish that probability. Contrary to what Gagnebin and Raymond claim, Rousseau thus opposes "money and market exchange" precisely because of its insufficient "utility and significance". A closer look at Starobinski's own cases makes this abundantly clear.

One particular problem is the character of Starobinski's evidence. He bases his conclusion about the "imaginative flight" into the "consoling dream of collective autarchy" on rather problematic evidence from a positional point of view. It is, although he never himself acknowledges or justifies this constraint – he is probably not even aware of it – entirely limited to texts and paragraphs

1 Grimsley 1974, pp. 42f. Bernard Gagnebin and Marcel Raymond, commenting on these lines in the Pleiade edition of the CONFESSIONS: OC I, p. 1250f.
2 OC I, p. 1250f.

concerning the sphere of domestic economy. Rousseau makes a strict distinction between "the domestic economy" and "the political economy".[1] The former concept refers to the housekeeping of the family while the latter concerns society at large. Therefore, it is problematic to draw conclusions about his thoughts on economic policy based only on the analyses of cases concerning domestic economy. The position of the writer must be a part of the analysis.

Starobinski, without discussion, turns Rousseau's mythical autarchy – originating in a certain psychic disposition and expressed in the context of domestic economy – into a political-economic principle. He focuses his discussion on three cases: in JULIE OU LA NOUVELLE HÉLOÏSE, in EMILE and in the CONFESSIONS. The attitudes to economic exchange are, in all three cases, expressed from the perspective of a single observer and concern economic units of a more limited size than in political economy. Still, these cases reveal a great deal about Rousseau's conceptualisation of the dynamics of market exchange.

### *The first case: debauched girls and poisoned wine*

In the CONFESSIONS Rousseau reports (or claims that he does) his personal emotional experiences. Mostly the book focuses on things very far from the foundation of political economy. But even here, among his introspective reflections, can we find keys to the construction of his thought on the relation between sentiment, autarchy and exchange. Some arguments for autarchy even in this personal context do not concern pure emotions at all. They are logically independent of his personal sentiments. One of these arguments illustrates the thin ice on which Rousseau would have been caught had his political-economic or personal-moral pleading for autarchy been based solely on the sentiments to which Starobinski refers.

For, is not the moral legitimacy of Rousseau's emotions before the act of buying in the pastry shop strikingly shaky – from the perspective of his own thought? What fundamentally makes him frightened is what the women in the shop will think of him, how he will appear in their eyes: how he will be *considered*. He fears to have to go home "like an idiot". But the drive to be well considered in the other's eyes is, of course, one of the prime symptoms of the degeneration and decay of society. This has been emphasised by many; for instance Starobinski, who however did not become troubled by his own interpretation that Rousseau defended his market avoidance by the wish to be well considered. And Rousseau, truly, as noted above, saw the separation of appearance and being ("paraître" and "être") as a threat to the happiness of the individual and to the prospects for friendship. If this were the only basis for his rejection of market exchange his argument would certainly be futile. The brilliant rhetorician, admired all over Europe, in the enlightened public arena of Europe — would he really be content with such a poor logical performance?

In order to legitimise his opposition to intermediary exchange Rousseau needs another argument. And, indeed, he has one of a much more compelling and persuasive nature; an argument which can even defend his reaction in the pastry shop. With this argument he can even face the modern microeconomist.

1 See p. 97 below.

He is about to describe the character of his personality. We are told about his shyness, his sensualism and passions, his dishonesty, his propensity to conceal, to lie, and even to steal. Then he explains how this, his "almost sordid avarice", is compatible with "the greatest contempt for money". Why does he not rather develop a terrible greed for money? An explanation is needed. Some complementary information about his personality must be exhibited. And, indeed, his relationship to money is given as the missing information. It is presented in three steps and paragraphs. Firstly, he explains something which is already apparent: that he only likes goods produced as use values, because they are not poisoned by money. Then, in the second paragraph, he presents a more general argument, parts of which appears in the Starobinski quotation about the poisoning money (noted above). This argument says that money is less precious than it is generally held to be. (Notice that this again contradicts Gagnebin-Raymond's proposition! Rousseau does not uncritically acknowledge the "utility and significance" of money.) In the third paragraph he describes his personal experiences of discomfort and humiliation, as in the pastry-shop, when involved in market exchange.

It is mainly the second and third paragraphs that are of interest here. The second paragraph begins with the argument we might recognize from Starobinski's quote: money has no value in itself but must be transformed. But Rousseau continues by explaining what he finds to be the problem with this kind of transformation:

> One must bargain and purchase and often be cheated, paying dear for poor services. I want an article of quality; but my money is sure to obtain a poor one. I pay a lot for a new laid egg and it proves stale; for a ripe fruit, and it is green; for a girl, and she is debauched. I enjoy good wine, but where can I get it? At a wine merchant's? Notwithstanding all my precautions, he will poison me.[1]

This does not describe the appearance of a negative value-added. Neither has it much to do with the psychic disposition of the customer. Rather, what is to be expected from the seller is the problem here. And it is not the fantasy of some paranoid neurotic. To the contrary, Rousseau's fear seems rather well-grounded. He is, in fact, saying that in market exchange we stand the risk of being cheated, the risk that all the seller's nice-sounding promises about the quality of the product may not hold. That they may quite well turn out to be no more than empty words. Whatever precautions are taken by the individual (or the collective), a dishonest pastry baker might very well sell bread from yesterday or a cake that will be stale when you have reached home. It seems clear that Rousseau is truly arguing against market exchange with propositions entirely independent of his or any other buyer's private feeling of uneasiness before the act of exchange.

1 OC I, p. 37. [Rousseau 1984, pp. 44f] "...il faut le transformer pour en jouir; il faut achetter, marchander, souvent être dupe, bien payer, être mal servi. Je voudrois une chose bonne dans sa qualité; avec mon argent je suis sûr de l'avoir mauvaise. J'achette cher un oeuf frais, il est vieux; un beau fruit, il est verd; une fille, elle est gâtée. J'aime le bon vin; mais où en prendre? Chez un marchand de vin? Comme que je fasse il m'empoisonnera."

The basis for his preference of "transparent" goods in this case, is not any such personal emotion at all, but rather the fact that significantly less *access to information* about the product and its quality is available in market exchange than in subsistence production. And in this case the asymmetrically little access to information for the buyer in relation to the seller is decisive.

Indeed, information problems of this kind are not unfamiliar to modern consumers. They often have reason to distrust the seller or producer; for example, regarding their affirmations of the impact of the good on our health or on the environment. Intuitively, Rousseau is even touching on a problem explored by Akerlof and others in the context of modern welfare economics, the problem of the presence of *asymmetric* access to information. In Rousseau's case, the seller who knows the quality of his product, like the girl knowing her virtue, can exploit the poor uninformed buyer. Akerlof describes in a famous essay the economic consequences of the asymmetric access to information between seller and buyer on the market for used cars.[1] The risk the consumer faces tends to cause inefficient price equilibria and inefficiently low demand. The buyer is unwilling to pay as much for the car as he would have considered appropriate – less than what he would have been willing to pay – had he been convinced in advance of the quality of the product. The consequence is that the equilibrium price is lower, and the quantity supplied less, than if consumers were fully informed. For this reason the implied resource allocation is not optimal for society.

Neither in the next step of his argument, in the third paragraph, does Rousseau employ his own emotional experiences as the prime argument. Again he presents a general economic problem connected with market exchange.

> Supposing I insist on getting what I want. What trouble and embarrassment I must put myself to! I must use my friends and correspondents, give orders, write, go hither and thither, wait; and often I shall be cheated in the end. What a trouble my money is! I am not fond enough of good wine to disturb myself to that extent.[2]

This argument is also fully understandable in the context of modern welfare economics and does not need to be legitimised by any personal sentiment. A market transaction carries additional costs, over and above the market price. In order to avoid the uncertainty of a market transaction, Rousseau explains, the buyer would have a number of costs, "troubles", and "embarrassments", would be required to spend considerable time communicating, would have to "wait" and "disturb" herself in order to get the appropriate information. These are transaction costs of a certain kind, namely costs of obtaining information. And Rousseau ends with the conclusion, perfectly persuasive also for the modern welfare economist, that he does not find the pleasure, the value of the good thus acquired, worth its price, these costs included. With the "disturbance" over and above the monetary price of the good, total cost would exceed its value.

1 Akerlof 1967.
2 OC I, p. 37. [Rousseau 1984, pp. 44f] "Veux-je absolument être bien servi? Que de soins, que d'embarras! avoir des amis, des correspondans, donner des commissions, écrire, aller, venir, attendre, et souvent au bout être encor trompé. Que de peine avec mon argent! Je la crains plus que je n'aime le bon vin."

These two instances show that Rousseau indeed legitimises his personal inclination to avoid market exchange with arguments valid independently of his sentiments. These arguments have a distinctly ***non-basic*** character (unlike the transparency interpretation). This is so although both instances are embedded in a description of his private feelings about market exchange. He does this to show – with an argument fully perceptible to welfare economic theory – something which must be foreign to it: that the expected utility of a good, net of all costs, might depend on its mode of distribution (market exchange or redistribution within the household).

## *The second case: the dazzling apparatus of pleasure*

Starobinski refers, secondly, to an example in EMILE, book 3, where he claims that the ideal of "a closed, autarchic, essentially agricultural economy is proposed".[1] Rousseau describes in his typical way the virtue of the subsistence economy; we are presented with a wonderful meal Emile is about to experience:

> This white bread that you like so much comes from the wheat harvested by this peasant. His wine, dark and crude but thirst-quenching and healthy, comes from his vineyards. His clothes come from his hemp, which his wife, daughters and servants spin during the winter. The dishes on his tables are prepared by no one outside his own family. The nearest mill and the nearest market are the limits of his world.[2]

To Starobinski this, again, is a case where Rousseau expresses his warm feelings for a transparent and closed subsistence agriculture, although here on a large scale. And the idyllic picture is truly painted with warm feelings. But, Starobinski fails to observe that the reader does not come across this idyllic home scene as a ***tabula rasa***. On the contrary, Rousseau has prepared her quite well some pages earlier. He has planted the motif of the wine and meal dramaturgically in advance. When the reader encounters the words about the dark and crude wine he is hit right in the heart by a technique to secure a "sympathetic reading".[3]

Thus, a few pages before the description of the wonderful meal, Rousseau tells of an experiment he contemplated for Emile's education. He would have poured a little wine from the vineyard of his own landlord and some wine from a wine-seller's into two glasses. Then he would have added an alkaline solution to both glasses. As a result, a layer of lead would soon have been visible at the bottom of the glass containing the wine from the wine-seller. In this way Emile would have discovered how the merchandised wine "is rarely free from lead".

1 Starobinski 1971, p. 131 n.1
2 OC IV, p. 464. Starobinski 1971, p. 131, [1988, p. 105 (note 63)] "ce pain bis que vous trouvez si bon, vient du bled recueilli par ce paysan; son vin noir et grossier, mais désalterant et sain, est du cru de sa vigne; le linge vient de son chanvre, filé l'hiver par sa femme, par ses filles, par sa servante; nullee autres mains que selles de sa famille n'ont fait les apprêts de sa table; le molin le plus proche et le marché voisin sont les bornes de l'univers pour lui."
3 Obviously not unique to Rousseau: cf. Marshall 1988.

Typically, the lead had been added in order to cover the acidity and low quality of the original wine. In contrast, the darkness and pleasant flavour of the landlord's wine would have been shown to be entirely natural, containing no lead.

Not even this idyllic intimacy of the meal, then, is free from the information cost problem. When Rousseau describes a pleasant consumption without intermediate exchange, the words are perceived by a reader aware of an unattractive contrast, signified by the adulterated wine. Rousseau again explains how a transparent self-sufficiency economy makes it possible to avoid the risk of being cheated, which is present on the anonymous market.

Moreover, this risk is not his only target. So far, the criticism of market exchange from the individual consumer's point of view is similar to that in the paragraphs of the CONFESSIONS already discussed. But here, in EMILE, a further problem is introduced. The meal example also aims at something else: the emptiness of luxury consumption. The reader's perception is also prepared by a second incident, also likely to cause sympathy when the reader encounters the simple, warm and harmonious table. The reader is introduced to another meal – as part of EMILE's educational plans – which is a "magnificent but tedious" meal, a dinner for wealthy people where "course follows course". It takes place in an "opulent house" with all the apparatuses of feasts and pleasure. "All that apparatus of pleasure and feasting brings something dazzling which carries away the head as long as one is not accustomed". But the teacher (the narrator) of the book interrupts dazzling state of Emile's head by a question:

> How many hands do you suppose the things on this table passed through before they got here?

Rousseau vividly describes how Emile's imagination will be captured and moved by this thought. But this is no mere random pedagogical example. It resounds from a passage in the well-known treatise by Mandeville: THE FABLE OF THE BEES, and anticipates those in the NATURE AND CAUSES OF THE WEALTH OF NATIONS.[1] And if Emile were to discover the truth he would know that:

> every quarter of the globe has been ransacked, so that some 2,000,000 men have laboured for years, and many lives have, perhaps, been sacrificed...[2]

1. Mandeville 1924 (1732), pp. 169f. (I: pp. 182ff) and Smith 1976, p. 22, (I:I.11). Mandeville: "A man would be laugh'd at, that should discover Luxury in the plain Dress of a poor Creature that walks along in a thick Parish Gown and a course Shirt underneath it; and yet what a number of people, how many different trades, and what a variety of Skill and Tools must be employes to have the most ordinary Yorkshire Cloth?"

2. OC IV, p. 463. [Rousseau 1984b, p. 153]: "Par combien de mains estimeriez-vous bien qu'ait passé tout ce que vous voyez sur cette table, avant que d'arriver?"
"toutes les régions du monde ont été mises à contribution, que vingt millions de mains, peut-être, ont longtems travaillé, qu'il en couté la vie, peut-être à des milliers d'hommes., et tout cela pour lui présenter en pompe à midi ce qu'il va déposer le soir dans sa garderobe?" Rousseau's English translator obviously found that Rousseau exaggerated and dramatically moderated the number of hands and dead.

Is all this suffering really worth it just to present "pompously at noon what he would have to depose in his garderobe at night?" the teacher may ask his student. So, in this second context, the description of the simple meal in the self-sufficient household functions as a contrast not only to the poisoned commercial wine, but also to the senselessly orgiastic luxury meal. The closed subsistence economy would possibly suit Rousseau's emotional "malaise". But it would also make it possible to diminish the information risk and information cost problems as well as the human tragedies imposed on people all over the world for the sake of the marginal and temporary pleasures of a few wealthy people.

## *The third case: the dual market for bread and toys*

A third case claimed by Starobinski can be found in JULIE OU LA NOUVELLE HÉLOÏSE. The writer here again takes his position within a domestic economy. A traditional estate of a considerable size is described, not unlike the autarchic household of EMILE. It is called Clarens and is owned and managed by De Wolmar and his wife, Julie. Clarens is a manorial household with peasants performing dues in kind or by corvées. The idyllic estate is, of course, basically self-sufficient. In portraying the estate Rousseau uses such evaluative expressions that it is impossible to miss the point: he obviously wants to portray a kind of ideal domestic economy. The nature of this ideal economy seems to confirm Starobinski's thesis beautifully. Wherever in the novel the estate is portrayed it is done according to a rather fixed pattern approximately as follows. The speaker or some other person compares his or her feelings about consuming a certain good achieved via the market with consuming a good produced within the estate. Again and again the conclusion is that consumption acquires a more pleasant flavour when the genesis and the history of the good are transparent, i.e. when it is acquired by one's own production, within the estate.

The reader's sense of pleasantness with respect to the estate is reinforced by a contrast similar to the one just described in EMILE:

> I don't think that any thinking human being can observe a prince's palace and its shining splendour for even an hour, and not become melancholic and cry for the fate of humanity. But the sight of this house and the unitary and simple life of its inhabitants implants an ever-increasing peaceful delight into the soul of the observer.[1]

The inhabitants are experiencing not merely a temporary ("until one gets accustomed") dazzling as in the previous case, but rather "an ever increasing peaceful delight". This pleasant absence of the desire to be well considered by others, the absence of "conspicuous consumption" is, as in the two previous cases, closely connected with economic self-sufficiency. And the importance of avoiding intermediary agents is again explicitly explained:

1. OC II, p. 547 (V:II).

> The big secret behind our becoming rich, is not that we possess a lot of money, but that we, as far as possible, avoid intermediary agents between production and consumption by using our own resources. No intermediary can enter, but at our loss, and if these our losses were multiplied, they would reduce considerable fortunes to next to nothing ...[1]

Whenever exchange is unavoidable it should be in kind, not through money. Intermediaries cause extra costs. Thereby the practical utility rather than the search for profit is decisive.

But the extra costs of using intermediary provision is not the only problem described. Also another problem is avoided by a self-sufficiency economy. It is described in a rather puzzling formulation:

> Nothing is contempted because it is common and nothing is overvalued because it is rare. Because everything coming from afar happens to be deformed or adulterated, we limit ourselves as much by good taste as by modesty to choose the best of what is supplied in the neighbourhood and is not of low quality.

In this passage, a fourth argument for self-sufficiency is invoked, an argument that will reappear in Rousseau's defense of international autarchy to be discussed later in this essay.[2] It maintains that self-sufficiency is to be preferred because market valuation is in some sense deficient or perverted. Goods that are rare or "from afar" are adulterated or at least over-prized in relation to their "real" value. Or, as in De Wolmar's formulation:

> There is a big difference between the value that people ascribe to things and that which they really possess.[3]

The origin of the "difference" is to be found in the evaluation made by the consumers. Rousseau seems to regard what today would be called the preference ranking of the consumers, as, in a certain sense, false. According to De Wolmar's evaluation scale, the general public gives rare, foreign, and fashionable goods an unjustly high evaluation. On what mandate can Rousseau base this curious proclamation about the "difference"?

One explanation and interpretation might be that Rousseau's idea is similar to that of some of his mercantilist predecessors. Some goods are *a priori* defined as natural but others as artificial and less useful. I shall return to this question later in the context of Rousseau's discussion of genuine and false needs. Another explanation would be that Rousseau prefers the simple, traditional or transparent, for a kind of aesthetic reason. In the perspective of modern microeconomics both would be no more than one consumer's (Rousseau's) judgment about the preference ranking of other consumers. In an apparently naïve way, Rousseau here, so to speak, prophetically rejects the future Paretian

1. OC II, p. 548 (V:II).
2. Chapter 5 below.
3. OC II, p. 550 (V:II).

claim that the equilibrium price on the competitive market represents the true social value of a product. Is it rejected on the basis that consumers do not understand the true value of commodities? Do they need a Platonian interference (by a philosopher like Rousseau?) to enlighten them about the real values? Welfare economics would treat his argument as just a question of taste about which economics should keep silent: *de gustibus non dispandum est*.[1] That would, to its theorists, perhaps, be an interesting piece of information for a biography or an anecdotal story, but hardly a persuasive argument for market avoidance. And as the basis of an economic philosophy it would seem oddly ad hoc.

There is, however, considerably more bite than that in Rousseau's argument even in this case. It appears in a revealing exposition of how Rousseau views the market price in the third book of EMILE. As in the previous passage in JULIE, Rousseau reflects about the "value set by the general public". He criticises this value in even stronger terms than in the paragraph just quoted.

> The value set by the general public on the various arts are in inverse ratio to their real utility.

Here the argument is more general and concerns the market evaluation of the products of different industries rather than different goods. And it is remarkable: the higher the price, Rousseau seems to claim, the lower the real social value of a good. And to really emphasise his point, to prevent the reader from having the slightest chance to glance past its extremely radical implications, he repeats the argument again in even more unmistakable and provocative words,

> They are valued directly according to their *uselessness*.

That this astonishing affirmation is not to be taken only for an emotional outburst by a pseudo-romantic lover of transparency and paradox is evident from the explanatory passage that follows. It reflects a very conscious idea of the price mechanism.

> This might be expected. The most useful arts are the worst paid, for the number of workmen is regulated by the demand, and the work which everybody requires must necessarily be paid at a rate which puts it within the reach of the poor.[2]

1. One should not dispute taste.
2. Italics added. OC IV, p. 457. [Rousseau 1984a p. 149]: "Il y a une estime publique attaché aux differens arts en raison inverse de leur utilité réelle. Cette estime ce mesure directement sur leur inutilité même et cela doit être. Les arts les plus utiles sont ceux qui gagnent le moins parce que le nombre des ouvriers se proportionne au besoin des hommes, et que le travail necessaire à tout le monde reste forcément à un prix que le pauvre peut payer." The same thought is already present in a note to the DISCOURS SUR L'ORIGINE ET LES FONDEMENTS DE L'INÉGALITÉ. "De la société et du luxe qu'elle engendre, naissent les arts libéraux et mécaniques, le commerce, les lettres; et toutes les inutilités, qui font fleurir l'industrie, enrichissent et perdant les États. La raison de ce dépérissement est très simple. Il est aisé de voir que par sa nature l'agriculture doit être le moins lucratif de tous les arts; parce que son produit étant de l'usage le plus indispensable pour tous les hommes, le prix en droit être proportionné aux facultés des plus pauvres. Du même principe on peut tirer cette règle, qu'en general les arts son lucratifs en raison invers de leur utilité et que les plus nécessaires doivent enfin devenir les plus négligés. Par où l'on voit ce qu'il faut penser des vrais avantages de l'industrie et d'effet réel qui résulte de ses progrès." OC III, p. 206.

This passage is remarkable. According to this quote, Rousseau claims that because the number of producers (that is, supply) is regulated by demand, the price is perverted. This is, however, not the formulation in the French original. The quoted translation by Foxley misses the whole point of the argument. Rousseau in fact claims that prices are low because the number of workmen is regulated by the "besoins" of people, and hence the price is low. What does this mean? Many workmen who produce the most useful products, those that everybody needs, cannot charge more than what the poor – whose demand is to satisfy their "besoins" – can pay, while those that produce for the few rich can charge more.[1] The argument is, however, more precise than that. In a following paragraph Rousseau compares this price behaviour with that generated by the rich. He explains that the prices on goods consumed by the rich are set on a different basis, that they, in contrast, are arbitrary. As an example he uses the high prices on the services by the artists serving at the high courts.

Adam Smith discusses the same example in the WEALTH OF NATIONS. He claims that the prices on artists' performances are determined by: a), "the rarity and beauty of their talents"; and, b), by the discredit of employing them. The last rather odd cause refers to the thought that "the exercise of their talents for the sake of gain" in the eyes of public opinion is considered "as a kind of publick prostitution" and that the artists must be compensated by a generous pay for this discredit.[2]

Rousseau's explanation is, however, different from Smith's (but not less perceptive):

> On the contrary, those self-important persons, who are not called artisans but artists, working exclusively for the idle [the '*oisifs*'], and the rich, set an arbitrary price on their lapri, and as the merits of these vain works exist only in the opinion, and the price itself is part of their merit, one estimates them in proportion to what they cost.[3]

The real point in Rousseau's argument is not that the luxury consumption of rich people is disgusting in view of the unsatisfied needs of the poor. (It is, of course, in view of the discussion of the sacrifice for the dazzling, probable that Rousseau would argue that too. But it is, nevertheless, not the main point here.) Veiled by the unfortunate mistranslation of the first passage the issue of concern is the *function* of demand. In the former case demand is generated by "besoins" – which is more properly translated as "need" or necessities rather than "demand" – and in the latter case demand is generated by "toys" – that is *lapri*, or non-necessities.

1. Chabert 1964, p. 354. A similar phrase occurs in the long note to the second Discours. OC III, p. 206 (note IX).
2. Smith 1976, p. 124.
3. OC IV, p. 457. I here use my own translation because I find that Foxley's says something entirely different, dubious and misleading. "Au contraire, ces importans qu'on n'appelle pas artisans mais artistes, travaillent uniquement pour les oisifs et les riches, mettent un prix arbitraire à leurs babioles, et comme le mérite de ces vains travaux n'est que dans l'opinion, leur prix même fait partie de ce mérite et on le les estime à proportion de ce qu'ils coûtent."

It is not the demand of the poor that perverts prices but the fact that in one case the allocation of labour is directed toward providing *necessities* and in the other case non-necessities, *toys* or lapri for rich adults.

How is it that prices are lower because the allocation of labour is determined for the provision of "necessities", rather than "toys"? Should we not expect it to be the other way around? If something is necessary for your survival, would you not be willing to pay any price for it? The price elasticity of demand should be very low. A small reduction in the supply of, say bread, would cause a very big increase in prices. Or conversely, a big change in prices would cause a small change in the demanded quantity. The price would not matter much; people would buy just about the same amount anyway. But that presupposes that there is a margin in people's budgets above expenses for necessities. Here Rousseau observes that there isn't. The prices must be payable for the many poor. The price elasticity of demand is – for that reason – on the contrary, very high: regardless of the amount supplied people would be able to pay just about the same sum. The amount of money paid is inflexible rather than the amount of goods consumed.[1]

On the other hand, if production is directed to the provision of "*toys*" (for wealthy adults) the price behaviour is different. Rousseau explains very clearly why. Here, the quotation says, the prices are "arbitrary". The reason is that they are consumed not as necessities but because "the merits of these vain works exist only in the opinion". Rich people demand goods that show that they are different, that they posses something not owned by everybody else. Then, what is better than things that are known to be expensive? "...the price itself is part of their merit, and one estimates them in proportion to what they cost", Rousseau concludes.

That which the wealthy demand, that which they will value highly, is, thus, precisely the high price of the good, its unattainability. It is the fact that it is, in Harrod's terms, oligarchic or, in Veblen's, feasible for conspicuous consumption, that gives the good its high value. The rich consumers are said to have a propensity to pay much for certain goods – just *because* they cost much. This polarisation of the different functions of demand is Rousseau's point.

> The rich think so much of these things, not because they are useful, but because they are beyond the reach of the poor. *Nolo habere bona, nisi quibus populus inviderit*.[2]

It is precisely just because they are not for all, not really necessary, that they are so dear for the rich. The third example shows, then, that Rousseau apprehends the market as dual, disfavouring the most important branch of the economy, the provision of necessities, or, in other words, agriculture. This causes a lack of diligence in caring for agriculture. Boisguilbert had expressed similar ideas. He

1 This is a very important economic problem that may cause serious famine catastrophes. Cf., Sen 1982d.

2 Italics added. OC IV, p. 457. [Rousseau 1984b p. 149]. My translation of the Latin: "I only want a good if the people envy it.". "Le cas qu'en fait le riche ne vient pas de leur usage, mais de ce que le pauvre ne les peut payer. Nolo habere bona nisi quibus populus inviderit."

had argued that agricultural products were undervalued. Because of divergent elasticities of income in the demand for necessary goods and goods of affluence, prices were perverted. But differently from Rousseau, Boisguilbert had suggested that the perverted prices had exogenous causes, and that the legal limitations in the corn trade were "partly responsible" for the early 18th century crisis in corn provisions.[1] Rousseau finds that the impetus is the market exchange stimulating luxury consumption. De Wolmar's estate and other households based on a self-sufficiency economy suffer a minimal risk to indulge in luxury consumption with all its destructive moral consequences.

* * *

The idea that the net value of the good is dependent on whether or not it is acquired through exchange appears so odd today, so distant from the most self-evident and least controversial premises of almost all economic discourses that it is nearly inexpressible, using conventional, formal language. But as Amartya Sen points out, such an idea may very well be perfectly realistic, at least in a predominantly agrarian society.[2]

Contrary to what Gagnebin and Raymond claim, there is more to find in Rousseau's confession about his visit to the pastry shop than what is captured in Starobinski's careful discussion of transparency. There are, beside Rousseau's aversion to "intermediate exchange", beneath the moving story of the malaise, other ingredients that are much more familiar to modern welfare economists.

It may be that Rousseau perceives an intrinsic, negative quality in goods enjoyed after market exchange; and suggests that an autarchic economy would support social harmony in society. But this is not all he says to legitimate his rejection of market exchange. Several arguments of an instrumental and conditional character consider the properties of market exchange per se. Market exchange increases the risks of information deficiencies or asymmetric information. The market for goods and services is dual and prices are perverted by the division of income, set by differing principles for goods necessary for survival, and for toys.

1 The expression is Lars Herlitz'.

2 One of the rare cases where a modern welfare economist has defended such a position can be found in Sen's critique of Gunnar Myrdal's Asian Drama. In his analysis of the contemporary Indian economy Myrdal claimed that in parts of the subcontinent the marginal labour productivity of agricultural work was zero or even below. Therefore he found that members of peasant households who resisted moving to towns for wage labour acted irrationally because their wage would, of course, be higher than their net marginal productivity in the peasant household. It was from society's point of view a waste of productive resources. Sen replied to this by indicating that entitlement rights to certain utilities might be connected with participation in family household work. (To be able to live and work in the household might even have an intrinsic utility e.g., the satisfaction to work with or for people one likes). These rights and utilities would be lost to those who went to the city for wage labour. The fruit of the rural subsistence labour was, therefore, not limited to the mere physical crop produced and consumed. Myrdal's calculus was incomplete. The physical marginal product of subsistence farming was merely a partial component in its entire social marginal product. Sen 1975.

## 4. EVERYONE MUST LIVE

# *Blueprint for an Autarchic Economy*

ROUSSEAU WAS SCEPTICAL about market exchange for substantial, economic reasons. But how did he imagine the alternative? How did he figure it when his proposals were not as restricted by his position as those in the CONSIDÉRATIONS? There is one unique text where Rousseau sets himself the task of proposing an economic policy in some detail. It was to be realised in a democratic setting; and because of his broad popularity among the receivers there were probably considerable possibilities that his proposals would be tried in real life. He could expect readers willing to read "with their hearts". The text is the PROJET DE CONSTITUTION POUR LA CORSE. In this text the project for a lovely self-sufficient autarchic economy is outlined.

### *Rousseau and Corsica*

The PROJET was written on request. In early September 1764 Jean-Jacques received a letter from a surgeon captain of Régiment Royal Italien at the Mézières garrison in France[1] asking for a "plan of gouvernement" for Corsica. At the time, Rousseau lived in exile at Neuchâtel after two years of turbulence since the publication of the CONTRAT SOCIAL and EMILE. The surgeon captain, Matthieu Buttafoco, a Corsican nobleman, served in the French army which had intervened with troops at his island.

Rousseau hesitated to answer affirmatively. He tells us in the CONFESSIONS that he felt insecure about the true purpose behind the request from Buttafoco and therefore asked to meet him in person. He was also hesitant because the work might interfere with his plans to make Corsica his home if the situation in mainland Europe became impossible. If that would happen he contemplated a calm and peaceful life on the island. He feared that the publication of the PROJET would make this solution impossible. But, despite all, he started working on a manuscript about the constitution of Corsica. The work was never completed, al-

1. Mély 1985, p. 205.

though it is possible that Rousseau never gave up his plans of doing it. It is said that, wherever he went, he always brought a dossier with his notes and documents on Corsica. His correspondence shows that he continued to keep himself informed about events at the island.[1]

What is the date of origin, then, of those notes that constitute what has posthumously been published as the PROJET DE CONSTITUTION POUR LA CORSE? His commentator in the Pleiade edition of the text, Sven Stelling-Michaud, supports Vaughan's earlier conclusion that they were written between January and September 1765.[2]

At the time of Buttafoco's letter, Corsica was unique in Europe in being ruled on the basis of a general vote. But to get a glimpse of the circumstances of the request it is necessary to start the story already in 1729. Genoa at that time ruled the island. But in that year, at San Pancrazio, representatives of the Corsican people came together and denounced Genoa's rights to the country. This started an armed resurrection against the Genoan troops and authorities which continued well into the 1730s. During the general confusion around this uprising many odd events occurred; a German baron (vainly) declared, for example, himself king of the island. In the years 1738-41, French troops were present at the island. In 1747 the European powers sided with the Genoese occupant and pronounced, in a peace treaty, Corsica a part of the republic of Genoa. In 1751, a new insurrection took place and the Corsicans again declared themselves a free nation. During the period from 1751 until the French annexation of the island in 1769, the country was ruled by a radical general, Pasquale Paoli, elected by popular vote. The PROJET was written during this democratic period.

Rousseau never lived on Corsica, never even went there. Several explanations are mentioned in the CONFESSIONS.[3] He was afraid that people would demand of him an "active life" he disliked and even feared. Therefore, he thought of offering to the surgeon captain that he write the history of Corsica rather than its constitution. Such a project would, he hoped, make it easier for him to "be his own master". Nevertheless he never did that, but rather began working on the constitution project.

At this same time he was working on the CONFESSIONS. In them, he reflects on writing about and going to Corsica in a way that reveals something of how he looked at the island. He feared that the journey to Corsica would be difficult and that he, on his way there, would be impeded and harassed by all the hostile nations he would have to pass. But even when safe on the island, he was worried:

> I should have none of the simplest comforts of life there, unless I brought them: linen, clothes, crockery, kitchen utensils, paper and books, all these I should have to carry with me.[4]

1. Stelling-Michaud, OC III, p. CCVIIIf.
2. Ibid., p. CCVII.
3. One reason was that he wanted peace and time for solitary meditation, but expected that the people of Corsica would engage him - with all justification - in an intensive work, collecting information for the construction of their constitution. Book XII. OC I, p. 651. [Rousseau 1984, p. 601].
4. Book XII. OC I, p. 651. [Rousseau 1984, p. 601]. "Je n'y devois trouver des plus simples comodités de la vie que celles que j'y porterois linge, habits, vasisselle, batterie de cuisine, papier, livres, il falloit tout porter avec soi."

The poverty of the island scared him:

> the thought of finding myself in the end alone and without resources, at my age and far from all acquaintances, at the mercy of the cruel and savage people that M d'Astier described...[1]

## *The Perspective*

The text did not appear as a singular work on the situation of Corsica. Moreover, Rousseau was far from the only author to write about the constitution of the island. The island was liberated decades before the North American settlement, after centuries of struggles for freedom; and lay wide open, as a carte blanche for the application of old and new political ideologies. It became one of the rudiments for mastership specimens in the arena of political philosophy in the Europe of the Enlightenment. Thus, it was a test case for the potentials of various post-feudal, absolutist or post-absolutist political ideologies. Correspondingly, several intellectuals visited the island or presented from afar their plans, patterns and outlines for the ruling of it. Besides Rousseau, there were Giuseppe Gorani, who drafted plans for an absolute monarchy; Dalmazzo Vasc, who spoke for an enlightened despotism; James Boswell;[2] and the remarkable whig historian Catherine Macaulay who brought plans for constitutionalism and democracy.[3]

The perspective from which Rousseau's text was written, then, was widely different from the CONSIDÉRATIONS SUR LE GOUVERNEMENT DE POLOGNE. The basic question was not, as there, limited to what could be done "leaving the deeper levels of your laws virtually untouched". Rather, it was: how should a society in its entirety construct its economic and social institutions in the interest of the people? We are entitled to assume the settings to be democratic in the sense of the DISCOURS SUR L'ÉCONOMIE POLITIQUE.[4]

Rousseau was clearly held in high esteem in wide circles on the island. This is testified to by Boswell and other visitors.[5] The CONTRAT SOCIAL had, a few years previously, apostrophised Corsica as the only named nation where its ideas could be implemented.

It does not seem entirely clear, in the literature, in whose interest or on whose commission Rousseau was consulted. One possibility is that it was part of an attempt at a dirty plot in which Rousseau's good name on the island was to be used, without his knowledge, to further the interests of Buttafoco himself or even

1. Book XII. OC I, p. 651. "L'idée de me trouver enfin seul sans ressource à mon age et loin de toutes mes connoiassances à la merci de ce peuple barbare et feroce, tel que me le peignoit M Dastier étoit bien propre è me faire rêver sur une pareille résolution avant de l'exécuter." Concerning M. d'Astier, see Stelling-Michaud , OC III, p. CCIV.
2. Stelling-Michaud, OC III, p. CXCIX.
3. Beretti 1988, p. 172f. Concerning Catherine Macaulay, a new biograhy has recently appeared: Hill 1992. A brief notice on this biography can be found in Social History, Vol 18, no 2, May 1993.
4. See below, p 98.
5. Beretti 1988, p. 38f. Boswell himself tells that he asked Rousseau to make him his envoyé to Corsica in order that he, Boswell, would get in contact with the leaders of the island - an offer Rousseau responded to with some sarcasm: "Boswell:'I offer you my services; Mr Boswell, Ambassador Extraordinary of Monsieur Rousseau to the Isle of Corsica.' Rousseau:'Perhaps you would rather be King of Corsica?' Boswell:'On my word! Ha! Ha! Not I. It exceeds my powers' (with a long bow). All the same I can now say, 'I have refused a crown'."

the French cause on the island.[1] Boswell, however, states in a letter that Rousseau had been asked by "the Corsicans" to "give them a set of laws" and had answered with the words: "it exceeds my power but not my zeal."[2]

So this may be a case where Rousseau had reason to expect – and even fear – that his text would be read with the readers' "hearts". This is also evident from the worries he felt about moving to Corsica. He feared that he would be

> compelled, as soon as I landed in Corsica, to yield to popular pressure and to hold frequent conferences with the leaders.[3]

That he must have had in mind readers very favorably prejudiced to what he would have to say is also obvious from the following very candid reflection from the CONFESSIONS of what would happen if he went to Corsica:

> I should lead a life quite contrary to my inclinations, and should always show myself at a disadvantage. I foresaw that in the flesh I should disappoint the expectations of my capabilities which the Corsicans had probably formed from my books; I should discredit myself in their eyes, as much to their detriment as to my own; and that I should lose the confidence they had placed in me, without which I could not successfully carry out the task they expected of me ...[4]

If Rousseau really – which is not perfectly certain since he never published the text – had intended the text on Corsica for the readers described in this last quotation, he should have had in mind precisely his ideal, friendly reader.

The assumptions that constitute the clay to be modeled, the context for the proposals, are, of course limited by Rousseau's information about Corsica. After all, he was not asked to propose a constitution for a society of his own making, but for a living people, badly tormented by decades of struggle, a people who could not afford further bloodshed because of mistaken premises. Here he had to modulate his proposals according to a crucially realistic restriction; he had to assume precisely those restrictions that were feasible in view of the intended use of the text. Thus he was confronted with extreme requirements on valid and relevant information. Now, we know that he never visited the island – so wherefrom came his essential picture of Corsica's predicament?

He gained his understanding from reading literature on Corsica, through his correspondence with nationalists on the island (he corresponded, for example, with the nationalist leader Pascal Paoli), and through live conversations and correspondences with visitors to Corsica, as exemplified by Boswell's description.

1. Mely 1985, p. 205.
2. Beretti 1988, p. 38.
3. Book XII. OC I, p. 650. [Rousseau 1984, p. 600]. "je sentois que, sans prendre part directement aux affaires publiques, je serois necessité sitot que je serois en Corse de me livrer à l'empressement du Peuple et de conférer très souvent avec les Chefs."
4. ibid. "Il étoit clair que je ne pourrois plus disposer de moi-même, et qu'entrainé malgré moi dans un toubillon pour lequel je n'étois point né, j'y montrerois qu'à mon desavantage. Je prévoyois que, soutenant mal par ma présence l'opinion de capacité qu'avoient pu leur donner mes livres, je me décrediterois chez les Corses, et perdrois, autant à leur préjudice qu'au mien, la confiance qu'ils m'avoient donnée, et sans laquelle je ne pouvois faire avec succés l'œuvre qu'ils attendoient de moi..."

But he had an even more ambitious plan for how to keep informed. For Buttafoco, who towards the end of 1764 was to return to the island, he put together an introductory questionnaire covering all kinds of aspects on the life of Corsica.

The PROJET is less well organized than, for example, the CONSIDÉRATIONS or the discourses. It shows clear signs of being unfinished. There are for example no subtitles. The main body of the text, the "projet", is preceded by a brief preface. The "projet" starts with a short description of the historical preconditions, followed by two short paragraphs determining Rousseau's task in view of the restrictions set by these historical preconditions. Thereafter, a longer section of the text presents "the first reflections"[1] on the local situation. The remaining part describes "what needs to be done".[2] It contains three main sections. Firstly, there is a subsection on the moral situation on the island and thereafter a large subsection on how to arrange the internal economy in view of the autarchy of Corsica in relation to other economies. Thirdly, there are suggestions on how to finance the public sector.

Rousseau opens the text by telling the reader about the situation of Corsica. Thereby, we get an unusually explicit description of how he views the preconditions for his own proposals. Already here, at the beginning of the text, Rousseau gives several specific reasons why Corsica should try to develop an economic policy of self-sufficiency. The necessary preconditions for autarchy were present on the island and there were no good alternatives.

These necessary preconditions were material and moral. It was, firstly, obvious that Corsica possessed enough natural resources to be self-sufficient. The land of the island had not been fully appropriated; fertile and cultivable land still lay in constant fallow. Genoa had purposely isolated Corsica in order to prevent all trade to the island. Thereby, Corsica had been forced to become economically independent. Especially during the war, the island had been isolated and many young men left the fields in order to go to combat against Genoa. In spite of fields laying idle at this time there had been enough food available to provide the people with basic necessities.[3] This proved that there were domestic resources enough to feed the country, and that Corsica could support an even larger population with its own agriculture.[4] Secondly, the people of Corsica possessed the necessary moral qualities to build a self-sufficient economy. The island had attained only an early stage in its social development, and had not yet acquired the "vices" typical of later stages in the "civilisation" process.[5]

Furthermore, there were no good alternatives to self-sufficiency; although the two preconditions present on Corsica could have been, writes Rousseau, very advantageous in international trade. Corsicans could easily have become one of Europe's flourishing peoples. But 40 years of continuous warfare had caused poverty, devastation and depopulation. Although during their free periods in the past the Corsicans had learned a social morality: to "obey their equals", much of

1. OC III, p. 913. "les premieres reflexions que m'a suggerées l'examen rapide du local de l'Isle".
2. Ibid , "ce qu'il doit faire".
3. Ibid., p. 921.
4. Ibid., p. 907.
5. Ibid., p. 902. "Le peuple corse est dans l'heureux état qui rend une bonne institution possible..."

this was lost during the judicial chaos under Genoese rule.[1] During that time, violence and other social problems increased. One particularly serious problem was the prevalence of vendettas which had been nurtured by the Genoese. In the future, combat between fractions may not easily disappear but rather escalate. Groups would deploy against one another the strength and armoury earlier aimed at Genoa. Such problems, as well as lack of finance, would prevent Corsica from having an administration and social cohesion necessary for successful participation in foreign trade.

## *Proposals*

Rousseau's text on Corsica does not very distinctly delineate the central goals for a political economy. But two concerns seem to dominate. The people of Corsica needed, firstly, to search "peace in liberty".[2] To economise for independence was, no doubt, important for the Corsicans, in Rousseau's opinion. It is indicated right in the historical introduction that this might have to be at the cost of "richesse".[3] Everyone's right to live has, secondly, higher priority than some people's right to "richesse". The economy must give priority to bread before providing for the toys of infantile adults.

> It is necessary that the whole world lives and nobody enriches himself. That is the fundamental principle of a nation's prosperity. And the policy I propose works for that purpose as directly as possible.[4]

The text includes a rather extensive political program whose most significant components, thus, concern the *right to live* and *peaceful independence.* According to this program, Corsica's constitution should serve the preservation of liberty. The island, therefore, had to strengthen itself with resources of its own, through a policy of self-reliance. International trade should be impeded. But this proposal is conditional. Such a policy should last as long as the constitution of the country was unstable and as long as there was no more to gain from *internal* trade.[5] But a population increase should, on the other hand, be encouraged. And when no room was left for land clearing, intensified exploitation of the land and the establishment of new farmsteads on the basis of subsistence agriculture, another policy must be applied.[6]

In order to know how to implement such a policy, the figures of imports to Corsica for a sequence of years should be closely studied, as should the

1. Ibid., pp. 916.f. "les haïnes de famille et les projets de vengeance" OC III, p. 903. "Les Corses ont beacoup gagné depuis qu'ils sont libres, ils ont joint la prudence au courage, ils ont appris à obéir à leurs égaux, ils ont acquis des vertus et des mÏurs, et ils n'avoient point de loix, s'ils pouvoient d'eux-mêmes rester ainsi, je ne verrois presque rien à faire."
2. Ibid., p. 904. "Il faut . . . qu'il cherche le paix dans la liberté".
3. Ibid., p. 903. "pour vouloir conserver vos richesses vous auriez perdu vôtre liberté".
4. OC III, p. 924. "Il faut que tout le monde vive et que personne ne s'enrichisse. C'est la [le] principe fondamentale de la prosperité de la nation, et la police que je propose va pour sa partie à ce but aussi directement qu'il est possible." For the historical context of the "right to live"-concept, see Thompson 1971, and later comments to that essay.
5. Ibid., p. 908.
6. Ibid., p. 904. "s'enrichir en hommes".

consequences of the year-long blockade in 1734-35. A policy of import substitution (not for export purposes as the mercantilists demanded, but for the home market) should eliminate the need for imports.[1] Subsistence peasantry should be supported by all means in order to secure international independence and for other reasons. To that purpose, it was urgent that agricultural work be made attractive. It was even more important, he claims, than the development of agricultural techniques.

The people should be as equally spread out over the territory as possible[2] in order to secure the optimal usage of the resources of the island. This proposal is a further indication that Rousseau was well-informed about the economic thinking of his time. The suggestion seems inspired by the Presbyterian minister Robert Wallace, a populationist who proposed this kind of arrangement out of a kind of proto-Ricardian analysis.[3] Rousseau advocates a system that:

> gets the people to spread over the surface of its territory, gets them to stay there, to cultivate everywhere, to love the rural life and every work that is connected with it, and so well find the necessities and satisfactions of life that they don't ever want to leave it.[4]

This dispersed allocation of inhabitants is necessary for democracy. In small congregations people know one another, and those who make the decisions are forced to observe their consequences. The public administration should be as flatly organized and decentralised as possible, which would be facilitated by such a land policy. Policy should be based on small local units where the inhabitants know one another and can have a direct influence on the government.[5]

Government should, if necessary, intervene to ensure that everybody gets her necessities for life, and that the unequal relation in the exchange between a seller with a surplus and a buyer with an urgent need for food is not exploited at the cost of the buyer. This means that the government should, if necessary, be prepared to regulate prices and to open public corn magazines which could also be used to stabilize the economy against economic conjunctures.[6] In addition, the use of land should not be regulated by land rents since no one should be denied her entitlement to land. Monetary exchange should be avoided since allocation by means of money would push labour and resources towards more "lucrative" uses and thereby disfavour agriculture.[7] This proposal is fully consistent with the idea of the dual economy, discussed in the previous chapter and in Chapter 6 below. An entitlement structure based on money facilitates the accumulation of private property, and thereby inequality.

1. Ibid., p. 926.
2. Ibid., p. 904.
3. Steuart 1966 (1767), p. 87. Wallace's most important works were published in 1753 and 1761. Hutchison 1988, p. 400, note 12.
4. OC III, p. 904. "une constitution qui porte un peuple à s'étendre sur toute la surface de son territoire, à s'y fixer, à le cultiver dans tous ses points, à aimer la vie champêtre, les travaux qui s'y rapportent, à y trouver si bien le necessaire et les agrémens de la vie qu'il ne desirent point d'en sortir."
5. Ibid., p. 906.
6. See Chapter 6 below. OC III, p. 923.
7. See p 85 below

With respect to representation the text advocates that all citizens should have equal opportunity to be appointed to public offices[1] and no class should be allowed unique privileges or unique power – legally or economically. Rousseau's view on aristocratic privileges is apparent in his reaction to Buttafoco's "mémoire" in response to Rousseau's quest for information. Buttafoco answered in December 1764 with a "mémoire" including some criticism of Paoli's "constitution" for its anti-aristocratic principles. He wanted the former privileges of the Corsican nobility restored.[2] However, Rousseau's way of handling Buttafoco's plans shows that he comes very close to Paoli's ideas. He spends several pages explicitly combating all ideas of a "necessary" reactionary restitution of the Corsican nobility. In a personal letter of reply to Buttafoco he very straightforwardly declares that, after having looked at the "mémoire", he finds his own ideas immensely[3] divergent from the captain's. And, he adds that he now understands that his own future proposals might possibly meet with considerab-le discontent, "and perhaps above all from yourself".[4]

Finally, the text contains some proposals concerning taxation. They are interesting because they reveal how Rousseau weighs the collective need of finance for public administration versus the entitlement to private property. Public administration should be financed, and becomes for that reason a threat to private property. The text is not exact concerning the rights to private property, but at least it rules out certain extreme alternative interpretations. Firstly, Rousseau defends the existence of private property. A certain amount of private property is necessary, he claims. Public rights should not expand to the point where this minimum would be endangered, but below that they should be as large as possible and private property consequently as small and weak as possible. Private property should then be regarded as necessary but secondary to the public good.[5]

Three kinds of taxation could be used to finance public administration depending on the situation of the moment. Rousseau distinguishes between two phases in the development of public administration: a phase of build-up, and a phase of maintenance. During the former phase, land laying idle should be used to establish public estates, and income from these estates should be the only source of public revenue. Peasant land should, however, never be transformed (for example, by expropriation of land) to public estates. Later, when society is more developed, a production-related tax like the tithes can be introduced. The experience from ecclesiastical tithes shows that their administration can be rather simple. For a third source of revenue, Rousseau suggests corvée taxation. Its advantage is that it requires an active popular participation in the public

1. OC III, pp. 909f.
2. Stelling-Michaud, OC III, p. CCIIff.
3. "prodigieusement"
4. Stelling-Michaud, OC III, p. CCVI.
5. OC III, p. 930. "il suffit de faire entendre ici ma pensée qui n'est pas de détruire absolument la proprieté particulière parce que cela est impossible mais de le renfermer dans les plus étroites bornes. de lui donner une mesure, une règle, un frein qui la contienne, qui la dirige, qui la subjugue et la tienne toujours subordonnée au bien public. Je veux en un mot que la proppriété de l'ètat soit aussi grande, aussi forte, et celle des citoyens aussi petit, aussi foible qu'il est possible."

administration. By being actively involved, citizens could more easily become committed to the public good. This kind of revenue, from the direct use of the labour power of the people, should be preferred as a source of public finance – their "hearts rather than their purses". The example of Switzerland showed that it could be used in a democratic way, claimed Rousseau.[1]

## *Ecological equilibrium*

The political economy of the island should be organised so that the government could control the exploitation of natural resources, for it was important that the natural environment be well conserved. Although the supply of wood for carpeting and shipyards was presently superabundant, no one should trust that this affluence would last. Hence, it should not be left to the "private discretion of the proprietors" to determine the lumbering of the forests. In step with population growth, a fast devastation of the forests could likely take place. The result would be damage which could be repaired only in the very long run. Soil erosion in France and Switzerland offered alarming examples of what could happen if this type of problem was addressed too late. A firm conservation policy should regulate the exploitation of the woods so that consumption and reproduction balance.

> The island abounds with wood, as well for building material as for fuel, but one should not confide in this abundance and leave the usage and cutting of the forests to the sole discretion of the proprietors. In the same measure with which the population of the island grows and the cultivations multiply, a rapid devastation of the woods will take place which will only be repairable very slowly.

In order to counter this prospect "it is necessary to establish in good time an exact policy for the forests, and regulate the cuttings in such a way that reproduction equals consumption."[2] The economic policy must be concerned with the future of society. The capability of the citizens to survive as well in the future must be protected.

1. OC III, pp. 931f. The idea has appeared now and then in political philosophy and practice, sometimes in perverse form (as in the Khmer rouge violence). A democratic example may come from the time of the formation of the Swedish welfare state where it was represented by the minister of social welfare Gustaf Möller.

2. OC III, pp. 926f. "L'Isle abondoit en bois tant pour la construction que pour le chauffage mais il ne faut pas se fier à cette abondance et abondonner l'usage et la coupe des forets à la seule discretion des propriètaires. A mesure que la population de l'Isle augmentera et que les defrichements de multiplieront il se fera dans les bois un degât rapide qui ne pourra se réparer que trés lentement." "Il faut établir de bonne heure une exacte police sur les forets et en régler tellement les coupes que la reproduction égale la consommation."

## *The Right to Live*

Corsica was, as mentioned above, a kind of virgin soil, a test case for grand ideological constructions. At the time, the island was in a very special situation in Rousseau's eyes. It was poor in monetary terms, but rich in resources for subsistence. It was unspoilt by civil society but suffered from the effects of war. Uncultivated land was still available for land reclamation and intensified exploitation. Rousseau suggested a policy of economic self-reliance based on subsistence agriculture. The farmsteads should be dispersed as evenly as possible over the entire island., resulting in the outcome of steady population growth.

But such a proposed economic structure is dependent on a small population. By proposing a policy that would increase the size of the population Rousseau in fact advocated a policy that would remove the basis for subsistence farming. If this is taken into consideration, subsistence farming was consequently advocated merely as a temporary policy, as a non-basic judgment offered as legitimate only during a transient historic interval.

With respect to the modernisation process, Fetscher compares Rousseau unfavourably with the physiocrats and ends up in a position close to Galliani's. He finds Rousseau "understanding for the importance of the high nobility".[1] This position is hard to accept with respect to the PROJET. Writing from a different rhetorical position than that in the CONSIDÉRATIONS, Rousseau (as I tried to show above) ends up very far from the *idéologie nobiliaire* of Galliani. He accepts unambiguously that the protection of everybody's right to live is one of the most basic duties of government. The high priority Rousseau gives to this right is also evident, for example, from an ethical reflection in EMILE:

> Everyone must live; this argument, which appeals to every one with more or less force in proportion to his humanity, strikes me as unanswerable when applied to oneself.

The basic-ness of this "right" also appears in an example. If a man has no other option than to commit a crime in order to survive he should not be held responsible. If conditions are so awful, it is those responsible for such a perverse state, and not the poor, who should be punished.[2]

1. Fetscher 1960, p. 258. ". . . der Republikaner Rousseau, weit mehr Verständnis für die Bedeutung des Hochadels aufbringt, als die scheinbaren Anwälte des adligen Großgrundbesitzes, die zwar die soziale und wirtschaftliche Bedeutung der 'propriétaires' gewaltig übertrieben, nich aber ihre Unabhängigkeit von der Krone verlangt haben, sondern im Gegenteil für einen 'despotisme légal' eintraten, der ganz im Sinne der geschichtlichen Tendenzen lag. So gesehen sind die Physiokraten verglichen mit Rousseau auch in politischer Hinsicht 'moderner' gewesen."

2. OC I, p. 467. [Rousseau 1984b p. 156] "Il faut que tout homme vive. Cet argument auquel chacun donne plus ou moins de force, à proportion qu'il a plus ou moins d'humanité, me paroît sans réplique pour celui qui le fait, relativement à lui même." Rousseau applied this principle to his own case when he tried to defend to Mme. Dupin that he had sent his children to an orphanage.

* * *

There are, no doubt, some peculiarities in Rousseau's position on Corsica, besides those already mentioned. What does he mean by his narrow balance between private property and public rights? And what about local autarchy: why should every family be as self-sufficient as possible, but never *fully* independent? And, it seems that his proposals are largely constructed to secure the mere physical survival of the inhabitants, their "right to live", and their independence. So what about the quality of life beyond survival? Before tackling the last question, I shall discuss two questions which both concern the right to live: the role of international trade, and the character of trade with that most necessary of all goods: corn. The former question will be attacked first.

# 5. STARVING FOR CANDY

# *The Futility of Mercantilism*

IN THE CASE OF CORSICA, Rousseau proposes a policy of national self-sufficiency. This policy is legitimised by the specific situation of Corsica at the time. But what does he have to say about international trade more generally? How does he, for instance, treat this issue in his other case study, that of Poland? The answer is that, again, international exchange is rejected. If Poland were to apply the same internationalist economic policy as the other nations of Europe, then violence, greed, servility, inequality and other social problems would result.[1] Such a policy would be infantile:

> ...and then, like Pyrrhus, like the Russians, which is to say like little children – you will be able to say: 'When the world is mine, I am going to eat lots and lots of candy'.[2]

Such an imitation of "the other peoples of Europe" is deemed unworthy of adults. It would merely be to "make a great splash". This chapter discusses the reason for and character of this rejection.

## *Counting People like a Herd of Cattle*

In the CONSIDÉRATIONS SUR LE GOUVERNEMENT DE POLOGNE[3], Rousseau very clearly declares that he proposes another policy. It is, in the strongest possible words, contrasted to the "candy" option. The two policies are "mutually exclusive" and any reader wanting to find out how to develop or perhaps reform the "candy" policy is strongly dissuaded from trying to learn anything from Rousseau's analysis. It is necessary to choose either one.

1. OC III, p.1003. [Rousseau 1985, p.67]. A similar warning can be found in the long note IX of the second DISCOURS. OC III, pp. 202ff.
2. Ibid., p. 1002.
3. In the 11th of the 15 chapters, the chapter on "political economy".

> Since the two plans of action I speak of are for the most part mutually exclusive, you must, above all, not try to combine them. By attempting both, through some sort of mixed policy, you would cut yourself off from success with either. Choose the one or the other, then. But if you prefer the first, do not read what follows; for all the proposals I have still to offer relate exclusively to the second.[1]

What does Rousseau refer to by the "first" plan of action? What are the characteristics of his rejection? Is it an unconditional rejection of international trade motivated by basic values or does it refer to some specific economic strategy? Is the rejection basic or instrumental to a more general principle? It seems again that the latter is the case.

The rejected policy is explicitly characterised as a mixture of principles. Some of these principles seem rather trivial and uncontroversial, others more specific and disturbing. It is a policy to stimulate culture, military power and trade. The Polish people (through their noblemen) are, in that policy, advised of several lines of action:

> Cultivate the sciences, the arts, commerce, industry; have regular troops, fortified places, academies, and, above all, a fine financial system, which will make money circulate smoothly and so multiply and greatly enrich you! Strive to render money absolutely necessary so as to keep your people highly dependent – which calls also for fomenting material luxury and the luxury of the spirit that is inseparable from it![2]

The most important property of the rejected plan of action is the establishment of "a fine financial system". This concept is rather obscure but has to do with monetarisation and constructing an institutional frame favourable for the circulation of money. Some of the obscurity of this concept can be minimised because of the fact that the idea appears rather frequently in other parts of Rousseau's "text". These other instances can enrich the basis for our interpretation and may, therefore, be worth looking at initially.

## *The "financial system"*

The concept "financial system" seems stable, consistent and well-defined wherever it appears in Rousseau's "text". It plays an important catalytic role, and seems mostly to refer to a *specific* doctrine to which his own philosophy is presented as an alternative. Often, when he characterises his own views, it is

1. OC III, p. 1004. [Rousseau 1985, p. 68]. "Ne tentez pas surtout d'allier ces deux projets; ils sont trop contradictoires, et vouloir aller aux deux par une marche composée, c'est vouloir manquer tous deux. Choisissez donc, et si vous préférez le prémier parti cessez ici de me lire; car de tout ce qui me reste à proposer, rien ne se rapporte plus qu'au second." See also a passage in the Projet de Constitution pour la Corse, OC III, p. 905.
2. OC III, p. 1002. "Cultivez les sciences, les arts, le commerce, l'industrie, ayez des troupes reglées, des places fortes, des Académies, surtout un bon système de finances qui fasse bien circuler l'argent, qui par là le multiplie, qui vous en procure beaucoup; travaillez à le rendre très necessaire, afin de tenir le peuple dans une grande dependenace, et pour cela fomentez et le luxe matériel, et le luxe de l'esprit. qui en est inseparable!"

evident that he contrasts them to some rather well-defined policy, as in the quote from the CONSIDÉRATIONS. In the FRAGMENTS POLITIQUES[1], Rousseau refers, for example to "the system that I attack":

> Firstly, even in the system I attack, it is evident, concerning commerce and the arts, that they are only means ...[2]

These words appear in a context without prior reference; and thus it seems that Rousseau must have regarded it as self-evident that his readers understood what he meant by "the system I attack", and that it was so obvious that no further explanation was necessary. That the *"financial system"* is a rather consistent and precise concept in his "text" is notable from the fact that it usually appears as a single rhetorical figure. The "system" – or sometimes "systems" – is generally contrasted to the political economy of classical antiquity. In the PROJET DE CONSTITUTION POUR LA CORSE Rousseau claims that:

> The financial systems are modern inventions. The word 'finance' was hardly better known among the 'anciens' than 'taille' and 'capitation'.[3]

It is expressed almost identically in the first DISCOURS and in the CONSIDÉRATIONS. Here is its presentation in the CONSIDÉRATIONS:

> The financial systems are modern. I can see nothing good or great coming out of them. The ancient governments didn't even know the word 'finance'.[4]

These three examples represent Rousseau's entire productive life, from the late 1740's to the early 1770's. Hence it appears that this rhetorical figure of "the system" was remarkably stable.

The details of his characterisations of the "system he attacked" show, further, that he was well-informed about the prevalent economic doctrines of his time. There are several examples of how texts are spiced, under their surfaces, with allusions to other treatises. Some of these allusions give more than a clue to what the target of the attack might be.

The earliest example can be found in the DISCOURS SUR LES SCIENCES ET LES ARTS. In this example, Rousseau does not yet use the actual words "financial system", but the characterisation of the policy he criticizes is the same. He contrasts the "ancient politicians", not to the "the financial system", as he does in the later formulations, but to "our" modern politicians, who care about nothing but "commerce and silver". An example is provided of the perverse consequences of this modern attitude:

1. Fragment VII:2.
2. OC III, p. 519. "Premièrement quant au commerce et aux arts, il est de la dernière evidence même dans le systême que j'attaque que ces choses sont plustôt les moyens . . ."
3. OC III, p. 929. "Les système de finances sont des inventions modernes, Ce mot de finance n'étoit pas plus connu des anciens que ceux de taille et de capitation."
4. Ibid., p. 1004. "Les systèmes de finances sont modernes. Je n'en vois rien sortir de bon ni de grans. Les Gouvernemens anciens ne connoisoient pas même ce mot de finance..."

> The ancient politicians spoke endlessly about 'moeurs' and virtues; ours only talk about commerce and silver: One tells you that a human being in a certain country is worth twice what they sell him for at Algiers.[1]

Others, he continues,who calculated in a similar way, found countries where "a man is worth nothing", and even those where he is "worth less than nothing"[2].

> They evaluate human beings like a herd of cattle. According to them a man is worth no more to the state than his consumption. One Sybarite, then, would have been worth 30 Spartans.[3]

These lines include clear references to other treatises. The idea of calculating the value of a human being in terms of her consumption was formulated in a work to which Rousseau himself explicitly refers in connection with this DISCOURS. In the DERNIÈRE RÉPONSE: A. M. BORDES which was published in May 1752, he mentions the ESSAI SUR LE COMMERCE, written by Jean-François Melon in 1734-6. Melon had presented a detailed method for calculating the value of "land, humans and shipping". In Rousseau's words, he had counted humans "like a herd of cattle".

The comparison with the value of a slave at Algiers does not appear in Melon's essay. It is, however, used in an older work to which Melon in his turn refers (with a critical remark): Sir William Petty's FIVE ESSAYS IN POLITICAL ARITHMETICK, published in French (before the English edition) in 1686. Petty calculates the value of a human being in England to be a little more than 80 Pounds sterling and compares this to the "intrinsic value" of a person in Paris, to the victims of "unnecessary deaths in Paris" and to the *"slaves in Algiers"*. The FIVE ESSAYS may have become known to Rousseau through Abbé de Saint-Pierre whom Rousseau probably met in the early 1740s, and who mentions them with enthusiasm. He could also have received the information through Diderot or through Melon's reference. But Diderot's reference to Petty[4] is less detailed and accurate than are the lines by Rousseau. And Rousseau obviously knew Petty's ideas so well that he came to a different opinion from the Abbé, whose judgments he otherwise appreciated.[5]

Rousseau attacks the "financial system" by contrasting it with classical antiquity. But he also uses another argument: it is not efficient. This can be seen

1. OC III, pp. 19f. "Les anciens Politiques parloient sans cesse de moeurs et de vertu; les notres ne parlent que de commerce et d'argent. L'un vous dira qu'un homme vaut en telle contrée la somme qu'on le vendroit à Alger."
2. Rousseau, as we have seen above, later used the same expressions to characterize the social polarisation of Poland (OC III, p. 972.)
3. OC III, pp. 19f. "un autre en suivant ce calcul trouvera des pays où un homme ne vaut rien, et d'autres où il vaut moins que rien. Ils évaluent les hommes comme des troupeaux de bétail. Selon eux, un homme ne vaut à l'État que le consommation qu'il fait. Ainsi un Sybarite auroit bien valu trente Lacédémoniens."
4. The Encyclopédie, Vol II, the article on "celibacy".
5. Havens 1940, pp. 499f. On Melon, see also Hutchison 1988, pp. 219f. Another interesting possibility is, of course, that this formulation was so well known that it was common knowledge in the intellectual circles of Europe.

from an example, the international success of "a handful of herring fishers". Neither of these arguments (that of classical antiquity nor of the herring fishers) was new. Both examples had appeared before; for instance, in the debate on Bernard Mandeville's FABLE OF THE BEES OR PRIVATE VICES, PUBLICK BENEFITS, published in 1724. In the DISCOURS SUR LES SCIENCES ET LES ARTS, Rousseau explains the success of the "handful of herring fishers" (the Netherlands) against the Habsburg empire and all its tresors. The Dutch people, Rousseau claimed, were successful because of a strong social morale, not because of a political arithmetic that calculated the value of the people.

> Finally all the power and all the wisdom of the heir of Charles the fifth, supported by all the tresors of the Indias came to be annihilated against a handful of herring fishers. Would our politicians condescend to suspend their calculations to reflect about their example, and that they would once learn that one has got everything with silver, except mœurs and citizens![1]

In THE FABLE OF THE BEES Mandeville countered the claim (contrary to his own view that private vices could sum up to public opulence) that the Netherlands had acquired its strength and success by being a virtuous and frugal people. Mandeville, born Dutch,[2] was not, of course, able to deny the success of the Netherlands. Neither could he deny that domestic consumption (luxury) in the Netherlands was minimized by comparatively heavy taxes and large savings. But he could argue that this "frugality" was involuntary. Mandeville ascribes the "grandeur" of the Dutch to "their political wisdom", their encouragement of trade and the "unlimited liberty of conscience" among them.[3] Mandeville had himself referred to the futility of the Habsburgian Indian treasures. These treasures were obtained with cruelty and at great cost. They took:

> the Lives of Twenty Millions of *Indians*; as soon, I say, that Ocean of Treasures came rolling in upon them, it took away their Senses, and their Industry forsook them...[4]

The Habsburgs cared about nothing but "the Conquest of the World". Their economic policy was characterised by bullionism, Mandeville claims. And Mandeville's critique served the argument in favour of a modern mercantilist policy based on the stimulation of each individual's wish to gain.[5] Rousseau could, in his turn, in the formulation about "the handful of herring fishers" exploit Mandeville's anti-bullionist critique against Habsburg in order to show the importance of collective morality. He, however, contrasted the Habsburg

1. OC III, p. 20. "Enfin toute la puissance et toute la sagesse de l'héritier de Charles-quint, soutenües de tous les trésors des Indes, vinrent se briser contre une poignée de pêcheurs de harang. Que nos politiques daignent suspendre leurs calculs pour refléchir à ces examples, et qu'ils aprennent une fois qu'on a de tout avec de l'argent, hormis des mœurs et des Citoyens."
2. Kaye 1924, p. xvii.
3. Mandeville 1924, p. 185.
4. Ibid., 1924, pp. 195f.
5. Like several other mercantilists (e.g. Thomas Mun) Mandeville was not a bullionist. Cf., Herlitz 1989.

"tresors", not to the Dutch "political wisdom" mentioned by Mandeville, but to their "mœurs and citizens". And those qualities were far beyond the reach of the calculations of the mercantilists (even of modernists such as Mandeville). Rousseau's extension of Mandeville's example struck at the very core of Mandeville's thesis.[1] In another sense, however, Rousseau agreed with Mandeville: success in the international competition for favourable bargaining positions was not the result of virtue. On the contrary, the successful "financial systems" were closely connected with the lack of a certain virtue: true citizenship.

With regard to these issues, references to ancient culture were often used in moralist condemnations of the search for wealth and luxury. It pays to be virtuous, was the message.[2] Bernard Mandeville tried to show that this message was hypocritical. In his "defence" of the thesis that "private vices" create public opulence, he had to counter the argument that ancient Sparta was feared and esteemed in spite of the frugality and exemplary virtues of its people. It had been argued, for example by the Danish playwrite Ludvig Holberg,[3] contrary to Mandeville, that frugal Sparta's wealth proved that virtue and not luxury would cause economic success. To that, Mandeville responded in several ways. Here is one formulation:

> But certainly there never was a Nation whose Greatness was more empty than theirs: The Splendor they lived in was inferior to that of a Theatre, and the only thing they could be proud of, was, that they enjoy'd nothing.[4]

In order to prevent luxury, Mandeville continues, the Spartans even had their meals in common. It is, however, to be noted that Mandeville does not question the existence of wealth in Sparta. His argument rests, rather, on a notion of the general unpleasantness of Spartan society.[5] So perhaps also Rousseau's comparison between the minimal value of a Spartan and the higher value of a Sybarite is aimed at Mandeville. The Sybarites were referred to for their alleged "vicious" indulgence in pleasure. Rousseau, however, nowhere in his argument claims that virtue *per se* causes wealth, which is the doctrine Mandeville reveals as hypocritical. Nor does Rousseau even question Mandeville's claim that private vices may cause opulence (in the sense of possession of bullion) for successful nations.

## *The two systems*

The idea about the two systems appears for the first time in the DISCOURS SUR LES SCIENCES ET LES ARTS in the late 1740s. The comparison of systems is not unique. It appears later in AN INQUIRY INTO THE NATURE AND CAUSES OF THE

1. Launay (1989, pp. 199f) contrasts Rousseau's position to Mandeville's.
2. Kaye 1924, p. xcif.
3. Holberg writes in the Epistles (Ed Bruun 1865-75: Vol I, letter 21): "The Lacedæmonian lawgiver Lycurgus has by his constitution shown, that a Country without such vices, the necessity of which Mandeville preaches, not only can defend itself from others, but also can become a considerable power." Mandeville 1929, p. 430.
4. Mandeville 1924, p. 245.
5. As pointed out by Kaye, Mandeville's editor. Mandeville 1924, p. 247.

WEALTH OF NATIONS. There Smith contrasts "the commercial or mercantile system" with "the agricultural system". Smith claims that the different economic conditions in the past have generated "two different systems of political economy, with regard to enriching the people". Smith, like Rousseau, attacks the "modern system". His great work is basically designed as a great attack against the mercantilist system. He characterises its fundamental maxim in this way:

> To grow rich is to get money; and wealth and money, in short, are, in common language, considered as in every respect synonymous.[1]

Smith's characterisation and critique of the system is, of course, elaborated to an extent which Rousseau's discussion is not. But nevertheless the two arguments have, largely, the same target.

Like Smith, Rousseau claims that mercantilist policy – "the financial systems" – is constructed to suit particular groups in the different nations. It aims to realise certain "particular wills";[2] not the general will of all, the best for, or the choice of, the people. The same "Christian nations" which, in the CONSIDÉRATIONS SUR LE GOUVERNEMENT DE POLOGNE, are said to apply the "economic systems", are described as governed by the cunning greed of a small group of people in power.[3] The mercantilist quest for silver and commerce is not rational from the point of view of the people at large, but only for individual, privileged agents. It generates a political "fanaticism" which even constitutes a threat to that European political stability which is in the "true interest" of the European peoples:

> because all depends now on the economic systems, most of them quite bizarre, which pass through the heads of the ministers.[4]

Rousseau's negative attitude to mercantilism has occasionally been observed. Galliani states (without any detailed argument) that Rousseau in the PROJET DE CONSTITUTION POUR LA CORSE, "condemned" mercantilism.[5] Fetscher, likewise

1. Smith 1976, p. 429 (introduction to book IV).
2. For this concept, see below p. 98f.
3. OC III, pp. 1037f. [Rousseau 1985, p. 111]. "Elles ne connoissent d'autres liens que ceux de leurs intérests . . .", ". . .l'intérest momentané d'un Ministre, d'une fille, d'un favori", ". . . et toute cette belle doctrines des intérests des Princes est un jeu d'enfants qui fait rire les hommes sensés."
Smith 1976, p. 438.
4. EXTRAIT DU PROJET DE PAIX PERPÉTUELLE DE MONSIEUR L'ABBÉ DE SAINT PIERRE. OC III, pp. 572f. "tout dépend maintenant des systêmes économiques, la plûpart fort bizarres, qui passent par la tête des Ministres." Rousseau did not share the contemporary idea that foreign trade would civilise the nations. The commentator in the OC III, Sven Stelling-Michaud points out, in a note, the difference to Montesquieu and Mirabeau but also the similarity to the concepts of the former French minister of foreign affairs, d'Argenson. OC III, p. 1547.
Galliani regards d'Argenson as a leading exponent of the aristocratic ideology he claimed Rousseau shared (See chapter 2 above). According to a reference in the Contrat Social (Book II, chapter XI) D'Argenson had an even more pessimistic view than Rousseau on the virtue of foreign trade: "Quelque branche de commerce extérieur, dit M. d'A., ne répand gueres qu'une fausse utilité pour un royaume en général; elle peut enrichir quelques particuliers, même quelques villes, mais la nation entiere gagne rien, et le peuple n'est pas mieux." OC III, p. 392.
5. Galliani 1989, p. 3.

without closer examination, notices that Rousseau's theory in several ways "differed" from mercantilist thought.[1] But the precise character of Rousseau's criticism has hardly been brought to light. Here, I try to show that his rejection is consistent throughout the "text", well-informed and reasonably argued. The CONSIDÉRATIONS SUR LE GOUVERNEMENT DE POLOGNE sheds some light on the argument.

## *The Case of Poland*

In the royal election of 1762 Stanislaw August Poniatowski was elected king of Poland. Apparently the choice was dictated by the Russian empress, Catherine the Great. It is said that Poniatowski had served as her lover. The newly elected king proved, however, to be far from that toothless marionette the Romanov dynasty might have intended him to be.

Influenced by the Enlightenment, Poniatowski tried to initiate political reform, causing a certain discomfort among the Russian rulers.[2] Their violent reaction to reform initiated an increased anti-Russian militancy among the Polish nobility. It materialised in the Confederation of Bar which demanded unconditional Polish independence and, in its turn, gave occasion to a Russian armed intervention resulting, in 1772, in the "first partition" of Poland. Three slices of Polish territory were cut off and redistributed to Russia, Austria and Prussia, respectively.[3]

In the middle of this dramatic development, a Polish convention congregated in 1769 decided to ask three foreign "experts" for advice on how to construct a new constitution. Rousseau was to be one of them, Mably another. The request was remitted to Rousseau by Count Wielhorsky. The experts were to consider in particular a reform program earlier proposed at the Bar convention.[4] The modernist reformers in the congregation wanted above all four fundamental changes of the Polish political system: that the elective monarchy be replaced by a hereditary monarchy, that a professional army be raised, that the imperative mandates to the Diet, and the *liberum veto* in it, be abolished in order to make parliamentary work more efficient.[5] In Western Europe, such archaic properties of the constitution, which the modernists opposed, had been swept away centuries earlier with the reign of absolutism. Besides these constitutional demands, the modernists wanted to open up Poland economically to the West.

Rousseau seems to have written his answer some time before April 1772, probably even before November 1771.[6] At this time, Poland was not definitely partitioned, but the cause of the Confederates was in mortal danger. It was not even in high regard everywhere among the Western European intelligentsia. Voltaire, for instance, had recently attacked the "fanaticism" of the confederates.[7]

1. Fetscher 1960, p. 249.
2. Grochulska 1982, p. 249.
3. Fedorowicz 1982, pp. 241ff.
4. OC III, p. 1735.
5. Kendall 1985, pp. XXIIIf.
6. OC III, p. 1734 and pp. CCXXXVIIf. (Stelling-Michaud).
7. OC III, p. 1735 and p. 1739.

The CONSIDÉRATIONS was not published until after Rousseau's death, in 1782.[1] It was, however, almost immediately after its delivery, circulated in manuscript form both in Paris and even, secretly, in Poland. Several manuscripts have been identified, with corrections and changes successively inserted. Rousseau was initially ignorant of this circulation and, as he had delivered the CONSIDÉRATIONS to Wielhorsky against an explicit promise that it would not be circulated in public without his concent, he was naturally upset when informed about it.[2]

## *Rousseau's interpretation of Poland's predicament*

How did Rousseau understand the context of the text? Firstly, regarding its political context, it is crucial to keep in mind the very fragile and specific political situation of Poland. It had been more or less constantly occupied for a long time and there was not much hope of liberation in the near future. According to one commentator, Kendall, the basic political problem of the text was: "How can the Poles remain 'free' even under a Russian occupation?"[3]

Secondly, Rousseau thought that the economic predicament was such that Poland had enough natural resources for a safe provisioning of its own, with food, clothing and shelter.[4] Beyond that, however, the country was in poor condition. But despite its miserable situation, Poland (like Corsica) possessed one startling resource, its moeurs, undisturbed by developments elsewhere in Europe. The cultural heritage was still vital. This was in the last instance the only true protection against all foreign dangers.

Thirdly, Rousseau in fact realized the tragic class structure of Poland. He found that the people could be divided into three social classes: the nobility "who counts for everything", the middle-class "who counts for nothing" and the peasants "who count for less than nothing". Nevertheless, he did, as mentioned,[5] make his proposals on the basis of the existing social system.

Rousseau did not side with the modernists. Poland should not become a modern nation state like France or England.[6] The strive for modernity was dangerously connected with a hunger for *"false goods"*. Instead he proposed institutions suitable for provisioning the nation with "genuine goods"[7] so that international trade could be avoided and the country less dependent on the West. The reform proposals of the modernists deserved, then, to be rejected.

Rousseau argued for his own proposals versus the "plan of action" of "the other nations of Europe" along four lines. The former policy (1) would guarantee the people a safe corn supply and thereby international independence. The latter strategy, on the contrary, would cause a ***vulnerable bargaining position*** in international trade because it would make the country dependent on others for

1. Ibid., p. 1889.
2. Ibid., p. 1885 and p. CCXIX.
3. Kendall 1985, p. XIII.
4. OC III, p. 1005.
5. P. 29 above.
6. Kendall 1985, p. XXV.
7. Ibid., p. XXVII.

corn. Further, in Rousseau's proposal, the productive resources should (2) be directed towards providing the people with genuine goods and *true abundance* rather than "false riches", i.e., goods consumed in order to impress others. This proposed policy would create (3) good preconditions for a just division of riches in society, while the monetisation necessary for the latter choice would have caused *social polarization* whereby a few would live in "opulence" and others in "misery", or even "slavery".[1] Finally (4) a strong social morale would be conserved while the latter policy would develop *"venality of hearts"*.

In considering the conditions under which Rousseau's proposal was drafted, it is conceded that the "candy" option may be successful in maximising opulence, given favourable trade conditions. But, even then, it may be a bad choice because of other consequences of the policy. The rejection has a non-basic character. Let us look at the four arguments in the light of a rich "text" reading.

## *Bargaining and Waiting*

The mercantilist policy is characterised as a policy to gain a strategic position within the international trade race: like a pole position in racing. When achieved, that policy will give maximum entitlement to unknown goods, "candy". But such blind position-seeking has its price. Without food "everybody's right to live" is threatened and the country may find itself in an awkward bargaining position that may also deprive it of its freedom. In his argument against the mercantilist policy of bullionism, Rousseau thus reveals that he finds the provision of food primary to the position for maximuml gains from international trade. This argument is based on an understanding of an 18th century version of the quantity theory of money and on an analysis of the role of food in bargaining.

The most extensive discussion on this subject concerns the nature of national wealth. It takes place in two short pieces included in the FRAGMENTS POLITIQUES in the Pleiade edition of Rousseau's work.[2] In these fragments Rousseau is again warning against dependence on international exchange. This gives cause, as so often is the case, to the interpretation that Rousseau's economic philosophy is naïvely aged. Derathé finds here, for example, support for his thesis about the "archaism" of Rousseau's economic philosophy. Rousseau's reflections about the properties of a rich nation express his reveries about a rural paradise.[3] But a close reading of the fragments reveals that such an interpretation is unduly simplistic, and that Derathé's treatment of Rousseau's call for subsistence agriculture as basic, is incorrect. Rousseau does propose a policy favouring subsistence agriculture because it would serve two superior goals: national independence and a secure "conservation"[4] of the people.

1. OC III, pp. 1003f.
2. Fragments VI:8 and VII:2.
3. Note by Derathé, OC III, p. 1526.
4. That is to say: preservation. Conservation is the term Rousseau uses.

## *Money and richness*

The two fragments were written to determine what constitutes a flourishing nation. In this context, mercantilist views were discussed. The cause for the discussion seems to have been a prize questions proposed by the Societé économique de Berne in 1762, at the time Rousseau was working on the proposals for Corsica. One of their questions asked precisely about the properties of a happy and flourishing nation. Rousseau never worked out a specific text in reply; but, in a polite letter to the Societé, he approved of the questions, yet apologized that he lacked the time necessary for an answer.[1] Nonetheless, he seems to have started to work on them. Among the Rousseau papers at Neûchatel there is a dossier with miscellaneous fragmentary texts which also includes some with quite carefully worked out statements on exactly these questions. One of them[2] is even explicitly addressed to the Societé, while another is obviously a more elaborated version of the first.

The argument in the two FRAGMENTS is logically and systematically organised according to a well-known pattern: the structure of the argument in Aristotle's NICHOMACHEAN ETHICS. In this manner, a number of candidate answers are proposed and tried, one after another, until the final standpoint is determined. In order, he explains, to spell out his argument as clearly as possible, Rousseau assumes that the interests of the people and the government are identical. Rousseau tries four optional characteristics of a flourishing nation: a) the arts, b) trade, c) silver and d) the three candidates taken together. In conclusion, all are rejected.

Firstly, a) and b) are easily dismissed. Arts and trade are only means, not ends. The presence of silver is no sure sign of a flourishing nation, he continues – not even under his simplifying assumption. The reason is that the value of a given stock of specie depends on several things besides the stock itself. It depends, for example, on the supply of food within the country and the international terms of trade influenced by that. The enormous Habsburgian treasures acquired in Latin America melt before "a handful of herring fishers" as he expresses it elsewhere.[3] Treasures are worthless in the absence of food. This argument is significant. Consequently, it is not up to the rulers to establish the value of the currency. Rather, it reflects the bargaining position of the nation. The value of silver depends on internal and external conditions. It reflects the conditions of the home market and the terms of trade for the international trade exchange.

One way to capture how internal conditions influence the value of money is through the quantity theory of money. This theory states that the prices times the volume of goods equal the volume of specie times the velocity of its circulation. If $P$= prices of goods, $Q$= the quantity of goods available at the market, $M$= the amount of currency available and $V$= the velocity of the circulation of money then $P \times Q = M \times V$. Rousseau seems to deny this law by saying that "silver by itself has no real value". This contradicts the quantity theory, which claims that the supply of bullion influences its value. Gold and silver are merely "representative signs" for those goods, "matières", for which they are exchanged, Rousseau claims.

1. Note by Derathé, OC III, p. 1526.
2. Fragments VI:8
3. OC III, p. 20.

The fact that Rousseau denies silver and gold any value of their own could be a clear indication of his poor knowledge of economics. At least since the appearance of scholastic Aristotelian theory it was clear that silver as a medium, measurement and conservor for exchange of other goods had an exchange value and use value of its own.[1] During Rousseau's time it was formulated by Cantillon.

When continuing the exposition, Rousseau, however, contradicts himself. He shows, in fact, precisely the opposite of what he claims to; he shows that silver has a value and even presents a rather accurate formulation of the quantity theory. Writing about the value of silver, he states:

> it takes one [a value] by tacit convention in each country where it is in use, and this true value is according to the concurrence of those causes that determine it. These causes could be reduced to three Principle ones, namely: 1. the abundance or rareness of specie, 2. the abundance or rareness of food and other merchandise, 3. the degree of circulation which depends on the quantity of exchanges, which is to say the vigour of the commerce.[2]

As the last lines show, Rousseau in spite of his own assertion, in fact assumes that silver has a value, determined by its supply. The passage is a rude formulation of the quantity theory of money.[3] This again shows that Rousseau was remarkably well-oriented in the economic literature of his time.[4] Perhaps Rousseau knew the writings of Cantillon[5] because of his correspondence at the time with Mirabeau, to whom Cantillon was an influential teacher and source of inspiration[6].

A country with much silver may be poor because it is short on necessities or rich although it is destitute with regard to silver.[7] And to the contrary: with no bullion a country may be affluent "on all those things other peoples would have to use their specie to get." The three candidate determinants do not suffice even if they are present together.

1. For example, in Oresme's treatises from the 14th century. Cf., Langholm 1983.
2. OC III, pp. 520f. "Quoique l'argent n'ait par lui même aucune valeur reelle il en prend une par convention tacite dans chaque paìs où il est en usage et cette valeur vraie selon leconcours des causes qui servent à la déterminer. Ces causes peuvent se reduire à 3 Principles, savoir: 1) l'abondance ou la rareté de l'espéce, 2) l'abondance ou la rareté des denrées et autres merchandises, 3) le dégré de circulation qui dépend de la quantité des échanges c'est à dire de la vigueur du commerce."
". . . dépourvu d'argent et cependant se trouver fort riche par l'abondance de toutes les choses à l'acquisition desquelles les autres peuples sont contraints d'émployer leurs espéces."
3. The quantity theory of Rousseau determines $P$ (the value of money expressed in other goods) by 1) $M$, 2) $Q$ and 3) $V$.
4. It is true that the formulation appears in an unpublished fragment, which calls for some caution. As mentioned above, however, the origin of it seems rather clear.
5. Cantillon 1952. See, e.g. p. 74 and p. 90.
6. Fox-Genovese 1976, pp. 145f.
7. This was in accord with Mandeville. (Mandeville 1924, p. 147.)

## *Dependence on others for food*

Rousseau, however, puts even greater emphasis on a second argument against bullionism, besides that of the quantity theory of money. The essence of this argument is (in modern terminology) that international trade relations must be treated not as parametric but as *strategic* relations: the outcome of the choice of action is dependent on how others choose. Such a situation exists where there is no market, no competition. Then the conditions for exchange are determined, not by a unique market equilibrium which is ideally not influenced by an individual agent, but rather the conditions for exchange are determined by bargaining strength. While in perfect competition, "the discipline of a market ... allows each agent to behave as a solitary decision maker", in bargaining the outcome "is determined entirely by the strategic strength of the bargainers".[1]

This is illustrated by the case of Poland. Active participation in international trade was probably quite feasible for Poland, although the future in general of the country had to be painted in very pessimistic colors. This was in contrast to the situation of Corsica, which, on the contrary, had, at least in the long run, a real chance to reach both independence and economic welfare. But because of 40 years of warfare, the island could not in the short run enrich itself by trade.[2] "Corsica can hardly enrich itself on silver" Rousseau wrote.[3]

As in his advice to Poland, Rousseau again stresses the strategic role of agriculture. Even if international trade had been a feasible alternative for Corsica there was an additional reason why self-sufficient agriculture was necessary for its independence:

> The only means to maintain a nation in independence from others is agriculture. Had you all the riches of the world, but didn't have anything with which to nourish yourselves, you would depend on others.[4]

More precisely, it is the price of bread or grain that matters. In a bargain, that party which is the least dependent, which *"can wait"*, is in a position to "read the law" to the other. By being able to decide the price of the currency and thereby of bread, those with relatively greater autonomy can dictate the terms of trade. Whereas, conversely, there is always a limit to how long the party which needs to buy food can wait. The text continues:

1. Roth 1985, p. 1.
2. OC III, p. 904. "Voici donc les principes qui selon moi doivent servir de base à leur legislation: tirer parti de leur peuple et de leur pays autant qu'il sera possible; cultiver et rassembler leurs propres forces, ne s'appuyer que sur elles, et ne songer pas plus aux puissances étrangéres que s'il en existoit aucune."
3. Ibid., p. 902 and p. 904. "L'isle de Corse ne pouvant s'enrichir en argent doit tâcher de s'enrichir en hommes."
4. Ibid., p. 903. "Le seul moyen de maintenir un Etat dans l'indépendance des autres est l'agriculture. Eussiez-vous toutes les richesses du monde si vous n'avez de quoi vous nourrir vous dépendez d'autrui."

> Your neighbours can set the price for your currency as it suits them, because they can wait, while the bread which for you is necessary, has for you a price that you have no possibility to dispute; for in the entire species of commerce it is always the least pressed who reads the law to the other.[1]

What is portrayed here is a monopolistic bargaining situation far from the Smithian idyll of free, independent agents bidding on a competitive market. The criterion used – "the ability to wait" – resounds from another contemporary economic treatise. It has much of the flavour of how sir James Steuart tried to capture the character of the market as determined by the "degree of eagerness". When the "degree of eagerness" of the sellers was different from that of the buyers, a perverse price equilibrium resulted.[2] Therefore, insecure food provisioning is dangerous not only per se, but also because it weakens the bargaining power and influences the outcome of bargaining between nations.

> Whichever the systems are, the commerce which tends daily to find an equilibrium, in depriving certain Powers of those exclusive advantages which they drew from it, at the same time deprives them of one of their great means by which to read the law to others.[3]

Switzerland was once a poor country, but self-sufficient in provision of foods and could for that reason "read the law for France". But due to mercantilist policies, agriculture was increasingly neglected and the domestic supply of food insufficient. Consequently, the republic became dependent on other nations and "trembled whenever a French secretary of state frowned".[4] Corsica had a choice; once trade had been impeded by the Genoese policy, yet now it was up to Corsica herself. But the island should not try to reopen trade until the constitution was in equilibrium and interior provisioning appeared insufficient: "not until your constitution has reached its equilibrium" and "not as long as the interior provides you".[5]

It is evident from the rest of the treatise that the "until" and "as long as" were seriously intended conditions, and, as mentioned, Rousseau even proposed policies to stimulate population growth. But he found the food market crucial, for dependence on monopolistic food suppliers could be fatal since it could cause a vulnerable bargaining position.

1. OC III, p. 905. "Vos voisins peuvent donner à vôtre argent le prix qu'il leur plait parce qu'ils peuvent attendre; mais le pain qui nous est necessaire a pour nous un prix dont nous ne saurions disputer et dans toute espéce de commerce c'est toujours le moins pressé qui fait la loi à l'autre."
2. Steuart 1966, pp. 167ff. Steuart did, however, not use it as an argument against international trade. Already Thomas Mun in his great discourse on trade distinguished a kind of competitive equilibrium from a monopolistic one. But, as far as I know, neither of them emphasized the importance of self-sufficiency of food for the bargaining situation, as did Rousseau. Cf., Mun 1949.
3. Extrait du projet de paix perpétuelle de monsieur l'abbé de Saint Pierre. OC III, pp. 572f. "Quoi qu'il en soit, le Commerce qui tend journellement à se mettre en équilibre, ôtant à certaines Puissances l'avantage exclusif qu'elles en tiroient, leur ôte en même tems un des grandes moyens qu'elles avoient de faire la loi aux autres."
4. OC III, pp. 916f.
5. Ibid., p. 908. "Ils vous ont ôté presque tous commerce et en effet ce n'est pas maintenant le tems d'en avoir. S'il étoit ouvert au dehors il faudroit l'interdire jusqu'à que vôtre constitution eut pris son assiete et que le dedans vous fournittout ce que vous pouvez en tirer."

## *False Riches*

Mercantilist policy cannot provide a nation with true riches, in Rousseau's opinion. By monetising the economy, it impedes the creation of "true riches". A monetised nation may have "an edge over one with less", but still the citizens may be poor, "because the prosperity of a nation does not depend upon money."[1] This is not only a question of the quantity theory of money and of bargaining power. It refers to something else too: perverting the true value of goods. As I discussed in another context above, Rousseau claims that market prices misrepresent the "true" value of goods. Here he compares the prices of natural resources (like agricultural products) and of manufactured, and finds that the latter tend to be overvalued. He has two criteria for the "true" value of an art: its necessity and its independence of other arts.[2]

As market prices tend to pervert the economy, other inducements must be used to promote the supply of "genuine goods". For that reason the farmers should be encouraged by moral incentives and by an entitlement structure[3] that makes their work agreeable. The necessary or "useful industry" must be strengthened by extra-market means. In particular, importation of manufactured goods should be avoided and manufactured goods necessary for domestic consumption should be facilitated by the establishment of domestic manufacturing, supported by a policy of import substitution.[4]

What does Rousseau mean by "true riches"? Firstly, it is not, as Derathé claims, merely synonymous with or instrumental to a nation's "independence or economic autarchy". The causation is rather the opposite: international independence is urgent because it is the best way to secure "true riches" for the people. In fact, Rousseau gives us more than a hint that this secure availability is what he means by the "happiness of a people". In the unfinished answer to the Societé économique de Berne, a final candidate for describing a happy and flourishing society appears. Such a society is one:

> where everything necessary for life is collected in the country in such a quantity that everyone with his work easily can get all that he needs for his subsistence.[5]

In this explicit statement there is no direct reference either to an intrinsic value of autarchy or to the necessity of peasant life. Society is to create abundance: a secure subsistence for all inhabitants. Derathé thinks that Rousseau in this paragraph merely "wanted to deliver the world from idleness and express a preference for industriousness". It is, of course, possible that Rousseau would dislike a society filled with Oblomovs,[6] but that is hardly the real point here. The

1. OC III, p. 1008. "De peuple à peuple, celui qui a plus d'argent a de l'avantage; mais cela ne fait rien au sort des particuliers, et ce n'est pas là que git la prosperité d'une nation."
2. OC IV, p. 459.
3. The concept is Sen's (Sen 1982d, Chapter 1).
4. OC III, p. 1008.
5. OC III, p. 524. "celui où toutes les choses necessaires à la vie se trouvent rassemblées dans le païs en telle quantité que chacun peut avec son travail amasser aisément tout ce qu'il en faut pour son entretien."
6. The hero of Gontjarov's famous novel OBLOMOV.

statement is not an expression of a moral style but rather an urgent political necessity in a world of strategic bargaining that threatens people with starvation.[1] Moreover, the point is that the creation of this kind of richness is a realistic option and not merely a utopian dream "where the whole world finds under its hand, without work and pain, enough to satisfy all its needs."[2]

What, more exactly, does Rousseau mean by "everything necessary for life"? And what does he imagine that such a realistic policy should look like? I shall return to those questions towards the end of this essay.

### *Polarisation*

The third problem is that mercantilist policy and monetarisation in particular stimulates economic polarisation in society. An egalitarian flavour is discernible in the very concept of happiness or "abundance". In the Bern paper Rousseau approaches this concept by stating what it is not. Thus, "abundance" is not:

> a situation where some individuals overflow with everything while the rest of the people are forced to flee to them in order to receive their subsistence, at a price that the former could set as they please.[3]

In a remarkable passage of the DISCOURS SUR L'ORIGINE ET LES FONDEMENTS DE L'INÉGALITÉ Rousseau gives his interpretation of "happiness" a natural law-legitimation. It is odd since the DISCOURS is a furious attack against natural law theory and particularly against its use as a legitimation of social institutions.[4]

> it is contrary to the law of nature that ... the privileged few should gorge themselves with superfluities, while the starving multitudes are in want of the bare necessities of life.[5]

Social and economic polarisation is not only bad in itself but also dangerous for the secure provision of the people with "everything necessary for life". The argument is that mercantilism, by monetarising the economy, supplies a form of riches that in itself causes inequality and insecure provision with the necessities for life. Monetary wealth is by nature relative. It can be accumulated only as a sign of relative wealth. The *only* use, Rousseau even claims, of monetary richness, is its value relative to that of others.

1. For modern examples, see Sen 1982d. For historical examples, see, e.g., Abel 1971.
2. OC III, p. 523. "où tout le monde trouveroit sous sa main sans travail et sans peine de quoi satisfaire à tous ses besoins".
3. Ibid., p. 523. "je n'entends pas par ce mot une situation où quelques particuliers regorgentde touttes choses tandis que tout le reste du peuple en contraint de recourir à eux pour en recevoir sa subsistance au prix qu'il leur plait d'y mettre..."
4. See below p. 108.
5. OC III, p. 194. [Rousseau 1983, p. 105]. "il est manifestement contre la Loi de Nature, de quelque maniére qu'on la définisse . . . qu'une poigné de gens regorge de superfluités, tandis que la multitude affamée manque du nécessaire."

> Pecuniary wealth is purely relative. According to the circumstances (which may change for any of ten thousand reasons), one can with one and the same amount of money, be rich one moment and poor the next. But with one and the same amount of real goods, no such thing can happen: they are directly useful to man, and so have always an absolute value that the operations of the market cannot effect.[1]

Derathé observes that it is not riches *per se* which are relative, but pecuniary riches.[2] I think this is a reasonable reflection, but still not correct. As Derathé points out – and as the quote shows – Rousseau draws a strict borderline between pecuniary wealth and possession of fortunes in kind. That is true. Rousseau claims that pecuniary wealth must be relative, but does not deny that other items too can be relative. On the contrary, he admits that all goods can be accumulated (except perhaps people) and thus create relative wealth.[3]

Rousseau explicitly admits that the concept of richness is ambivalent and that his interpretation of it is not the only possible one. But the two FRAGMENTS POLITIQUES concerning the Bern price question allow us to follow the argument more closely, although the fragments themselves are complex and not always easy to understand. It is often only because of the difference in the amount of "fortunes" that a person is judged "rich" or "poor, he starts. The term "rich" is used for someone who "has more goods than the great number usually have."[4] Richness is here obviously a relative concept. To be poor is not to have less than "enough goods to live" but to have less than "others".[5] It is tempting to think that Rousseau deviates from his earlier-mentioned concept of richness as "everything necessary for life"; and that he either conceives of poverty as relative deprivation,[6] or refers to what Harrod 200 years later called "oligarchic wealth".

The first concept measures or describes poverty as one person's lack of endowments in comparison to someone else's or people in general. To earn *x* £ less than the mean income makes a person poor according to this concept. Such a concept focuses on the fact that relative deprivation excludes the poor from many of those activities that belong to a normal social life.

The Harrodian concept says that certain consumable goods which constitute the richness of rich people do so because the non-rich cannot have them. These goods can be enjoyed as objects of conspicuous consumption. One kind of pleasure or utility in consuming them lies in the status or privilege they give to the consumer. The fact that one can consume something that most people

1. Ibid., p. 1008. [Rousseau 1985, p. 73]. "La richesse pécuniaire n'est que relative, et selon des rapports qui peuvent changer par mille causes, on peut se trouver successivement riche et pauvre avec la même somme, mais non pas avec les biens en nature; car comme immédiatement utiles à l'homme, ils ont touchours leur valeur absolue qui ne dépend point d'une opération de commerce."
2. Ibid., p. 1530.
3. The Considérations, OC III, p. 904.
4. OC III, p. 521. "On donne le nom de riche a un h[omme] qui a plus de bien que le plus grand nombre n'a accoutumé d'en avoir." The insertion is added by the editors in OC.
5. Italics added. Rousseau was not the first to speculate about the implications of relative richness. Hörnigk did for example, in a text from the 1680s. Somewhat similarly to Rousseau, Hörnigk concluded that because of the implications of the relativity of richness dependence should be minimized. Hutchison 1988, p. 94.
6. See, e.g., Sen 1982d, p. 30.

cannot, for example an exclusive car, *is* the use of the good. Other goods may be oligarchic because they lose their enjoyable properties if many people are to consume them, (homes on a unique, beautiful site, close to a city).[1]

Rousseau is aware of the importance of oligarchic consumption. But still neither of these two interpretations captures the point. The argument continues in a way that makes both highly problematic. Suppose, proposes Rousseau, that a nation in fact succeeded in accumulating all the silver and gold of the world! What would that mean to its inhabitants? He discusses two different cases.

If the new wealth would be equally distributed, which Rousseau concedes is highly unlikely, it would be worthless. It could entirely disappear during a night and nothing would be changed. The reason, he claims, is that the only function of "fortune", in this sense, is to manifest the difference between the sizes of the possessions of people. In terms of the quantity theory of money, the only effect of the sudden increase in the supply of money would be to change the numbers on price tags by a fixed factor.

If instead the fortunes were unequally distributed, there would by a kind of multiplier effect causing secondary increases in inequality. The difference by itself would multiply inequality. Here we find again the familiar argument: the more you need something, the less you can wait, and the more you can be exploited in the bargaining process. Therefore, it is the relative richness in itself that is fatal to the poor. It is not because the rich need the resources of the poor that they threaten the poor, but on the contrary, precisely because they do not need them:

> It is the superfluity itself among the rich that puts them in a position to deprive the poor of their necessities.[2]

This is something other than oligarchic goods or relative deprivation. To be poor compared to someone else is dangerous because of its consequences for the bargaining terms. Not only does a country striving for positional advance among other nations risk causing a "difference" that can be dangerous to itself, but the presence of silver inside the country, necessary for such a policy, seems, in Rousseau's eyes, to, cause a similar progressive process of increasing "difference" within the country. In that way, it is doubly dangerous for the poor to be dependent on exchange for the provision of food.

* * *

Instead of accepting the monetary incentives generated by mercantilist policies, society should apply "more powerful and dependable" ones based on a strong social morale, means which are impeded by these policies.[3] I shall return to this problem in Chapters 8 and 9 below.

1. Hirsch 1977. Fetscher in a related spirit perceives that Rousseau here talks about "conspicuous consumption" in the sense of Veblen. Cf., Fetscher 1960, pp. 215f.
2. OC III, p. 521. "la difficulté d'acquérir croit toujours en raison des besoins et que c'est le superflu même des riches qui les met en état de depouiller le pauvre de son necessaire."
3. OC III, p. 1008. The economic importance of social morale has, of course, been emphasised by a number of economists with very different perspectives. See, for example: Sen 1983; Morishima 1982.

6. THE IRON LAW OF PEASANT MISERY

# *The Maladie of the Corn Market*

SEVERAL TIMES already in this essay the food market has been identified as a very important issue in Rousseau's economic thinking. Firstly, it has appeared as a *right,* perhaps even a natural right, which entitles everybody to food enough for her survival. Food provisioning is therefore a prime concern in his economic philosophy. Secondly, it has been given a crucial role in the trade bargaining between countries, influencing terms of trade. Thirdly, food prices have been characterised as perverted. They are said to be determined on a dual market where prices of necessities are set on a different basis than prices of lapri.

The dominant component in the food of most people at Rousseau's time was corn. For that reason the corn market is especially important and must be penetrated in more depth. That is the task of this chapter.

Corn policy was a very urgent and intensely discussed topic in the Parisian mid-century salons. Grimm called it *"la maladie à la mode"* and noticed that the "whole world" was passionately engaged in it. At the time, there were regular grain shortages in France in spite of a traditional interventionist policy to secure the supply of bread and corn in years of low yields. In the 50s this policy was questioned by the physiocrat treatises. Quesnay's Encyclopédie article "Fermiers" was published in 1756, Mirabeau's TRAITÉ DE LA POPULATION in the same year, and the TABLEAU ÉCONOMIQUE in 1758.[1]

Rousseau's reaction to the physiocrat treatises is not wellknown. Mirabeau, in an invitation letter, in fact tried to convert his friend to the doctrine.[2] An unpublished but preserved note taken by Rousseau proves that he had read at least parts of Mirabeau's THEORIE DE L'IMPÔT no later than in 1761.

1. Fox-Genovese 1976, pp. 24f.
2. Jedryka 1952, p. 251; Gossman 1964, p. 337.

The book itself was published in 1760.[1] In his declining answer to Mirabeau, Rousseau accused the physiocrats of being unrealistic. In particular, he demanded more realistic assumptions about human nature:

> Messieurs, permit me to tell you, that you give too much weight to your calculations, and not enough to the propensities of the human heart and the play of passions.[2]

Rousseau did not present any elaborated critique in the letter. But his various comments in other texts show that he was far more pessimistic than the physiocrats about the potentials of market exchange. In his view it was corrupt and perverted.

## *The Ideal Market*

Rousseau does have a conceptualisation of what uncorrupt market exchange would be like. He presents it in EMILE. In order to understand the problem of market exchange, Emile needs to understand how it would function ideally, in pure theory, Rousseau explains. Firstly, he has to understand a fact that is remarkable in view of Rousseau's bitter criticism and his readers' comments. Market exchange of some kind *has to* exist in every society:

> There can be no society without exchange, no exchange without a common standard of measurement, no common standard of measurement without equality. Hence the first law of every society is some conventional equality either in men or things.[3]

Such an equality should preferably be money. Money facilitates exchange by functioning as a common measure.

> It is difficult to make a direct comparison between various things, for instance between cloth and corn; but when we find a common measure, in money, it is easy for the manufacturer and the farmer to estimate the value of the goods they wish to exchange in terms of this common measure.[4]

1. Namer 1969, pp. 239ff.
2. Fabre (in an annotation), OC III, p. 1750. "Messieurs, permettez-moi de vous le dire, vous donnez trop de force à vos calculs et pas assez aux penchants du cœur humain et au jeu des passions."
3. OC IV, pp. 461. [Rousseau 1984b, p. 156]. "Nulle societé ne peut exister sans échange, nul échange sans mesure commune, et nulle mesure commune sans égalité. Ainsi toute societé a pour prémiére loi quelque égalité conventionelle soit dans les hommes soit dans les choses."
4. OC IV, pp. 462. [Rousseau 1984b, p. 157]. "Il est difficile de comparer immédiatement des choses de différentes natures, du drap, par example, avec du bled; mais quand on a trouve une mesure commune, savoir le monnoye, il est aisé au fabricant et au laboureur de rapporter la valeur des choses qu'ils veulent échanger à cette mesure commune."

The presence of this common measure is central to the very existence of society:

> ...in this sense, money is the real bond of society; but anything may be money; in former days it was cattle; shells are used among many tribes at the present day; Sparta used iron; Sweden leather; while we use gold and silver. [1]

So, at least in theory, some measure is necessary whereby incommensurable things can be made commensurable. By capturing the value to society of a certain good, the price provides such a measure. Still, in real life, it is obvious that prices, according to Rousseau, deviate from value. What is the relation, then, between value and price? Why does not the price express the true value of the goods?

Rousseau does in fact answer; although, to our frustration, not in a very elaborate way. There are only two non-arbitrary laws of value, he explains in EMILE.:

> These are the true laws of the value in arts; all others are arbitrary and dependent on popular prejudice.[2]

The character of these laws indicates that his theory of value is not a pure labour theory of value. It includes other production resources besides labour costs, but it is not a pure production cost theory either. It is rather a combined theory wherein value is determined by a kind of use value which constrains the set of feasible resource costs. We get a closer glimpse of it when Rousseau compares the different arts (in the abstract context of Emile's education). First, one scale of values is presented:

> It is in relation to his use of them, his security, his conservation and his wellbeimg that he should judge all substance in nature and every work of man: Thus he should value iron far more than gold, and glass more than diamonds; in the same way he has far more respect for a shoemaker or a mason than for a Lempereur, a Le Blanc, or all the jewelers of Europe. A pastry maker is always an important person in his eyes, and he would give the whole Academy of Science for the least confectioner on Lombard Street.[3]

The non-"arbitrary" laws of value, then, are again based on everybody's right to live. That art which is "most generously useful and necessary" is also the most valuable. Immediately however, after this statement, a secondary, complementary evaluation criterion is introduced, which is independent of the use value of the

1. OC IV, pp. 462. [Rousseau 1984b, p. 157]. Rousseau is here influenced by Aristotle's thought. "...en ce sens la monnoye est le vrai lien de la societé; mais tout peut être monnoye; autrefois le bétail l'ëtoit, des coqillages le sont encore chez plusieurs peuples, le fer fur monnoye à Sparte, le cuir l'a été en Suede, l'or et l'argent le sont parmi nous."

2. OC IV, pp. 460. [Rousseau 1984b, p. 155]. "Voila les véritables règles de l'appréciation des arts et de l'industrie; tout le reste est arbitraire et dépend de l'opinion."

3. OC IV, pp. 459. "C'est par leur rapport sensible avec son utilité, sa sureté, sa conservation, son bien-être, qu'il doit apprécier tous les corps de la nature et tous les travaux des hommes. Ainsi le fer doit être à ses yeux s'un beaucoup plus grand prix que l'or, et le verre que le diamant. De même il honore beaucoup plus un cordonnier, un masson, que l'Empereur, un Le Blanc et tous les joüaillers de l'Europe; un pâtissier est surtout à ses yeux un homme très important, et il donneroit toute l'Academie des sciences pour le moindre confiseur de la rë des Lombards."

good. That art which "requires the least help from other arts", that which is "the freest and most independent", has the highest value:

> There is an order no less natural and even more accurate, by which the arts are valued according to the bonds of necessity which connect them; the highest class consists of the most independent, the lowest of those most dependent on others.[1]

Both scales are non-arbitrary, but tend to become perverted by popular opinion:

> so that the use of raw material is the work of the worst and lowest paid trades, while the more frequently the material changes hands the more the work rises in price and in honour.[2]

But, the categorical statement that the two non-production-cost "laws" are "*the* true laws of the value in arts" and all others "arbitrary", is hard to reconcile with a statement presented in one of the FRAGMENTS POLITIQUES. The fragment deals with the relation between prices and supply and demand. The conclusion is that prices are determined by production costs. By comparing the movement of corn and meat prices when corn productivity increases the argument ends up in a kind of production cost theory.

> If some means were found to make the tilling of the fields easier, and to save the number of oxen that one employs, this invention would by necessity result in a diminuation of the corn price and an augmentation of the meat price.[3]

This statement implies that lower costs of production (easier tilling of the field, fewer oxen needed) cause a reduction of the corn price. It also implies that increasing opportunity costs influences oxen prices. Through the increased productivity of the soil carrying the yield and of the oxen employed in tilling, the prices of alternative uses of these two resources will increase.

It is hard to reconcile these three price determinants. Perhaps the first two (the relative independence of the industry and the use value of the product) are thought of as value determinants and the latter as price determinants. Or, perhaps, Rousseau's idea is that, within the frames given by the social valuation of the arts based on necessity and independence, production costs influence the price and value. Necessity and independence constrain the feasible production cost interval. One thing, however, is clear: when he claims that the true values may be distorted by actual market prices he refers to all three: to "the true laws of value in arts" and to the influence of the production costs on prices.

1. Ib. "Il y a un ordre non moins naturel et plus judicieux encore par lequel on considére les arts selon les rapports de nécessité qui les lient, mettant au prémier rang les plus indépendens, et au dernier ceux qui dépendent dún plus grand nombre d'autres.
2. Ib. En sorte que l'emploi des matiéres prémiéres se fait dans des métiers sans honneur, presque sans profit, et que plus elles changent de mains, plus la main d'œuvre augmente de prix et devient honorable.
3. OC III, p. 525, (Fragment VIII: 3). "Si l'on trouvoit quelque moyen de rendre le labourage plus facile et d'épargner le nombre de Bœufs qu'on y employe il resulteroit nécessairement de cette invention une diminution de prix pour le blé et une augmentation pour le viande."

## *The Iron Law of Peasant Misery*

Production costs on the basis of necessity and independence are not always identical with the real prices on the market. In Chapter 3 above, I referred to the idea that prices of goods, lapri, produced for the entertainment of the rich, are "arbitrary". Now we can add that they are "arbitrary" in the sense that they are not set according to production costs, necessity and independence. Rousseau writes about the "arbitrary prices" on the "lapri" of artists when employed by the rich. In particular these "arbitrary prices" disfavour peasant agriculture.

The idea that agricultural production is disfavoured by market exchange appears already in the DISCOURS SUR L'ÉCONOMIE POLITIQUE[1] and later in the PROJET DE CONSTITUTION POUR LA CORSE.[2] Robert Derathé here merely detects a reflection of Plato's hostility to entertainment industries and luxury crafts.[3] Rousseau does, however, present hard economic arguments when contrasting trade and the interests of agriculture; as in his discussion of corn taxes. In the DISCOURS SUR L'ÉCONOMIE POLITIQUE, the proposition that taxation on agricultural production is a good by itself is rejected. Taxing the peasants' produce would impose a disincentive to an efficient peasant agriculture. An excessive taxation would, moreover, ruin agriculture by perverting the market.

The most interesting part of this discussion is that Rousseau describes a price mechanisms whereby peasants are caught in a cycle of eternal economic misery. It is obvious that this discussion does not concern tax in general, but rather feudal tax. It is clearly supposed in this fragment that, contrary to the case in other parts of Rousseau's text, we have to deal with a non-democratic revenue possessor: a seigneur. And it is not only a question of the character of demand for necessities compared to "lapri".

### *Tax*

Peasant agriculture is threatened by two mechanisms on the existent corn market. As a result of these mechanisms, peasants' market incomes will always be very low. They work like an iron law, similar to the iron law for wages later described by Ricardo. The first mechanism implies that agricultural products are undervalued compared to other goods. The second impedes corn prices from responding adequately to changes in supply. Taxation plays an important part in both. I shall begin with the former mechanism.

Taxation on agricultural products favours industry and commerce, because a considerable part of the revenue is transformed into a demand for industrial and commercial goods. "The revenue passes from the hands of the prince or financier to those of the artists and merchants." Taxation reduces the circulation of species at the countryside. The consequence is a unidirectional flow of money from peasants to townspeople, which perverts the "proportion" between the "needs" of

1. OC III, p. 259. Rousseau explains what means a government should apply to prevent "an extreme inequality of fortunes". One is to prevent that agriculture gets "sacrifiée au commerce".
2. Ibid., p. 920. "Je regarde si bien tout système de commerce comme destructif de l'agriculture, que je n'en excepte pas même le commerce des denrées qui sont le produit de l'agriculture."
3. Ibid., p. 1399. "les arts d'agréments et les metiers de luxe".

the peasant and what he actually gets paid for his grain. "Money passes without end and never returns. The richer the town, the more miserable is the country." One interpretation of this is that demand moves to "luxury goods" and the terms of trade for agricultural products get worse. But the discussion concerns another relation: that between agriculture and production of craft for peasant consumption. "The cultivator who never receives more than the minor part, gets destitute by constantly paying the same for receiving less."[1]

If Rousseau had claimed that the prices of luxuries (far beyond the buying power of peasants) grew, relative to food prices, the argument would have been easily understandable. When buying power moves from consumers in the market for necessities where prices are set in "proportion", to consumers on the market for superfluities where prices are "arbitrary", prices must fall, relatively, on necessities. But why do relative prices on industrial goods ***demanded by peasants*** increase, why must peasants constantly pay the same for "receiving less". Why should the terms of trade for artisans, peddlers, and others in the towns, improve relative to peasants? The towns need food; their inhabitants cannot wait for it. On this matter, Rousseau offers an explanation that is completely reasonable and very revealing. The problem is that "that proportion that could still exist between the needs of the farmer and the price of his corn" is perverted. It is "destroyed" by the tax. The reason is that it influences the price on the market:

> ...the peasant who, whether or not he sells his food, is forced to pay at fixed terms for the land he cultivates,lacks the power to wait until the price he would like is set, because if he does not sell it how can he pay the tax? Why, it is often the enormity of the tax that maintains the food at low price.[2]

Rousseau's explanation is that the peasants are put in a situation where they are forced (in order to pay taxes and rents) to supply a large amount to the market. For that reason their bargaining conditions are poor. The urban buyers possess, because of the tax, a kind of monopolistic (or strictly speaking monopsonistic) privilege whereby they can wait for prices to fall.

Nor can the peasant get price compensation for the taxes because prices are influenced by international prices which are set independently of the national tax. "Grain is a good which taxes don't make more expensive even in the country which produced it."[3] The peasant cannot compensate for the tax by increasing the price because then he might not sell anything at all, and he is forced to sell. He

1. OC III, p. 274. "Le premier vient du défaut de circulation des especes car le commerce et l'industrie attirent dans les capitales tout l'argent de la campagne; et l'impôt détruisant la proportion qui pouvoit se trouver encore entre les besoins du laboureur et le prix de son blé, l'argent vient sans cesse et ne retourne jamais; plus la ville est rich plus le pays est miserable. Le produit des tailles passe des mains du prince ou du financier dans celles des artisteset des marchands; et le cultivateur qui n'en reçoit jamais que le moindre partie, s'épuise enfin en payant toûjours également et recevant toûjours moins."
2. OC III, p. 274. "Mais le laboureur qui, soit qu'il vende ou non, est contraint de payer à des termes fixes pour le terrain qu'il cultive, n'est pas le maître d'attendre qu'on mette à sa denrée le prix qu'il lui plaît? et quand il ne la vendroit pas pour payer la taille, de sorte que c'est quelquefois l'énormité de l'imposition qui maintient la denrée à vil prix."
3. Ibid. "Le blé est un denrée que les impôts ne renchérissent point dans le pays qui la produit . . ."

*cannot wait.* Rousseau is portraying a situation which Witold Kula in a study of the Polish medieval economy (with no reference to Rousseau) called "obligation to commercialize" and Amit Bhaduri described as part of modern development problems in Bengal.[1]

## *King's law*

Another problematic mechanism contradicts established economic wisdom. It is described in the DISCOURS SUR L'ÉCONOMIE POLITIQUE: the "quantity [of grain] diminishes and still the prices do not get higher, despite its absolute necessity".[2] Why is that?

Because of this comment Rousseau has been accused of being ignorant of economics. Robert Villers found Rousseau wanting in methodology and competence. He referred to Rousseau's pessimism about the potentials of economic growth, but worst of all, according to Villers, was Rousseau's ignorance of the true relation between supply and demand such as it was described already in the 17th century by Gregory King in "King's law".[3]

King's law was named after the well-known "genealogist, accountant and perhaps the most accomplished economic and social statistician of his time",[4] Gregory King (1648–1712). It stated in precise numbers "how a defect in the harvest may raise the price of corn". The larger the supply, the lower the prices and vice versa. Given that 1 = normal price and yield, prices will on average change with harvest rates as follows (Table 1).

*King's law (1= normal price and yield)*

| Harvest rate | Price rate |
|---|---|
| 1.0 | 1.0 |
| 0.9 | 1.3 |
| 0.8 | 1.8 |
| 0.7 | 2.6 |
| 0.6 | 3.8 |
| 0.5 | 5.5 |

Source: Fogel R 1988, p. 10: Table 2.

King's law is an attempt to depict the price elasticity in the demand for grain.[5] As can be seen from the table above, the price elasticity is somewhat decreasing with the harvests. At big harvest rates a 10% cut in the harvest causes a three times as

1. For a discussion of this concept and problems caused by the "obligation to commercialize" see Kula 1976, p. 43 and Bhaduri 1983, pp. 10f.
2. OC III, p. 274. "[le blé est un denrée dont que] malgré son absolue nécessité, la quantité diminue, sans que le prix en augmente . . ."
3. Villers 1964, p.335.
4. Hutchison 1988, pp. 47f
5. The price elasticity tells how much more or less of a good that will be demanded because of a certain price change, or how much the price will change due to a certain change in supply. A high price elasticity means that a small price alteration will cause a big change of the amount demanded, and that a big alteration in supply will cause only a small price change. A low, negative price elasticity means then, for example, that a small fall in supply will be enough to cause a big increase in the price.

big price rise (+30% ), while at smaller rates a 17% cut in the harvest causes a relatively smaller 44% price increase. Robert Fogel[1] calculated that King's law could, with some precision, be summarised in a constant elasticity demand function with e = -0.403. That means that if P = the price rate (with normal price = 1) and Q = the yield rate (with normal yield = 1) then

$$Q = P^{-0.403}$$

The precise origin of King's law seems rather obscure. It appeared in written form for the first time, not in a text by King, but in a work by Davenant published in 1699; although King without any doubt played an important part, at least, in formulating it.[2] It seems that the law is not based on empirical evidence but probably only on a hypothetical mathematical formula with diffuse origin, which in fact, could have been a formulation by King. Another suggestion is: "that Isaac Newton may have been responsible for the approach adopted".[3]

Since historical harvest information is rare and mostly of limited reliability, but price information more abundant, this relation has frequently been used by economic historians to estimate harvests from price observations – often and long before Fogel's formulation. In fact it was not until a few years ago that the three-centuries-old influential law was tested against empirical facts. The test was done by Robert Fogel on English pre-modern economic history and he found that the law fitted the historical facts very poorly. It could not possibly have depicted the true relationship between corn yields and prices in English early modern times. Fogel found that King's law would have left large segments of the population in some years of the 16th century with a caloric consumption "well below the requirement for basal metabolism". But the years so noted did not register the slightest evidence, in any records, of radically increased mortality, serious famines, or the like. So, after all, Rousseau may well have been wise not to use King's law. A close-up shows, moreover, that his statement contains a very interesting analysis of the early modern corn market and economy.

Fogel tried to fit to his numbers an alternative, truer, price elasticity in the demand for corn. The resulting figure suggested that the price elasticity in the demand for corn was far *lower* than that implied by King's law. The result also deviated, in that Fogel's price elasticity increased with the yield. This means that price elasticity is particularly low in years of want, and prices are responding to a given supply decrease with particularly steep rises in such years. The result also implies that the known price volatility reflects a far smaller variation in yields than what was to be expected from King's law. High prices may have been a worse threat to corn buyers than an actual deficit of corn.

As Rousseau had done in general terms, Fogel assumed that the market for grain had a dual character. The price elasticity in the demand for grain was far

1. Fogel 1988, pp. 9-11.
2. Essay upon the Probable methods of Making a People Gainers in the Balance of Trade. Cf., Hutchison 1988, p. 48.
3. Ib.

lower among the rich than among the poor grain buyers, simply because the poor could not afford to pay much, due to their tight budget constraint. This is what Rousseau claimed in the statement quoted above:

> The most useful arts are the worst paid, for the number of workmen is regulated by necessity, and the work which everybody requires must necessarily be paid at a rate which puts it within the reach of the poor.[1]

Fogel argued that when the grain yield was small, the rich buyers represented a larger share of the aggregate demand. For this and other reasons the price elasticity would decrease with decreasing supply. This is fully compatible with Rousseau.

Rousseau presents a reasonable argument in support of his view, one that, however, deviates from Fogel's analysis. Fogel attempts an explanation in terms of market power while Rousseau's attempt is more institutionalistic. It is not, according to Rousseau, only the different budget constraints, but the presence of rents and taxes which pervert the price mechanism by influencing the bargaining power through "the obligation to commercialize". While Fogel pities the poor corn buyers, Rousseau cries for the poor peasants.[2] Fogel detected a price elasticity that was problematically *low* (high price volatility in relation to a given supply volatility) causing prohibitive prices for poor buyers, Rousseau was worried about precisely the opposite reality: that the price elasticity in the demand for corn was too *high* (people soon stopped buying when prices went up) causing an insufficient income for the peasants. Who was right?

In fact, it is possible to reconcile the two views. Moreover, Rousseau's analysis may very well add an explanatory mechanism to Fogel's result. The two arguments present different elasticity problems but perhaps also different elasticity relations. Neither Rousseau nor Fogel are at all clear about what they mean by the "supply" they compare with prices. Let us try some possibilities. Suppose that the yearly yield of corn ($Y$) is distributed into three uses: peasants' own consumption ($O$) + what they are *coerced* to offer the market in order to pay the "enormous" tax ($C$) + what they offer the market voluntarily ($V$). Market supply ($M$) would consist of $C+V$. In this way, we get three reasonable measures of supply: $V$, $M$ and $Y\ (=M+O)$.

It is very probable that the demand for $V$ has a Rousseauan, high price elasticity, given a large $C$. One effect of the "enormity of the tax" is that the free part ($V$) is so small that it only marginally influences total marketed supply ($M$). Changes in the supply of $V$ only marginally influence M and moreover probably to a high degree concern those buyers who have a strict budget constraint – the poor townspeople. For this reason, buyers have little reason to buy if prices increase heavily on the free segment ($V$) and much reason to buy if prices

1. OC IV, p. 457. Compare p. 47 above.
2. They also write about cases with very different institutional settings: Fogel on English post-enclosure agriculture and Rousseau on French pre-enclosure agriculture of the "ancien régime". Regarding France, see e.g., Bloch 1930.

decrease. In other words, the quantity (of *V*) the consumers will buy is heavily dependent on the price: price elasticity of the demand is very high. The expended volume (of money) rather than the consumed volume tends to be constant. There is then a Rousseauan peasant trap.

On the other hand, the demand for *M* may very well be Fogelian. The volatility of *M* is very low, due to the enormity of *C*. The volatility is probably lower than that of *Y*. Peasants are forced to sell to pay their taxes, even at the expense of *O*. And when M diminishes, the rich (with a loose budget constraint) start to dominate the demand (decreasing price elasticity). But there may be another reason for the difference. In the 18th century France the peasants were sellers on the corn market while in Fogel's case probably the market supply was dominated by landlords or capitalistic farmers. In the English case sellers probably had a considerably ability "to wait" while the French peasants forced to sell had not. It is because the peasants *need* to sell that their prices are dear.

## *The Dazzling Sweet Voice of Nature*

Rousseau rejected Mirabeau's invitation to join side with the physiocrats. That his ideas diverged from theirs is evident from a checklist, compiled by Fetscher, comparing their respective positions. Both, Fetscher concluded, reject the mercantilist argentomania. But while the physiocrats advocated a policy for a maximal net product in agriculture, implying that its share of the total labour force should be optimal – so that labour productivity is maximum – and therefore as small as possible,[1] Rousseau prefers that a maximum share be allocated to agriculture. While Quesnay, for example, advocates attempts to exploit economies of scale in agriculture, with capital investment and efficient employment of labour (using as little as possible), Rousseau advocates an agriculture oriented towards self-subsistence and a maximum employment of labour.[2] For Rousseau, an agriculture penetrated by money would either end in misery (according to the iron law of peasant misery) for the peasants or in a manufacture-like structure with rent-paying farmers.[3]

While Quesnay assumes that there is an independent class of foncières, from which farmers could rent land, Rousseau's agriculture consists of many independent peasants. The one proposed a market-oriented agriculture, the other a market-avoiding one. The taxation proposed by the physiocrats was in the end most favourable for the manufacturers (who were to be exempted from tax) while Rousseau, as we have seen, warns against taxing the peasants. By low or no taxes they should be able to "tell the law" to the industrialists. The physiocrats argue for a capitalist agriculture whereby the farmers could get rich through high prices on corn. Such a policy was rejected by Rousseau.[4]

Finally, the physiocrats called for the people to follow the law of nature, the "ordre naturel", to let nature have its "laissez faire – laissez aller", while he who

1. On the Physiocrat opposition to the tradional mercantilist populationism and other aspects on this doctrine, see Herlitz 1989a.
2. For a summary and discussion of Quesnay's view, see Fox-Genovese 1976, p. 121.
3. Projet de constitution pour la Corse, OC III, p. 920.
4. This is discussed also by Denis 1951, pp. 46f.

was so often regarded as being romantic, even raving about the charms of nature, the botanist, critic of civil society, etc., warned against letting nature rule:

> the sweet voice of nature is no longer an infallible guide.[1]

The idea of letting nature herself regulate corn trade did not appeal to Rousseau.

## *The sacred right of property*

Rousseau was, indeed, not the only opponent of the physiocratic doctrine. People like Mably, Morelly, Necker and Galiani formulated different kinds of criticism. But Rousseau's opposition was different from them all.

Morelly proposed a centralized economy without private property, where an interventionist state controlled the distribution of corn, and where the state owned the land.[2] Mably advocated the establishment of common property.[3] While the physiocrats tried to legitimise entitlement inequalities by referring to "a natural inequality in the physical faculties", Mably and Morelly claimed that inequality in property is unnatural. By nature, they claimed, no one owned anything.[4] In spite of claims to the contrary by scholars such as Talmon[5] and Fetscher[6], Rousseau never sided with such ideas. On the contrary, he claimed private property to be "a sacred right" of the citizens:

> It is certain that the property right is the most sacred of all rights of the citizens, and in certain regards even more important than liberty itself.[7]

As will be shown below, in Chapter 8, this statement was far from being a mere declamatory phrase. It was supported by an extensive analysis.

Necker presented the merchant-capitalist agents as the strategic economic class. Without participating concretely in either production or distribution, they organised production so that a secure provision was maintained. In this way, Necker represented an opposite pole to Rousseau's perspective on the unequal exchange conditions of agriculture.[8]

Galiani represented a third kind of opposition to the physiocrats. He argued in a treatise written in 1772 that the physiocratic idea of a free corn trade is entirely

1. Fetscher 1960, pp. 250f; OC III, p. 283. "Ainsi la douce voix de la nature n'est plus pour nous un guide infaillible."
2. Regarding Morelly, see, for example: Coe 1961, pp. 141ff.; Faure-Solet 1964, p. 200f.; Talmon 1970, p. 60.
3. Airiau 1965, p. 126.
4. Faure-Solet 1964, p. 181.
5 Talmon 1970, pp. 60f.
6 Fetscher 1960, p. 248. Fetscher is, however, very cautious and careful in his argument.
7 OC III, p. 263. "Il est certain que le droit de propriété est le plus sacré de tous les droits des citoyens, et plus important à certain égards que la liberté même."
8 Grange 1973, p. 177f. "Le service des marchands devint plus grand, lorsqu'ils joignirent à la qualité d'agents dont nous venons de parler, celle de propriétaires considérables; ce qui leur donna les moyens d'entretenir sans cesse l'industrie, en se chargeant de nourrir les ouvriers." Necker argued from assumptions related to Rousseau's ideas or laws "that temper the harshness of property with a wise policy for guaranteeing their subsistence". For, both the existing political institutions had been constructed for the rich at the cost of the poor. But Necker advocated regulation of the existing market system, while Rousseau proposed market avoidance. Cf., Baker 1975, p. 63.

unrealistic. The physiocratic argument presupposed that legal restrictions were the only constraints on free market exchange, but they overlooked a number of impediments. But the corn market was far from free, even when all legal restrictions were removed. Furthermore, some of the remaining impediments could not be eliminated even in theory. Corn trade was, for example, highly dependent on local conditions, wrote Galiani. While the English example showed the physiocrats how beneficial free corn trade could be for France, Galiani denied that the results of the policy in one economy were automatically relevant for predicting its effects in another context. As an example of the particularity of the English economy, he mentioned that this nation "was so strange that it drew revenue from Bengal to indulge in the sport of racing at Nue Market".

Like Rousseau, he argues that society must not let nature rule. Nature can wait, he writes, but men cannot. Therefore, it is necessary to control nature. Nature is instrumental to man's economic needs. Nature is immense while people are "atoms", "insects", "nothing". Yes, he concedes, the grain price will find its equilibrium, but the problem is that it may take time and time is important. For that reason the "laissez faire – laissez aller" argument is for the "metaphysician", because it does not "take account of the long duration it takes to arrive" at the equilibrium. The physiocratic model is unrealistically abstract in ignoring practical problems. Nature cannot handle them: "She [nature] is a too big a Lady to be given the responsibility for our small problems". In particular, the lack of concern for the problem of time reveals that the theory is unrealistic. It makes for a very poor economic policy.

> Time is necessary to send the letters with the news of a shortage of wheat in a town, and more time is necessary for wheat to arrive there. If this length is fifteen days and you only have supplies for a week, the town is without bread for a week, and this insect called man can die in a week...[1]

Therefore the invisible hand or the "laissez faire laissez aller" naturalism must be regulated.[2]

* * *

Like Necker, Galiani, Morelly and others, Rousseau opposed the physiocratic call to let nature rule in the market for corn. But his analysis was different from theirs. Unlike some of them, e.g., Necker and Galiani, he did not believe that a traditional policy of government regulation and intervention would ever suffice to secure the necessary supply of corn. And unlike others, e.g., Morelly and Mably, neither did he support the idea of a centrally planned corn provision.

1. Galiani 1959, p. 222.
2. Hutchison 1988, pp. 267f.

> The corn market was, in Rousseau's view, inefficient in the sense that corn prices did not express the constrained production cost value. The reason was not that market exchange necessarily perverted prices in all circumstances, but that it did in a specific institutional context. Such a context consisted of a large sector of rent-coerced commercialisation. The consequent "enormous" forced supply caused two problems: it increased the market power of the rent-receiving classes and it influenced the relationship between demand and supply. Because of the presence of a stable forced supply beyond the choice of the suppliers, prices did not respond elastically to changes in the supply of voluntarily-marketed corn. But, on the other hand, relative to the low volatility of the total marketed supply, prices moved considerably.
>
> To an extent, Rousseau and Fogel provide reasons for both the peasants and the wealthy to avoid market exchange. This is interesting since we know that many rural households before and during the Industrial Revolution – as well as in modern developing countries – in fact did avoid market exchange.[1] Although people could gain by offering their products or labour power to the commodity market or the labour market,, they often preferred to secure their provision by means of subsistence agriculture.

Market avoidance is obviously no basic judgment. Rousseau's analysis is interesting in that it separates the market behaviour of necessities and lapri and of different segments of the aggregated demand. Some goods are in certain institutional situations better provided for by non-market modes of provision. Hence, in pre-revolutionary society the rents were perverting and the provision of food particularly endangered. This was even recognized by some landlords. Kula gives examples from Polish medieval, seigneurial estates, of how the market was to be avoided for the input in the production of the estate. "Both in the collections of instructions to bailifts, and in economic correspondence we find in every instance the golden rule of good economic management: avoid expenditure in money."[2]

Rousseau's proposals raises several questions. Why did he not support a policy of pure state management of the economy that would perhaps allow a division of labour and increased labour productivity? Why keep private property sacred? And why not allow the farmers full autarchy? These questions concern the interplay between market-oriented and household-oriented modes of provision[3] – a relationship of great importance when on the threshold of market economy, as well as today; although it has evoked only marginal attention in welfare economic research. I suggest that the answers have much to do with Rousseau's conceptualisation of dependence.

1. Fridén 1991; McCloskey 1975a and 1975b.
2. Kula 1976, p. 31.
3. Becker 1981.

# 7. THE SELF COMMON TO THE WHOLE

# *Democracy Necessary and Impossible*

AT THIS POINT, a number of problems connected with market exchange have been considered: information costs, environmental non-sustainability, increasing "difference" in income and bargaining power, deviance from the "true" utility-constrained production cost value, undervaluation and sticky prices of corn – all problems causing inequality and inefficiency. Some (at least) of these problems belong to a specific historical context. This is true, for example, with respect to the negative consequences of taxation on corn. The feudal rent system provided the wealthy with corn and enforced a large, constant market supply: rich people with a loose budget constraint became largely independent of a demand-driven market supply. In this way the price structure was "perverted". This problem may disappear or diminish when democracy rules and if market power is not too asymmetrically distributed. Some of the problems Rousseau discusses may be of this historically specific character. But others may be more general, and may even, in one way or another, be present in all market exchange. Rousseau discusses two means for democratic society of handling these latter kinds of problems. These means are market avoidance, and a democratic government that breeds a strong social morale.

Since market avoidance through the stimulation of self-sufficient peasant economies becomes less and less feasible over time, due, in Rousseau's opinion, to population growth, the securing of a democratic government which can intervene in the economy becomes all the more necessary. In Rousseau's formulation, the economy itself must be democratic, and governed by *"the general will"*. This concept will be discussed briefly in this chapter, based mainly on a consideration of the DISCOURS SUR L'ÉCONOMIE POLITIQUE.[1]

1. A second article on political economy appeared in Tôme IX of the great ENCYCLOPÉDIE. It was written by M. Boulanger. But this second article, according to Robert Derathé, concerns oriental despotism and thus has little to do with economic doctrine in a modern sense. The article is little known and the author's identity is even disputed. It might be understandable, then, that it is rarely discussed. OC III, pp. LXXIIf. According to Hubert the appearance of the second article in Tôme IX

## *A Blank Cheque for Dictatorship?*

Now and then Rousseau has been accused of not being a true democrat. In particular, his insistence that the concept of "the general will" connotes something other than "the will of all" – the aggregate of individual wills – has given rise to such interpretations.

J. L. Talmon is one such accuser. He treats Rousseau's philosophy as if it did not discriminate clearly between democracy and dictatorship, or between obedience and freedom. He regards the PROJET DE CONSTITUTION POUR LA CORSE as a "blueprint for dictatorship". Further, Talmon claims, the CONTRAT SOCIAL favours a tyrannical political economy. The "general will" becomes a "preordained will":

> The very idea of an assumed preordained will, which has not yet become the actual will of the nation; the view that the nation is still therefore in its infancy, a 'young nation', in the nomenclature of the SOCIAL CONTRACT, gives those who claim to know and to represent the real and ultimate will of the nation – the party of the vanguard – a blank cheque to act on behalf of the people, without reference to the people's actual will.[1]

Talmon thinks that Rousseau conceives of the contents of the general will as analytically deducible, as "something like a mathematical truth or a Platonic idea".[2] That this, however, need not be the case has been shown theoretically by means of non-cooperative game theory.[3] In the present chapter this point is to be made in another way, by reference to Rousseau's own explicit discussion, mainly in the Encyclopédie article. I shall also try to show how Rousseau regards the creation of a democratic economy as simultaneously necessary and impossible.

## *Popular Political Economy*

In the DISCOURS SUR L'ÉCONOMIE POLITIQUE Rousseau presents and determines his conceptualisation of political economy and sets the basic concepts, constraints, and aims. The article consists of four main sections: the first sets the stage, defines, introduces, and delimits the subject, while the three remaining parts treat three different aspects of what Rousseau regards as the subject of political economy. In the first part, the meaning of the concept of a democratic economy, "popular political economy", is determined.

Rousseau opens this first section with an etymology of the word "economy".

reflected that Diderot was disappointed with Rousseau's article. Robert Derathé claims, however, that Boulanger's article is a short discussion of a previous book by him, and thus in no sense competes with Rousseau's article. In any event, it seems clear that the editors of the Encyclopédie chose a distinctly pluralistic approach towards economic theory. Quesnay wrote articles on economic matters such as "proprieté", "fermiers", "grains." Turgot and Forbonnais also authored economic treatises with distinctly different ideological positions from that of Rousseau's. And Diderot himself wrote articles on agriculture and other economic subjects although he avoided aligning himself with any particular standpoint. Derathé, OC III, pp. LXXIIf. See also Wokler 1987, p. 98 and Denis 1951, p. 44.

1. Talmon 1970, p. 48.
2. Ibid., p. 41.
3. Cf., Cohen 1986 and further references there.

He finds that it originally referred to the good government of a family household, to the benefit of all its members, but was later extended to cover the good government of entire societies.[1] The concept developed, in Rousseau's presentation, progressively: parallel to and fully consistent with the development of society itself in his hypothetical[2] story.[3] In this story the family plays a decisive role in the transition from the state of nature.

The logic of the family economy must be carefully distinguished from that of society; for the two are as different as the state of nature is to the state of society.[4] The members of society are economically dependent on one another within a far wider network than are the members of a family household. The economy of the family household, the *"domestic"* or "particular" economy, belongs to a different species than the *"political"* or "general" economy. Since they require different rules and concepts, it is not possible to draw any conclusion about the management of the one from the functioning of the other. Some basic rules are even contrary: "In order to act right the first [the father] has only to consult his heart; the other [the magistrate] becomes a traitor the moment he listens to his."[5]

Rousseau makes it clear that his treatise exclusively concerns economy in the second, extended, sense, the economy of "la grande famille". He discusses four norms that should constrain its behaviour. Firstly, he determines its two aims, and secondly discusses two legitimate modes of governing. Political economy must have as its aims: (1) to conserve all individuals in peace; and (2) to maintain them in abundance.[6] And, with respect to governance, it must be managed according to (3) conventions and (4) law, rather than – as in a family – by any kind of paternal authority.[7] An arbitrary element is necessary within the family but should not be allowed in political economy.

The *"popular"* public economy is, further, distinguished from the *"tyrannical"*. A popular public economy exists where "there reigns a unity of interests between rulers and the people" and where the "magistrate belongs to the people" rather than the opposite. In the tyrannical economy government and people have contrary interests. Its forms are well known throughout history. Of a democratic economy, however, Rousseau can give no historical example, merely a reference to literature. For the maxims of the tyrannical economy have long since been

1. OC III, p. 241.
2. On the hypothetical nature of the transition story, see Chapter 8 below.
3. Especially in the DISCOURS SUR L'ORIGINE ET LES FONDEMENTS DE L'INÉGALITÉ PARMI LES HOMMES, just finished when Rousseau started to work on the Encyclopédie article.
4. An explicit aim within the DISCOURS SUR L'ORIGINE ET LES FONDEMENTS DE L'INÉGALITÉ PARMI LES HOMMES is to combat the idea that the state of nature and state of society were genetically related and that therefore normative political principles applicable to the latter could be deduced from the former (as in natural right ideology).
5. OC III, p. 243. [Rousseau 1983, p. 119]. "Pour bien faire, le premier n'a qu'à consulter son cœur; l'autre devient un traître au moment qu'il écoute le sien."
6. This principle is also expressed in the PROJET DE CONSTITUTION POUR LA CORSE.
7. OC III, p. 242. [Ibid.]. "la richesse du fisc n'est qu'un moyen souvent mal entendu, pour maintenir les particuliers dans la paix et dans l'abondance." Ibid., pp. 241f. "Dans la grande famille dont tous les membres sont naturellement égaux, l'autorité politique purement arbitraire quant à son institution, ne peut être fondée que sur des conventions, ni le magistrat commander aux autres qu'en vertu des lois." See also LE CONTRAT SOCIAL; OC III, p. 326 and OC III, p. 1390.

inscribed in "the archives of our history"[1] while the "rules" of the democratic economy can only be found in the writings of "those philosophers that venture to proclaim the rights of humanity".[2]

The democratic government must primarily attend to three tasks: (1) to realize the general will, (2) to teach the people to love their country, and (3) to guarantee that all citizens get their necessary provisions. The remainder of this chapter will address the first of these tasks. This task demands that decisions are democratic. But can collective decisions really be based on the people's free choices? And does not *any* execution of them constrain people's freedom? Can the true general will ever be realised?

## *Cato and the Character of the General Will*

The DISCOURS SUR L'ÉCONOMIE POLITIQUE tells nothing about the role of autarchic provision and international trade in a democratic economy. This absence is significant. How the economy should be organised is regarded as a feature of democratic choice. But the Discours does not, in any manner, prescribe what this choice is to contain. Nor does the text discuss how the democratic decision is to be reached.[3] Rousseau's emphasis is simply that the accomplishment of the "general will" demands the freedom of the people. The assumption is only that a social choice is made, democratically, but in a way that is not described. It is up to the government to follow and execute that decision, that "general will" – whatever it is.[4] The article discusses the necessary preconditions for the execution of any democratic choice regardless of its substance. Therefore, it is not directly known whether the general will is thought of as an analytical truth (as Talmon assumed) or as something else. But indirectly, via the assumptions put forth, it is clearly evident that the latter is the case.

To clarify the nature of the general will, Rousseau uses the idea of a hierarchy of wills.[5] For every association in society, formal or not, there is a general will, different from the particular wills of each of its members. But this general will of the *partial* association is just one of several particular wills in relation to the general will of the entire social body. An enormous hierarchy of collective units is outlined, each of which consists of many particular wills, and each constituting one general will in relation to its members, but simultaneously constituting only one of several particular wills in relation to the general will of a higher order, ultimately the social body or mankind. One of the tasks of political economy is

1. They are, for example described in the "satires of Machiavelli".
2. OC III, pp. 247f. [Rousseau 1983, p. 123]. ". . . ne se trouvent que dans les écrits des philosophes qui osent réclamer les droits de l'humanité." "Les magistrates appartiennent au peuple". The names of the philosophers are not mentioned.
3. See Sen 1986. The distinction between the decision making process (social choice function) and the execution of its result is an important issue in the politics of the Enlightenment. In Condorcet's historiography this separation constitutes the second stage in the development of political institutions. Cf., Arkhipoff 1989, p. 95.
4. Launay 1989, p. 223f. Launay defended Rousseau from Derathé's allegation that his economics were archaic and primarily moralist. Launay argued that Rousseau's view on economics, far from being disengaged and arbitrary, was very deliberately and carefully designed and that he was far from ignorant about economics.
5. An idea which was later to reappear in the CONTRAT SOCIAL.

therefore, according to Rousseau, to manage these hierarchically-related particular wills and govern them in accordance with the general will of society at large.

It must be carefully ascertained that this general will is completely distinguished from the particular wills of the politicians or officers running the public administration. The first and most important duty of a government truly serving "the good of the people"[1] is "to follow in everything the general will".[2] This is, to Rousseau, more than empty words. In later texts sarcastic statements ridicule claims by different rulers to represent the true general will of their people. To the Polish noblemen, for example, he writes that the policy of the dominating Christian states of his time is largely the result of intrigues within the courts: "the momentary interest of some minister, some wench, some favorite". The explicitly declared aims of their policies are not worth a penny: "And all the pretty doctrines concerning the 'interests of the crown' are a child's game, at which sensible men can only laugh."[3] Talmon is, of course, wrong when he claims that Rousseau hands out "a blank cheque to act on behalf of the people" to whomever lays "claim to know and to represent the real and ultimate will of the nation".

Still, an epistemological question is left unsolved: how is the general will to be revealed? According to Talmon, Rousseau pictured the general will as some preordained or metaphysical entity other than "the people's actual will".[4] But if that is true, why his insistence on the importance of civil liberty for the formation of the general will? Could not a few philosophers, with their professional competence, deduce the general will without interference from the people?

Rousseau in fact answers this question. He had, since his youth, been a deep admirer of the great classical sages like Plato, Socrates and Aristotle.[5] But when he, in the DISCOURS, compares the importance to society of the sage to that of the representative of democracy, the former loses. Rousseau ranks the virtuous defendant of democratic freedom as more indispensable to society than the sage whom we know he appreciates so highly. Who would be of the greatest use to society, he asks: a Cato, who sacrificed his own life for the happiness and freedom of the people, or a Socrates who taught truth, beauty and justice, and even sacrificed his life to that cause? Cato, he answers. Because it is he who expresses the general will of the people. He is a great citizen, since he defends the people and "its *liberty*".[6]

"The general will", then, is not an analytical truth which philosophers can deduce. The conception is democratic rather than expressing a Platonian epistemology. It is not something decided by "those who claim to know". Nor is it a simple aggregation of the votes of the people. What is it then?

1. Ibid. "le bien du peuple".
2. Ibid. "de suivre en tout la volonté générale".
3. OC III, pp. 1037f. [Rousseau 1985, p. 111]. "Elles ne connoissent d'autres liens que ceux de leurs intérests . . . l'intérest momentané d'un Ministre, d'une fille, d'un favori. . . . et toute cette belle doctrines des intérests des Princes est un jeu d'enfants qui fait rire les hommes sensés."
4. For a convincing criticism of this view, see Grofman and Feld 1988, p. 568.
5. Hendel 1962, pp.1ff.
6. OC III, p. 255.

## *Unity of Interests*

The character of the general will is illustrated by means of an analogy between the particular society and a human body. The analogy is used with reservations: "I shall take the liberty of making use of a very common and in some respects inaccurate comparison, which will serve to illustrate my meaning."[1] The general will refers to "the body politic", something which concerns the whole society, the whole "organized, living body", with all of its organs (citizens).[2] Life in both bodies, the physical and the social, consists of:

> *the self common to the whole,* the reciprocal sensibility and internal correspondence of all the parts.[3]

Like a human being, who has a will, the "organized living body" also has one: the general will:

> which tends always to the preservation and welfare of the whole and of every part...[4]

The innate character of the general will is parallel to the two aims (mentioned above) that Rousseau sets for political economy (to preserve peace and to maintain the people in abundance). The idea that it is the identical interest of "self" and "others" which constitutes and connotes the general will is later also established in the CONTRAT SOCIAL.

The undertakings which bind us to the social body are obligatory only because they are mutual; and their nature is such that in fulfilling them we cannot work for others without working for ourselves.[5]

But how can the "self common to the whole" be something other than the aggregation of the wills of the people? This question is, of course, investigated further in the CONTRAT SOCIAL. Rousseau, in a footnote, asks the reader to try patiently to understand, although he admits that his language on this point is poor and that it is unavoidable that he seems to contradict himself. He writes that when people discuss what they label "the interest of all", still they always guard their own interest.[6]

1. Ibid., p. 244. [Rousseau 1983, pp. 120f]. "Qu'on me permette d'employer pour un moment une comparaison commune et peu exacte à bien des égards, mais propre à me faire mieux entendre."
2. Ibid., "Le corps politique pris individuellement, peut être consideré comme un corps organisé, vivant, et semblable à celui de l'homme." "Body politic" refers to the metaphoric use of the body to demonstrate the interrelatednes of different parts of society and the fact that government functions poorly when other body parts aren't operating correctly. See, for example, Shklar 1985, pp. 197-214.
3. Italics in OC, but not in Rousseau 1983. Ibid., "La vie de l'un et l'autre est le moi commun au tout, la sensibilité réciproque, et la correspondance interne de toutes les parties."
4. Ibid., "Le corps politique est donc aussi un être moral qui a une volonté; et cette volonté géneárle, qui tend toûjours à la conservation et au bien-être du tout et de chaque partie . . ."
5. Ibid., p. 375. [Rousseau 1983, p. 186]."Les engagemens qui nous lient au corps social ne sont obligatoires que parce qu'ils sont mutuels, et leur nature est telle qu'en les remplissant on ne peut travailler pour autrui sans travailler aussi pour soi."
6. OC III, p. 373. "Pourquoi la volonté générale est elle toujours droite, et pourquoi tous veulent-ils constamment le bonheur de chacun d'eux, si ce n'est parce qu'il qu'il n'y a personne qui ne s'approprie ce mot chacun, et qui ne songe à lui-même en votant pour tous?"

The general will must not only be the will of the majority; it must "come from and apply to all".[1] But it is not synonymous with the majority choice. Rousseau argues that the best way to establish the general will is through democratic voting. But in voting the general will is often perverted by intrigues, missing information, strategic actions by interest groups. If the general will is neither an analytically deducible Platonian truth, nor a majority decision, then what remains? What delineates the general will, Rousseau explains, is the ***unity of interest***, shared by all.

> ...what makes the will general is less the number of votes than the common interest uniting them...[2]

Since (at least) the 1965[3] publication of a remarkable note by W. G. Runciman and Amartya Sen, it has been possible to regard the general will as the Pareto-optimal choice in a prisoner's dilemma game, while the "will of all" can be regarded as the equilibrium choice. The prisoners' dilemma can be illustrated in different ways.[4] One is by Hilal Gildin's fishing example: Suppose a number of fishermen use a fishing zone where the reproduction of the stock is in danger because of over-exploitation. In order to avoid a disaster all would gain if the fished volumes were to be limited (the Pareto optimum where no one would become better off except at the cost of others). Still, each fisherman would individually be able to gain by increasing his own yields, whether or not the others did likewise (equilibrium choice). The former choice could, in Rousseau's terms, be called their common general will, the second one, "the wills of all".[5]

Grofman and Feld in 1988 "complemented" this note in the same spirit by means of probabilistic theory and reference to Condorcet's jury theorem.[6] They claimed that Rousseau thought that certain institutional conditions and arrangements would impede the voters from forwarding their particular interest (the "wills of all"), but would incite them to vote for what they thought were the interests of all ("the general will"). Democratic voting would in that sense offer the highest probability that those truly common interests would be revealed.

That Rousseau takes democracy seriously is also evidenced by the space and efforts he dedicates to the conceptual problem of democracy, which has challenged political and social science for more than two centuries since. Rousseau was not naïvely optimistic in this regard. He realised that democracy was impossible. Such was also the irritating message of a great study in the 1950s.

1. Ibid. [Rousseau 1983, p. 187]. "la volonté general pour être vraîment telle . . . doit partir de tous pour s'appliquer à tous . . ."
2. Ibid., p. 374. [Rousseau 1983, p. 187]. ". . . ce que généralise la volonté est moins le nombre des voix, que l'intérêt commun que les unit."
3. Runciman and Sen 1965. In a sense this note gave the original impetus to the present essay. See also, e.g., Cohen 1986.
4. Regarding Rousseau and the prisoners' dilemma, see also the following chapter.
5. Grofman and Feld 1988, p. 572. See also Cohen 1986, note 7, p. 278 and the following discussion by Cohen of Gildin's interpretation.
6. Grofman and Feld 1988. On Condorcet's jury theorem, see below.

## *The Impossibility Dilemma of Liberal Democracy*

Kenneth Arrow's wellknown theorem of 1951 states and proves that it is logically impossible to construct a mechanism whereby two or more individuals' rankings of three or more optional states can be aggregated to a collective decision or a collective ranking that simultaneously satisfies four reasonable requirements.[1] The dilemma hits, for example majority vote procedures as well as the market mechanism. Unconditional democracy is, then impossible. Still today, a half century and an almost infinite number of commentaries later, nobody has been able to counter the core[2] of Arrow's argument. The problem he defined was known in rudimentary form during Rousseau's time as well.[3] It seems that much of Rousseau's analysis of the general will and the possibility of building a "popular political economy" is coloured by an awareness of the core of this problem.

Rousseau's conception of the impossibility dilemma pertains to the conflicting rights of the individual versus those of the common interests of all. Far from providing tyrants with "a blueprint for dictatorship", Rousseau treated this conflict of rights like an aprioristic synthetic category (in Kant's sense) embedded in the very essence of being a society.

The dilemma is treated not only in the CONTRAT SOCIAL, but also in other works, including the DISCOURS SUR L'ÉCONOMIE POLITIQUE. In order to be able to execute the general will, the government has to possess authority, and thereby the right to limit the liberty of its citizens and the right to use sanctions at the cost of property. But public liberty is an indispensable necessity for the formation of the general will:

> as, in order to will, it is necessary to be free, a difficulty no less great than the former arises that of preserving at once the public liberty and the authority of government.[4]

Rousseau's impossibility problem arises in that the *formation* of the general will necessitates the freedom of the people, while its *execution* necessitates a state of society incompatible with full liberty. How can, for example, the "holy right of

1. The four reasonable requirements are: that all voters are allowed all logically possible ranking orders; that if every individual in his ranking order prefers one alternative before another then that alternative must also be preferred to the other in the common, social preference ranking; that the social preference ranking of two options (among the three or more choices) must only be influenced by the individual preferences concerning precisely these two options and may not be influenced by the ranking of any others; and, that there must not exist any individual, "dictator", such that whenever he prefers one alternative before another, then this alternative will always be preferred to the other in the social preference ranking. Arrow argued in his 1951 essay that there is no aggregation mechanism that can satisfy all these four conditions simultaneously. Arrow 1963, p.1 and pp. 22ff.
2. A number of attempts at reformulations seems to have been successful. See e.g., Sen 1982a. On questions related to Rousseau's formulation of the problem see e.g., Sen 1982d.
3. Arrow's argument is usually labelled "the impossibility theorem". A primeval version of the theorem was formulated already during Rousseau's time by people connected to the Encyclopedie. It has been called "Borda's" or "Condorcet's jury theorem" and sometimes "the voting paradox". I have not been able to find any conclusive proof that Rousseau knew the paradox in its detail.
4. OC III, p. 248. [Rousseau 1983, p.123]. "Comme pour volouir il faut être libre, une autre difficulté, qui n'est guere moindre, est d'assurer à la fois la liberté publique et l'autorité du gouvernement."

property" be upheld against society's unconditional duty and right to protect its citizens, and thereby, if necessary, trespass on property in order to raise funds or save lives?

Rousseau formulates the dilemma as a legitimation problem. Society, the state, and its institutions exist and have legitimate rights towards the citizens because people need mutual protection for their property, life and liberty. The self, "common to the whole", therefore has a right to demand that the state fulfills this, its ontological task. But, how can any society protect these three rights for all citizens if it is never allowed to inflict itself on a single one of them? How can society, for example, defend the liberty of one person without ever constraining the freedom of another? And how can it provide for the "public needs" (for example of life-preserving food) without even once "alienating the individual property of those forced to contribute"? Rousseau answers that it cannot. In order to fulfill its task it has to abuse the very rights, the protection of which legitimates its existence.

> With whatever sophistry all this may be covered over, it is certain that if any constraint can be laid on my will, I am no longer free; and that I am no longer master of my own property, if any one else can lay a hand on it.[1]

* * *

In this way Rousseau, like Locke, formulates a historical legitimation of the rights of the individual (such as the right to property) versus those of society. But his formulation also contains a figure of reasoning which reverses Locke's. While Locke argues that history may legitimate the individual's claim to an absolute and inviolable right to his property, Rousseau here simultaneously argues both Locke's position and its opposite. True, the very society-creating event, the very rationale for individuals to accept the legitimacy of social institutions, is that their life, freedom and endowments be protected; and society (in contrast to the state of nature) is the only means by which this can be done. But if people's life, liberty and endowments would otherwise have been left unprotected, this means that neither the rights nor the people themselves may even have existed without society. This lays the basis for Rousseau's dilemma: in order to fulfill its societal task, the duty which constitutes its legitimacy, society might need to trespass precisely upon the exact values it purports to protect. The "self, common to the whole" is embedded, by necessity, in a conflict between self and others. Hence, if the individual's three "needs" (property, life and freedom) were absolute, deontological rights, they could never be "protected", and might get lost because of lack of protection.

Rousseau prefers the second of these new Scylla or Charybdis options, (encroachments into the three basic rights rather than having no protection). Without the constraints set by society, a state of nature would inevitably result.

1 OC III, p. 248, [Rousseau 1983, p.123]. "De quelques sophismes qu'on puisse colorer tout cela, il est certain que si l'on peut comtraindre ma volonté, je ne suis plus libre, et que je ne suis plus maître de mon bien, si quelqu'autre peut y toucher."

In that case, obedience would be prescribed "solely by necessity", while in society, members are "confining their wills by their own consent". The state of nature would, then, provide still fewer freedoms.

It is significant that Rousseau admits that the defence of liberty and property may conflict, and suggests an important restriction on how conflict should be resolved: that it must be according to general law.[1] But the basic legitimation dilemma remains – as an "impossibility problem" – unsolved. In other texts we can see that Rousseau also presumes that there may be a conflict between life and property: the right to survival and the right to trade freely with one's assets.

Arrow seems inclined to search the de-paralysing formula of his impossibility problem in the arena of social conventions.[2] Likewise, the importance Rousseau gives to citizenship and social morale reflects a related idea. He thinks that potentials of the general will must be tended by nurturing a kind of basic social consensus concerning fundamental moral principles. That is why he gives so much weight to citizenship, tradition and cultural heritage.[3] The impossibility dilemmas demand of a democratic society that democracy is conserved by means of culture.

1. Ibid.
2. By weakening his requirement. See Arrow 1961, pp. 81-86.
3. More about this in Chapter 9 below.

## 8. CHAINS OF DEPENDENCE

# *From Abuse to Use*

IN ORDER TO prevent individual interests from interfering with common interests, society should take care that no one becomes too independent. This is one of the messages of Rousseau's only concrete attempt to design a democratic and just economy: the proposals on Corsica. Although Corsica should strive for autarchy in its international relations, and although subsistence agriculture should be stimulated by all means, households should nonetheless be strongly discouraged from becoming totally autarchic in relation to the rest of the economy. For this reason, Rousseau proposes a policy for *conditional* autarchy. In pursuit of this goal governments may even have to manipulate prices "a little":

> ...it is best to revive them [prices] a little, from fear that the individuals having become too isolated, too independent, and too savage, no longer have enough government.[1]

This statement against autarchy should be disturbing to all who claim that old-fashioned subsistence agriculture is a basic goal in Rousseau's economic philosophy. The most astute scholar of Rousseau's economic thinking, Iring Fetscher, has noticed it, and is puzzled:

> It is extremely remarkable that Rousseau here opposes that very economic tendency in his constitution draft, which unambiguously aims at the creation of autarchic peasant enterprises.[2]

1 OC III, p. 935. "... il conviendra de la ranimer un peu de peur que les particuliers, devenus aussi trop isolés, trop indépendans, trop sauvages ne tiennant plus assés de gouvernement."
2 Fetscher 1960, p. 236. "Es ist außerordentlich bemerkenswert, daß hier Rousseau selbst der wirtschaftspolitischen Tendenz seines Verfaßungsentwurf entgegentritt, die eindeutig auf die Schaffung autarker Kleinbauernbetriebe abzielte."

After a long discussion, Fetscher concludes that Rousseau wanted people to remain dependent in order to make the state potent and indispensable. In particular, peasants had to be made dependent on those trades that were to be monopolised by the state. This policy of dependence would further the cause of étatism.[1] But Fetscher's solution and his ideas concerning Rousseau's étatism are not supported by evidence elsewhere in Rousseau's writings. Consequently, Fetscher's interpretation can hardly be reasonable. The concept of dependence is, nevertheless, puzzling. On the one hand, Rousseau argues that everybody should be kept dependent for the sake of the government; while, on the other hand, dependence is the very mark of Cain in his diatribes against the dehumanizing experiences of the civilisation process. In this chapter, an attempt is made to clarify the double function of the concept. The result will be relevant to the understanding of Rousseau's views on the option and foundation of a democratic economy.

## *The Tacit Contract*

The idea of a *terrorising* dependency is central to Rousseau's general views. One's ultimate dependence (for one's survival) on someone else marks the defining characteristic of the societal state. Moreover, in all societies throughout history, this condition has caused some to be unilaterally dependent on others and thereby easily exploited. To diminish this problem, societies should stubbornly support small scale subsistence farming to the greatest extent possible. But why, then, not encourage full independence? In order to find the answer, it is, I suggest, again of help to turn to Rousseau's contemporary, Sir James Steuart.

Sir James Steuart shared much of Rousseau's view on dependence. In his stage theory of historical development, dependency increases with the development of population (as it does in Rousseau's view of history). But his policy conclusions are the opposite of Rousseau's. While Rousseau wants to postpone the moment when autarchy has to surrender, Steuart concludes that the divorce between "parent earth and her labourious children" should be actively stimulated or even coerced by government calculation and planning. Every possible gain achieved by a division of labour would be beneficial because it would facilitate the provisioning of the people. For that reason a radical specialisation is unavoidable. Policies to strengthen subsistence agriculture should, consequently, be abolished.

In spite of their political differences, Steuart, like Rousseau, is concerned with the problems caused by the division of labour. Excluded from the traditional mode of provision by subsistence farming, the specialised non-agrarian labourer becomes ultimately dependent on others for her food provisions. Thereby, her very survival is endangered while society at large gains economic advantages of an order that would make it possible to save lives. The only reasonable compensation for the good these non-peasants do for society, and the risks they suffer, is that society guarantees their protection and provision. Their dependence implies a "general tacit contract", guaranteeing reciprocal support, Steuart claims.

1 Fetscher 1960, pp. 236-248.

Like Rousseau, Steuart nevertheless fears that this tacit contract will be abused and labourers will become exploited because of their unilateral dependence:

> Whenever, therefore, any one is found, upon whom nobody depends, and who depends upon every one, as is the case with him who is willing to work for his bread, but who can find no employment, there is a breach of contract, and an abuse. For the same reason, if we can suppose any person entirely taken up in feeding himself, depending upon no one, and having no one dependent upon him, we lose the idea of society because there are no reciprocal obligations between such a person and the other members of society.[1]

The mutual dependence between oneself and others implies "reciprocal obligations". The absence of such obligations threatens the very core of society. Therefore, not only unilateral dependence, but also its complement, unilateral *independence,* should be avoided.

I contend that Rousseau's view on "dependence" is very similar to that above. Two cases may illustrate the double problem of dependence in his thinking.

## *Friday's Iron Chain*

The first case describes how the possibility of sustained control over another person (like serfdom), is facilitated by the latter being ultimately and unilaterally dependent. A large population, efficient property rights, and the possibility of excluding others from fertile lands, are the necessary preconditions for keeping people permanently obedient. If free land existed, sooner or later the dominated person would be able to escape:

> A man, could very well seize the fruits another had gathered, the game he had killed, or the cave that served as his shelter; but how would he ever be able to make him obey, and what could be the chains of dependence among men who owned nothing?[2]

Rousseau offers a vivid example of his argument that could very well have been part of a novel:

> If I get chased away from a tree, I am free to go to another one. If they tormented me at one place, who would prevent me from moving elsewhere? Is there one single person with a force so superior to mine, and moreover so depraved, so lazy and so ferocious as to force me to take care of his subsistence while he remains idle?[3]

1. Steuart 1966, p. 88.
2. OC III, p. 161. "Un homme pourra bien s'emparer des fruits qu'un autre a cüellis, du gibier qu'il a tué, de l'antre qui lui servoit d'azile; mais comment viendra-t-il jamais à bout de s'en faire obéir, et quelles pourront être les chaînes de la dépendance parmi des hommes qui ne possèdent rien?"
3. Ibid. "Si l'on me chasse d'un arbre, j'en suis quitte pour aller à un autre; Si l'on me tourmente dans un lieu, qui m'empêchera de passer ailleurs? Se trouve-t-il un homme d'une force assés supérieur à la mineene, et, de plus assés dépravé, assés paresseux, et assés féroce pour me contraindre à pourvoir à sa subsistance pendant qu'il demeure oisif?"

And the hopeless and ultimate powerlessness, under such conditions, of the lord is described even more dramatically:

> He must resolve not to lose me from sight for one single instant, to keep me bound with very great care during his sleep for fear that I will escape or that I will kill him: that is to say that he is obliged to expose himself voluntarily to a pain much worse than that which he wanted to avoid, and than that he gives to me. ...I take five steps into the forest, my iron shackles are broken, and he will never see me again in his whole life.[1]

Do not these lines resound from a very particular piece of literature? Who does not have Robinson Crusoe and Friday in mind when reading them? Robinson is, in fact, Rousseau's grand example of the tragedy of dependence. In Defoe's novel, Robinson Crusoe forces Friday into obedience because he possesses an efficient monopoly of the means necessary for Friday's survival (the gun, the land and the tools found in the shipwreck). There are simply no means whereby Friday can subsist by himself. The very origin of Friday's dependence is telling, and very Rousseauan. It all started with Robinson saving Friday's life: Friday would doubtless have been dead had he been on his own. It is precisely this ultimate inequality that in Rousseau's thinking is the necessary and sufficient condition for the presence of those "ties of dependence" that create the state of society. As long as he is not dependent for his survival, nothing really prevents Friday from finding his subsistence elsewhere. As long as he is not bound by *chains of dependence* he cannot be permanently controlled. He would always have the possibility of exit: "If I get chased away from a tree, I am free to go to another one". To keep someone obedient would require a highly improbable amount of vigilance and ingenuity. When Friday had recovered and Robinson feared that he would flee and try to survive by himself, what precautions Robinson then had to take! At that point Robinson had to face a dreadful situation characteristic of the master's fate in the state of nature.

The state of nature is presented in a specific rhetoric context. In the first part of the DISCOURS SUR L'ORIGINE ET LES FONDEMENTS DE L'INÉGALITÉ Rousseau wants to counter Hobbes' attempt to legitimate certain non-democratic political institutions through a natural law argument. In particular, he attacks Hobbes' thought that a state of nature, where man could provide for his subsistence independently of others, is more likely to cause war and violence than is a civil society. Hobbes used this thought to legitimate the intervention of a civilising hegemonic authority, a Leviathan, a ruler. The sovereign would be entitled to power because he saved men from the deadly and chaotic war of the state of nature: without him they would not even have been alive. Contra Hobbes, Rousseau argues that, between a hypothetical pre-civil state and a civil society, no relevant similarity can exist which would permit that norms are deducible from

1. OC III, p. 161. "Il faut qu'il se résolve à ne pas me perdre de veüe un seul instant, à me tenir lié avec un très grand soin durant son sommeil, de peur que je ne m'échappe ou que je ne le tüe: c'est-à-dire qu'il est obligé de s'exposer volontairement à une peine beacoup plus grande que celle qu'il veut éviter, et que celle qu'il me donne à moi-même . . .
Je fais vingt pas dans la forêt, mes fers son bris'es, et il ne me revoit de sa vie."

the one to the other. Influenced by Pufendorf,[1] he emphasises that his description of the state of nature is purely hypothetical,[2] an arbitrary assumption made with a discursive or expository purpose, similar it seems, to the delimitations used in modern deductive economics. And secondly, it is not independent man's propensity to passion (as Hobbes thought) that threatens peace and freedom from violence, but rather that very *dependence* which constitutes civil society. Therefore, Hobbes is wrong:

> that Author should have said that as the state of nature is that in which the care for our conservation is the least prejudicial to that of others, it would consequently be the state the most proper for Peace, and the most feasible for Mankind.[3]

The real threat, the really war-provoking condition arises when individuals or families are dependent on others for their survival and conservation. The establishment of efficient and complete property rights removes the option of escape and independent subsistence. But such rights are not possible until population is so large that all land cultivable enough for someone's subsistence is occupied. From that moment on, some are ultimately dependent on others: he who owns the land, owns the people. It is precisely this expropriation of all land as private property that characterises the origin of the state of society. Here in the words of the second DISCOURS:

> some people cannot expand except at the cost of others, and the people left over which 'faiblesse' or indolence have prevented from acquiring anything... become obliged to receive or seize their subsistence from the hands of the rich.[4]

1 Pufendorf is a forerunner, both in his use of the state of nature as a "gedanklicher Fiktion" (discursive fiction) and in his portraying of it not as an Hobbesian state of war but as a state of peace. Cf., Dufour 1986, pp. 109ff.

2 In OC III, p. 123 he describes his use of the concept, the state of nature like this: "un état qui n'existe plus, qui n'a peut-être point existé, qui probablement n'existera jamais". And he admits that he is trying is to use the concept hypothetically: "Je ne pourrais former sur ce sujet que des conjectures vagues, et presque imaginaires." He illustrates his method by a comparison with the natural sciences, also in the same Discours OC III, p. 135: "Commençons donc par écarter tous les faits, car ils ne touchent point à la question. Il ne faut prendre les recherches, dans lesquelles on peut entrer sur ce sujet, pour des vérités historiques, mais seulement pour des raisonnement hypothétiques et conditionelles; plus propres a éclaircir la nature des choses, qu'à en montrer la véritable origine, et semblables à que font tous les jours nos physiciens sur la formation du monde."
The hypothetical nature of Rousseau's concept, the state of nature has been observed by authors such as Paul de Man and Suzanne Gearhardt (Cf., Gearhardt 1984, pp. 265f). It is mentioned also in an article by Gustaf Steffen published in 1913 (Steffen 1913).

3 OC III, p. 153. [Rousseau 1983, p. 65]. "cet Auteur devoit dire que l'état de Nature étant celui où le soin de notre conservation est le moins préjudiciable à celle d'autrui, cet état étoit par conséquent le plus propre à la Paix, et le plus convenable au Genre-humain."

4. Ibid., p. 175. "les uns ne purent plus s'agrandir qu'aux dépens des autres, et les surnuméraires que la faiblesse ou l'indolence avaient empêchés d'en acquérir . . . furent obligés de recevoir ou de ravir leur subsistance de la main des riches." A second characteristic of the state is that the people become mutually dependent for their subsistence. (The Contrat Social I:6). OC III, p. 360. "Je suppos les hommes parvenus à ce point où les obstacles qui nuisent à leur conservation dans l'état de nature l'emportent par leur résistance sur les forces que chaque individu peut employer pour se maintenir dans cet état. Alors cet état primitif ne peut plus subsister, et le genre humain périrait s'il ne changeait sa manière d'être.Or comme les hommes ne peuvent engendrer de nouvelles forces, mais seulement

## *The Stag Hunt and the Tragedy of Independence*

Rousseau's second case study concerning the dual-problem of dependence is provided by the well-known story of the stag hunt. It is one of the most revealing examples of how Rousseau thought about civilising dependence. Typically, it concerns the provision of necessities.

> Suppose we are in a wilderness without food. Separately we can catch rabbits and eat badly. Together we can catch stags and eat well. But if only one of us deserts the stag hunt to catch a rabbit, the stag will get away; so the stag hunters will not eat unless they desert too. Each must choose whether to stay with the stag hunt or desert according to his expectations about the others, staying if, and only if no one else will desert.[1]

The story of the stag hunt is told in the DISCOURS SUR L'ORIGINE ET LES FONDEMENTS DE L'INÉGALITÉ. In order to precipitate its tale of civilising dependence, it is necessary to look more closely at this example and how it has been read. It is here interpreted by David Lewis in a manner I shall discuss initially.

## *The need for assurance*

A short discussion of Lewis' reading is necessary since the tragic role of independence *cannot* appear in his version. His stag hunt is a tale of the need for coordination, assurance or conventions. My point about the tragedy of independence is based on a deviant interpretation. Here, I shall try to show that Lewis' reading is too narrow.

In Lewis' influential[2] interpretation, what is most rational for the hunter to do when he discovers the meagre rabbit depends wholly on how much he believes in the fidelity of others and in a successful stag hunt:

> Separately we can catch rabbits and eat badly. Together we can catch stags and eat well.[3]

In this story there is one motive only to desert: the fear that others will leave their parts so that one would be left hungry.[4] If everybody stayed and the stag was caught then everybody would be better off. No one would have any reason to run for the hare as long as he knew that the others would also cooperate. If the hunter could be assured that the others would stay, he would do so as well. A convention could easily create that assurance, since one would gain as little by breaking it as

unir et diriger celles qui existent, ils n'ont plus d'autre moyen pour se conserver que de former par aggrégation une somme de forces qui puisse l'emporter sur la résistance, de les mettre en jeu par un seul mobile et de les faire agir de concert."

1. Lewis 1969, p. 7. Compare R. Hardin 1982, p. 167ff, which suggests a diverging interpretation of the stag hunt.
2. It has caused considerable confusion in the literature. Many have followed it. A recent example is Hermansson 1992.
3. Lewis 1969, p. 7.
4. In gametheory it is pictured expressively in the so-called assurance game. (cf., Rapaport and Guyer 1966). It is a coordination problem with two equilibria one of which is Paretooptimal.

one would gain by driving on the "unconventional" side of the road. No policing would be needed to keep such a convention. The dilemma is to find a common rhythm, in David Hume's example:

> Suppose you and I are rowing a boat together. If we row in rhythm, the boat goes smoothly forward; otherwise the boat goes slowly and erratically, we waste effort and we risk hitting things. We are always choosing whether to row faster or slower; it matters little to either of us at what rate we row, provided we row in rhythm.[1]

In Lewis' story the creation of certainty is the decisive thing. Any operative convention is better than uncertainty.

> If Rousseau's stag hunters stay with the hunt every time, they do so by a convention. Each stays because he trusts the others to stay as they did before, and he will eat better by staying and taking his share of the stag when it is caught. ... But less obviously, if they always split up and catch rabbits separately, that is a convention too.[2]

The stag hunter can face three possible outcomes. Which will be the best depends on what the hunter believes the others will do, and what they actually do. It is a question of assurance. The best outcome would be that he stays at his post, correctly believing that others do the same. Then he will get a good piece of venison. The next best outcome is that he acts as if the convention is to desert. Then he gets a mediocre meal (hare), regardless of whether or not desertion really is the convention. The worst choice takes place if, thinking that the convention is to stay, he stays, while others abandon their posts. Then he remains hungry.

### *The tragedy of the stag hunt*

Lewis' reading is not the only one. Another reading is possible that is more tragic (and more reasonable). It is, admittedly, true that Lewis' non-assurance motive for desertion is well-known to Rousseau. Read for example these lines from the CONTRAT SOCIAL (1st version):

> 'It is useless', he might add 'for me to try to reconcile my interest with that of others; everything you tell me about the advantages of the social law would be excellent if, whilst I was scrupulously observing it towards others, I could be sure that they would all observe it towards me. But what assurance can you give me on this? Could I find myself in any worse situation than that of being exposed to all the harm which stronger men might wish to do to me without daring to get my

1. In Lewis 1969, p. 5.
2. Ibid., p. 47.

> own back on the weaker ones? Either you must give me guarantees against any unjust undertaking, or you must not expect me to abstain from similar actions in my turn'...[1]

But (as in fact this quote already shows) non-assurance is not the entire problem. For in Rousseau's tale there are two rational motives for deserting: a second one besides non-assurance. What Lewis ascribes to Rousseau:

> Separately we can catch rabbits and eat badly. Together we can catch stags and eat well.[2]

is, in fact, not really there in Rousseau's text. And this absence gives the tale far more bite. Here is a reference from the text in Rousseau's own formulation:

> but if a hare happened to come within the reach of any one of them, it is not to be doubted that he pursued it without scruple, and, having seized his prey, cared very little, if by so doing he caused his companions to miss theirs.[3]

Rousseau never states that the individual would eat better if the stag were captured. Rather, he seems to take the opposite for granted. Lewis' story in fact, firstly, contains an added degree of precision compared to Rousseau's formulation. Secondly, there is some uncertainty about the result of the stag hunt in Rousseau's text which Lewis' reading hides. Lewis' tinkering robs the story of much of its bite and tragedy. What if the hunter does not find the venison more attractive than the hare? The notable problem in Rousseau's text is that the hare meat may actually be preferable. It may be more attractive for several reasons. The meal may simply be more nourishing or tasty, or one may have a time preference of not caring to wait for the (possible) venison. The present value of a future steak may not be terribly great if one is very hungry right now. In fact, Rousseau explicitly declares that the hunters did not much care for future consumption. They *"know nothing of foresight", he explains.* That should mean that their time preference is high, and they therefore rate future consumption as relatively inferior. Another reason refers to the possibility that the hunters may be risk averse; for there is a considerable risk that, remaining faithfully at their posts, they will get neither stag nor hare. So understood, the story portrays not one, but

1. OC III, p. 285. [Rousseau 1983, p. 158]. "'C'est vainement', pourra-t-il ajoûter, 'que je voudrois concilier mon interest avec celui d'autru; tout ce que vous me dites des avantages de la loi sociale pourroit être bon, si tandis que je l'observois scrupupeusement envers les autres, j'étois sur qu'ils l'observeroient tous envers moi; mais quelle sureté pouvez-vous me donner là-dessus, et ma situation peut-elle être plus forts voudront donnez-moi des garants contre toute entreprise injuste, ou n'espérez pas que je m'en abstienne à mon tour.'"
2. Lewis 1969, p. 7.
3. OC III, p. 166f. [Rosseau 1983, p. 78] "S'agissoit il de prendre un Cerf, chacun sentoit bien qu'il devoit pour cela garder fidellement son poste; mais si un liévre venoit à passer à la portée de l'un d'eux, il ne faut pas douter qu'il ne le poursuivît sans scrupule, et qu'ayant atteint sa proye il ne se souciât fort peu de faire manquer la leur à ses Compagnons."

two reasons to leave and run for the hare: Lewis' non-assurance (one wants to protect oneself against losses caused by the possible non-cooperation of others); but also, secondly, the possibility of gaining something better.

A significant portrayal of the gain motive can be found in the second version of the CONTRAT SOCIAL. It refers to the relationship between individual citizens and the government, "the sovereign". The sovereign has here, by definition, no interest other than the common interests of all – the general will. Everybody can be fully assured and has no reason to desert because of the assurance motive. Only the former gain remains:

> The sovereign is entirely formed by the individuals that constitute it. Therefore he neither does nor can have any interest contrary to theirs. Consequently the sovereign power does not need to offer any guarantee in relation to his subjects, because it is impossible that the body would want to hurt all its members. And we shall see further on that it cannot hurt any individual.[1]

But on the other hand, Rousseau affirms, the sovereign still has reason to fear the motives of the citizens. Although they have an interest in common with the sovereign, representing the "general will", they may have nothing to lose by not cooperating. The "sovereign" would need "means to make sure of their fidelity".

> In fact, each individual can, as a human being, have a particular will contrary or dissimilar to that general will he owns as a citizen. His particular interest may speak to him quite differently from the common interest: *his absolute and naturally independent existence* may make him regard that which he owes to the common cause as a free [gratuitous] contribution, the loss of which will do less harm to others, than the harm of the payment is being burdensome to himself.[2]

In game theoretical terms the tragedy is not an assurance game but rather an example of the most well-known game of all, the prisoner's dilemma.[3] Thus, an equilibrium (a choice that is the optimum for each individual regardless of what the others choose) exists, unique or not, that is not identical with Pareto-optimum. In other words, the potential cooperators have rational reasons not to

1. OC III, p. 363. "Or le Souverain nétant formé que des particuliers qui le composent n'a ni peut avoir d'intérêt contraire au leur; par consequent la puissance Souveraine n'a nul besoin de garant envers les sujets, parce qu'il est impossible que le corps veuille nuire à tous ses membres, et nous verrons ci'après qu'il ne peut nuire à aucun en particulier."

2. Ibid.,"Mais il n'en est ainsi des sujets envers le souverain, auquel, malgré l'intérêt commun, rienne répondrait de leurs engagements s'il ne trouvait des moyens de s'assurer de leur fidélité.
En effet chaque individu peut comme homme avoir une volonté particuliere contraire ou dissemblable à la volonté generale qu'il a comme Citoyen.
Son intérét particulier peut lui parler tout autrement que l'intérêt commun; son existence absolue et naturellement indépendante peut lui faire envisager ce qu'il doit à la cause commune comme une contribution gratuite, dont la perte sera moins nuisable aux autres que le payement n'en est onéreux pour lui . . ." Italics added.

3. My interpretation is that the stag hunt pictures the state of nature as a noncooperative game with a suboptimal equilibrium, naturally causing failure to cooperate. Kenneth Waltz and Russel Hardin correctly understand it as the prisoners' dilemma. Cf., R. Hardin 1982, pp. 168f. See also, de Jasay 1989, p. 50ff.

participate, although cooperation would give the best gross result and all could be better off if they chose it. Strict individual rationality dictates a choice that is less than optimal. The prisoner's dilemma, and in another context Garret Hardin's "tragedy of the commons", are well-known examples of this situation.[1]

This interpretation contains more tragedy still. Here, communication and trust are urgent means for society in the presence of an agent that is strictly maximising personal gain. Whether or not the individual hunter knows for certain what the others will do, he will gain by deserting, by getting a meal he values higher than the stag meal; although the hunting team would gain as a group if all stayed at their posts. At the same time, the presence of the gain motive makes the non-assurance motive stronger: it is more difficult to feel assured that others will not desert. Society needs strategies to protect itself from such a problem.[2] Rousseau proposes two kinds of strategies. To keep everybody dependent is one of them. This will be discussed next. To implement *a* "republic of hearts" is the second strategy. The next chapter considers that approach.

## *The role of independence*

When Rousseau presents the possibility that the hunter may desert his post (in modern game theoretical terms, that the equilibrium choice may differ from the optimal) he points out one significant precondition. It is with the words just quoted

> his absolute and naturally independent existence...

that makes it attractive for him to exploit the gain motive. It is this condition which makes him regard goods that are due to the "common cause" as free – what we may call "free-riding".

And it is highly significant that the tale of the stag hunt appears in the (hypothetical) state of nature described in the DISCOURS SUR L'ORIGINE ET LES

1. G. Hardin 1968, pp. 1244ff. I shall recall the latter one. Imagine a common field which a number of herdsmen keep as pasture and where the number of animals is such that any increase, because of diminished pasturage per animal will decrease the total animal produce of the field! There are two reasons for each of the herdsmen to increase his number of animals on the field although the increase may cause the total amount of milk and flesh produced to decrease. "Adding together the component partial utilities, the rational herdsman concludes that the only sensible course for him to pursue is to add another animal to the herd. And another; and another ... But this is the coercion reached by each and every rational herdsman sharing the commons. Therein is the tragedy. Each man is locked into a system that compels him to increase his herd without limit – in a world that is limited. Ruin is the destination towards which all men rush, each pursuing his own best interest in a society that believes in freedom of the commons. Freedom of the commons brings ruin to all."
The first reason to increase the number of cattle is to compensate for the decrease of the produce in case a neighbour would add animals to the fields. The other reason is the potential gain. For a systematic treatment of the prisoner's dilemma and other fundamental games, see Rapaport 1989, and Rapaport and Guyer 1966.

2. Cohen (1986) discusses this problem in relation to recent interpretations of the thinking of Rousseau mostly by political scientists. He interprets Rousseau's general will as the optimal solution in the presence of suboptimal equilibria. The government trying to realize the general will encounters two: problems "to avoid arrangements that tempt people to subordinate the general will to their private advantage, and to assure those who are not tempted that their cooperation will not be abused." (p. 295).

FONDEMENTS DE L'INÉGALITÉ. Here, people are assumed to be taking care of their provisioning on their own, or with the help of other family members. Other "trees" are available toward which one can run, other game ready to be subdued, other caves exist wherein one can find dwelling, etc. In this situation it would be advantageous only *at times* to cooperate:

> Taught by experience that the love of well-being is the only force mobilizing human action, [man] found himself able to distinguish a few cases, in which mutual interest might justify his reliance upon the assistence of his fellows[1]

In these "few" cases only temporary associations were formed. They "lasted no longer than the transitory occasion that formed them."[2] But, as long as anyone could gain by not cooperating, there could be no certainty that agreements would be kept. And, if an individual could benefit by deserting, then nothing in the world might stop him. At this point, the tale of the stag hunt appears:

> If a deer was to be taken, each could see that, in order to succeed, he must abide faithfully by his post: but if a hare happened to come within the reach of any one of them, it is not to be doubted that he might pursue it without scruple, and, having seized his prey, cared very little, if by so doing he caused his companions to miss theirs.[3]

Cooperation would only be temporary, because man was not continually dependent on mutual assistence. The independence of people in the state of nature *impeded* cooperation.

In the state of society, however, nobody is by nature independent, except by means of power or property [EMILE]:

> Any one who wanted to consider himself as an isolated individual, self-sufficient and independent of others could only be utterly wretched. He could not even continue to exist, for finding the whole earth appropriated by others while he had only himself, how could he find the means to subsistence?[4]

1. OC III, p. 166f. [Rousseau 1983, p. 78]. "Instruit par l'expérience que l'amour du bien-être est le seul mobile des actions humaines, il se trouva en état de distinguer les occasions rares où l'intérêt commun devoit le faire compter sur l'assistance de ses semblables".
2. Ibid.,. "il s'unissoit avec eux en trupeau, ou tout au plus par quelque sorte d'association libre qui n'obligeoit personne, et qui ne duroit qu'autant que le besoin passager qui l'avoit formée."
3. Ibid.,. The character of this love of well-being in relation to nature and to man's natural and artificial, exogenous needs and desires are exposed in a very clarifying and stimulating way in an annotation by Bernard Gagnebin to this paragraph in OC III, p. 1341. The translation in this paragraph follows closely R. Hardin 1982, p. 167., also OC III, p. 166.
4. III. OC IV, p. 467. [Rousseau 198, p. 4 and p. 156]. "Sur ce principe, un homme qui voudroit se regarder comme un être isolé, ne tenant du tout à rien et se suffisant à lui-même, ne pourroit être que miserable. Il lui seroit même impossible de subsister; car trouvant la terre entiere couverte du tien et du mien, et n'ayant rien à lui que son corps, d'ou tireroit il son nécessaire?"

This formulation of the problem seems to harbour its solution. By eliminating the cause, the problem might well be avoided. If "independent existence" were, by some means, transformed, and the individuals were to become dependent on society, society could then protect itself from this source of uncooperative behaviour. In this way, the very essence of the tragedy of the state of society, dependence, could be transformed to a decisive advantage.

In the state of nature such a permanent, civilising dependency does not exist. It is for this reason that the behaviour of the stag hunters is reasonable. There is simply no reason:

> why in that primitive state, a human would have more need for another human being than that which a monkey or a wolf would have of its kind; or if this need is assumed, by what motive the other could be engaged to care; and, in the latter case, how the two parts would come to a mutual agreement about the conditions.[1]

This perspective is not simply about human concern and sympathy. Rousseau, like other contemporaneous authors (e.g. Adam Fergusson), assumes that man, like animals, possesses an original faculty for compassion with his likes. In his texts he repeatedly refers to the existence of a natural sentiment of sympathy among humans as well as animals, *pitié*. Even the horse refuses to step on a prone individual and the concierge interferes when someone is threatened by violence.[2]

Notwithstanding these points, the text is about something else: the option to permanently employ another being for one's own good: for one's survival or for indulging in luxury. The problem is that in the state of society most people are:

> subjected to a universal dependence, and obliged to get everything from those that are not obliged to give them anything.[3]

## *Bargaining and the ability to wait*

One way to counteract the temptation to desert, and thereby cause a sub-optimal result, would be to redistribute the gain by cooperation. If Norwegian fishermen were to lose out on the number of catch due to increased fishing by Icelandic fishermen, the Norwegians could pay the Icelanders to abstain and still end up better off than if they had simply let their suboptimal fishing continue. Or they could demand that the Icelandic fishermen compensate them for their decreased productivity. If a group of agents are dependent on the actions of each other, as in the stag hunt, then they may be tempted to blackmail one another. If the agents decide to cooperate, then the stag hunt points to the fact that, contrary to competitive market equilibria, the conditions for trading are arbitrary. This

1. OC III, p. 151. [Rousseau 1983, p.63]. "pourquoi dans cet état primitif un homme auroit plûtôt besoin d'un autre homme qu'un singe ou un Loup de son semblable, ni, ce besoin supposé quel motif pourroit engager l'autre à y pourvoir, ni même, en ce dernier cas, comment ils pourroient convenir entr'eux des conditions."

2. OC III, p. 154. Rousseau does not share the "New economic gospel" of Margaret Thatcher and others portrayed by Amartya Sen. Its assumption is that man is basically egoistical. Cf., Sen 1984b.

3. Ibid., p. 153. "de s'être soumis à une dépendance universelle, et de s'obliger à tout recevoir de ceux qui ne s'obligent à leur rien donner."

means that the terms of trade have to be bargained. Bargaining implies a kind of monopoly, where one aspect is in a sense unique: if the hunter leaves for the hare – then, no stag.

By choosing the Paretooptimal option all could gain. Instead of letting one hunter leave his post, the others could pay him with a little extra meat relative to what he would have got by catching the hare. Still, all the others would at least get something to eat (that is, more than by not cooperating). But this possibility also means that the cooperators can act strategically to get optimal conditions of participation. Merely the threat not to cooperate can, for example, be applied as a strategy to get an advantageous deal. Amartya Sen offers the following intuitive definition of "the essence" of the bargaining problem:

> The essence of the problem is that there are many cooperative outcomes – beneficial to all the parties compared with non-cooperation – but the different parties have strictly conflicting interests in the choice among the set of efficient co-operative arrangements. So the problem is one of 'cooperative conflict'.[1]

The situation of "cooperative conflict" is, as has been made apparent repeatedly above, a very important consideration in Rousseau's economic philosophy. The bargaining over the distribution of available gain that is generated by cooperation can potentially be exploited by those who need cooperation the least, those who "can wait". He/she who has the best fall-back position[2] can dictate the bargain. It is against this background that we can understand Rousseau's resistance to any policy that would increase "the difference", i.e., strengthen the fall-back position of the most privileged. The larger the "difference", the greater the risk that the rich might abuse others' dependence on them for food. Similarly, the more independent some privileged citizens are, the more they can demand from those who are ultimately dependent. In order to prevent abuse, then, all should be kept dependent on society.

## *Dependent on the City*

Such a strategy is described, in an embryo shape, in the context of the family. Social dependence is compared to that between father and children:

> The goods of the father, of which he is really the master, are the ties which keep his children in dependence, and he may bestow on them, if he pleases, no share of his property unless they merit it by constant deference to his will. But the subjects of an arbitrary despot are far from having the same favour to expect from their chief...[3]

1. Sen 1984a, p. 375. The best situation in case no cooperation would take place, or the best opportunity to "wait"
2. Ibid.
3. OC III, p. 182. [Rousseau 1983, p. 94]. "Le Pere n'est le maître de l'Enfant qu'aussi longtems que son secours lui est nécessaire."
"Les biens de Pere, dont ils est véritablement le Maître, sont les liens qui retiennent ses enfans dans sa dépendance, et il peut ne leur donner part à sa succession qu'à proportion qu'ils auront bien mérité de lui par une continuelle déférence à ses volontés. Or, loin que les sujets ayent quelque faveur semblable à attendre de leur despot . . ."

Being unilaterally dependent on a single individual is a situation which can easily be abused by the "arbitrary despot". But in the father-child relationship dependence can serve decent purposes because the father and the children have common interests. Rousseau assumes that the father cares for his children and will not abuse them. The same thing is the case – by definition – with the government formed by the general will. To prevent abuses of this tacit contract, society must create a father-child-like "general dependence between its members", Sir James Steuart claimed.[1] Rousseau's solution is that each should be dependent on democratic society, on "the city":

> each Citizen should be in a full independence of all the others, but in an excessive dependence to the City.[2]

An example of the general structure of Rousseau's dialectics of dependence can be found in the EXTRAIT DU PROJET DE PAIX PERPÉTUELLE, one of the texts resulting from Rousseau's work with the papers by l'Abbé de Saint-Pierre. Although this text concerns the relations between nations rather than the dependence of citizens, it nevertheless clearly illustrates this latter idea. In order to conserve peace, Rousseau (in presenting the thought of Abbé Saint-Pierre) argued, the European community should not allow any nation to become entirely independent. An all-European "solid and durable confederation" should be set up. For that to work:

> a solid and durable confederation is necessary to get all the members in a dependence so mutual that *none by himself is able to resist all others and that the particular associations that could hurt the grand one, meet sufficient obstacles* to prevent them from realizing that; otherwise the confederation would be empty ...[3]

This formulation expresses well how Rousseau treats mutual dependence also in society. Rousseau suggests several means by which the individual can be made mutually dependent. Firstly, governments must guarantee everybody's right to live. Secondly, households should be conditionally self-sufficient. Thirdly, society should guarantee private property. Fourthly, the accumulation of private property and the growth of inequality must be impeded.

## *A secure food supply*

The food supply is the key to Rousseau's dialectic of dependence. In order to glue the citizens to one another, government or society must be able to guarantee a secure corn supply even when the regular provision is insufficient. Thus, to the

1. Steuart 1966, p. 88.
2. OC III, p. 394. "chaque Citoyen soit dans une parfaite indépendance de tous les autres, et dans une excessive dépendance de la Cité."
3. OC III, p. 573, italics added. "car pour former une confédération solide et durable, il faut en mettre tous les membres dans une dépendance tellement mutuelle, qu'aucun ne soit seul en état de resister à tous les autres, et que les associations particulieres qui pourroient nuire à la grande, y recontrent des obstacles suffisans pour empêcher leur exécution; sans quoi, la confédération seroit vaine, et chacun seroit réellement indépendant sous une apparente sujétion."

Corsicans, Rousseau suggested that they keep a public stock of corn. As was often the case in his writings, he found his model in Geneva[1] and was inspired by the idea of creating the "new Geneva".[2]

Geneva's *chambre des blés,* its grain magazine, had several functions. It kept a secure stock of corn and provided credit; it was a major source of revenue of the government, and was uncorrupt. Its corn stock was supplied not by taxation but by trading.[3] Rousseau's flattering picture of the Chambre appears to have been supported by empirical evidence. The magazine was, for example, able to assist not only its own citizens but also neighbouring regions with grain during the disastrous famine of 1771.[4] Rousseau also proposed the establishment of a kind of public, proto-virtual corn magazine. Instead of being kept in large and expensive barns, the corn could remain within individual households; and the households could borrow from one another by means of a public register wherein each household would announce its needs and its surplus and the exchange would be equalised in the long run.[5]

## *Conditional autarchy*

There are some suggestions as to how a policy of conditionally autarchic subsistence agriculture would best be designed. In the PROJET DE CONSTITUTION POUR LA CORSE a principle for government intervention is proposed. It is proposed that peasants could choose whether to pay tax in cash or in corn. The government should then study the ratio between taxes paid in kind or in cash. If the share of cash surpassed an optimum ratio (defined by the government), that would indicate the situation was too advantageous to the peasants and too detrimental for the "useful arts"; and vice versa.[6]

Rousseau obviously supposed that taxes are converted between cash and kind according to a fixed ratio. When the price of corn is higher than the norm then peasants can gain by paying tax in cash, and also be able (because of high corn prices) to accumulate money. At times when the prices of corn are below the norm, the amount of cash available and disposable among the peasants for tax is correspondingly less. Peasants would lose by paying taxes in cash if they could avoid it. All in all, the aim of the public corn policy is well summarized in the following paragraph from the DISCOURS SUR L'ÉCONOMIE POLITIQUE.

1. Ferrero 1934.
2. He gave the "new Geneva", a status similar to the new Jerusalem or the mythological Rome or Sparta (cf., Ellis 1977, p.38 and elsewhere). This is the case although he, like his father, seems to have been rather harshly treated by his birth city, Geneva. His concern for Geneva and its reputation is, for example, indicated in the Lettre à d'Alembert, and in his reaction to d'Alembert's characterization of the city in the Encyclopédie-article on Geneva.
3. DISCOURS SUR L'ÉCONOMIE POLITIQUE, OC III, p. 267.
4. Blanc 1939, pp. 436ff.
5. OC III, p. 923.
6. Ibid., p. 935. "Comme les particuliers seront toujours libres de payer leur contingent en argent ou en denrées . . ." "le gouvernement ayant une fois calculé la meilleure proportion qui doit se trouver entre ces deuc espéces de contribution . . ." "Quand le recouvremens en denrées passeront leur mesure et que ceux en argent n'atteindront pas à leur ce sera un signe que l'agriculture et la population vont bien mais que l'industrie utile se néglige"

> The private certainty is so aligned with the public confederation that, apart from due regard to human weakness, that convention would be rightly dissolved, if a single citizen in the state perished who could have been aided...[1]

This is a policy to prevent the establishment of unilateral ultimate dependence whereby some peasants are independent while others (e.g., craftsmen and others) are unilaterally dependent on them.

### *Private property as a sacred right*

According to Rousseau, private property[2] is a very important right in society. Perhaps the most important of all:

> It is certain that the right of property is the most sacred of all the rights of citizens and more important in certain respects than liberty itself;[3]

However, the contrast is remarkable between this canonization and the well-known, burning prophetic condemnation of the devastating consequences of property in the DISCOURS SUR L'ORIGINE ET LES FONDEMENTS DE L'INÉGALITÉ:

> The first one who, having enclosed a piece of land, took it upon himself to say, 'this is mine', and found men foolish enough to believe it, was the true founder of civil society. What crimes, wars, murders, miseries and horrors would mankind have been spared by one who, uprooting the stakes or filling in the ditch, had cried out to his fellows: Beware of listening to this impostor: you are lost, if you forget that the fruits belong to all and the land to no one.[4]

Rousseau's divergent statements on property are not easy to reconcile.[5] One explanation of the contradiction is that Rousseau is describing two different epochs in history. The elegy about private property is normative and concerns its establishment at that point in time when man began to live "outside oneself" desiring, above all, to be considered by others (women). According to this interpretation, the canonization, on the other hand, describes the entitlement rights

1. OC III, p. 256. "La sûreté partuculiere est tellement liée avec la confédération publique, que sans les égards que l'on doit à la foiblesse humaine, cette convention seroit dissoute par le droit, s'il périssoit dans l'état en seul citoyen qu'on eût pu secourir.."
2. I am not trying to discuss Rousseau's view on property in its full complexity. For a more complete discussion, see for example such works as MacAdam 1988 or Derathé 1970 and further references there. Here, property is exclusively discussed in its relation to dependence.
3. OC III, pp. 262f. "Il est certain que le droit de propriété est le plus sacré de tous les droits des citoyens, et plus important à certain égards que la liberté même;" Robert Wokler claims that the article Discours sur l'économie politique represents a different view on property than the other treatments by Rousseau, and refers the former to an influence from Locke and Diderot. (Wokler 1987, p. 77, note 89).
4. MacAdam 1988, p. 112; OC III, p. 164.
5. MacAdam claims that they appear as "contradictions enough to warm the enthusiasm of any Hegelian." MacAdam J, 1988, p. 113. Chabert A 1964, p. 355, accused Rousseau of being inconsistent and opportunist because of his non-consistent attitude to private property.

of modern society. Property is *in fact* the most sacred of all rights.[1] This interpretation portrays the appearance of private property as a choice based on some socio-psychological folly; while, contrastingly, in Rousseau's conceptualisation it is rather a true tragedy: an unavoidable consequence of the population growth.

But the talk about the sanctity of property in the DISCOURS SUR L'ÉCONOMIE POLITIQUE could also be interpreted in a more reasonable way. This right is more important than anything else, including liberty, for the *"conservation of life"*:

> the true foundation of civil society, and the true guarantee for the engagement of the citizens: for if the goods were not responded for [possessed] by anybody, nothing would be as easy as to elude one's duties and mock the laws.[2]

By virtue of the property right, guaranteed by government, most people are made dependent on the government.[3] The important point is that citizens own private property, not that they own much. The amount of private property should be limited to what is necessary for the conservation of one's life, to what is needed to prevent the "mocking of the law"[4]

Hence, property is not treated as an unconditional, deontologic right. It is a necessary means whereby to keep citizens dependent on their government. But it is subordinated to the public good and should, for that reason, be limited. Government should

> enclose it within the closest possible limits, to give it a measure, a rule, a bridle that restricts it, directs it, curbs it and keeps it always subordinated to the public good.[5]

Private property is accepted because civil society with true citizens is impossible without it. In addition, Rousseau does not entirely exclude state property, but warns that this grants too much power to the government.[6] State property is not ruled out but must be limited too, in order to prevent excess power within the government. Rousseau, therefore, does not follow Morelly and others who claim that most moral, social and political evils are traceable to property.

1. Ibid., p. 118 and p. 121.
2. OC III, p. 263. "soit enfin que la propriété est le vrai fondement de la société civile, et le vrai guarante des engagemens des citoyens: car si les biens ne répondoient pas des personnes, rien ne seroit si facile que d'éluder ses devoirs et de se moquer des lois."
3. This is a descriptive statement, but is given normative implications. For, if property is so necessary, then it is important that nobody is left without. As the individual is morally entitled to live, he has, then, a kind of natural right to own property. OC III, p. 263. [Rousseau 1983, p. 138]. Diderot expressed that it is property that makes a citizen, that the relative right to property is a means for the government whereby social interests can dominate private. Cf., Fox-Genovese 1976, p. 62.
4. Discours sur l'économie politique, OC III, p. 271.
5. Projet de constituion pour la Corse. OC III, p. 931. "ma pensée qui n'est pas de détruire absolument la proprieté particuliére parce que cela est impossible mais de la renfermer dans les plus étroites bornes, de lui donner une mesure, [une] règle, un frein qui la contienne, qui la dirige, qui la subjugue et la tienne toujours subordonnée au bien public."
6. EMILE, OC IV, p. 241.

### *Money and the accumulation of fortune*

Finally, money presents an obstacle to the civilising dependence because it is easy to accumulate. Thereby it facilitates a privileged individual in becoming independent of society and potentially abusing the dependence of others. For this reason, government should try to avoid letting citizens have "too much control, such as money and silver that one easily hides from the public inspection."[1]

Money makes the resources that can be used for one's subsistence almost independent of conventional entitlement rights because it is an excellent medium to accumulate, to acquire.[2] This idea may have been inspired by Aristotle's characteristics of *chrematistike*: channeling money into a store which is to serve no envisaged purchase plans at all but is meant only to embody wealth.[3] The idea is that money, being such an efficient means of accumulating abstract entitlement rights without any necessary connections to particular use values, may stimulate and facilitate chrematistic enterprises.

Rousseau recognizes a legitimate use of money. It is not because of its primary function that monetisation should be avoided, but because of its secondary effects, because it facilitates abuses. Every society needs some standards whereby to make exchanged goods commensurable.[4]

* * *

The chains of dependence are terrible. But without mutual dependence, having an "absolute and naturally independent existence" the individuals will regard "the common cause as free" and desert the common cause when there is a possibility to gain. For that reason a policy of making everyone dependent on the city should be applied. Such a policy would provide everyone with a secure entitlement to food, the right to live in conditional autarchy, the protection of private property and it would avoid monetarisation of the economy.

1. OC III, p. 931. ". . . .le possesseur particulier est trop le maitre telles que la monnoye et l'argent que l'on cache aisement à l'inspection publique."
2. OC III, p. 916. "La pauvreté ne s'est fait sentir dans la Suisse que quand l'argent a commencé d'y circuler. Il a mis la même inégalité dans les ressources que dans les fortunes; il est devenu un grand moyen d'acquerir oté à ceux qui n'avoient rien."
3. Langholm 1983, p. 55.
4. OC IV, p. 462. [Rousseau 1984, p. 153]. "En toute chose il importe de bien exposer les usages avant de montrer les abus. Si vous prétendiez expliquer aux enfans comment les signes font négliger les choses, comment de la monnoye sont nées toutes les chiméres de l'opinion, comment les pays riches d'argent doivent être pauvres de tout, vous traitteriez ces enfans non seulement en philosophes mais en hommes sages, et vous prétendriez leur faire entendre de ce que peu de philosophes mêmes ont bien conceu."

## 9. THE JEWS ARE CITIZENS

# *The Realism of the Republic of Hearts*

BESIDES DEPENDENCE Rousseau holds forth a second strategy for promoting social morale: by the systematic *cultivation* of homogeneous interests, by the creation of a "republic of hearts". Like Kenneth Arrow, he emphasises the importance of "likeness in desires for social alternatives". Such a likeness is important both to attain a democratic social choice, a "general will" (Arrow's point), and to prevent individual rationality from interfering with the optimum: the problem of deserting hunters or free riding. For that reason, Rousseau stubbornly tries every means to further the homogeneity of interests. No way seems too odd or too insignificant. This urge overshadows almost all other concerns. And even such values for which he in his personal life cares most, may have to be sacrificed: theatre, political and intellectual exchanges with women, and musical performances.

Even bizarre opinions can sometimes tell us something important about what the author is vainly trying to achieve. Rousseau was, of course, influenced by his times and for that reason held one or two bizarre opinions.[1] But some of these are, I suggest, the result of his determination to find a means to promote the republic of "hearts". In this present chapter, two such opinions are focused upon. They have both, now and then, been found to be disturbing. The first concerns Rousseau's raving for Lycurgos, the mythical Lacedaemonian warrior-ruler; and the second is his resistance to the establishment of a theatre in Geneva.

### *Lycurgos*

Rousseau's admiration for Lycurgos is revealed in many contexts. One is in the CONSIDÉRATIONS SUR LE GOUVERNEMENT DE POLOGNE. Modern societies lack true legislators, he claims, while Israel, Sparta and Rome had their Moses, Lycurgos, and Numa (Rome's mythical founder). These figures

1. Like, for example, Aristotle who is characterised in this way by Zagorka Zivkovic. Cf., Zivkovic 1995, p. 20.

concerned themselves mainly with matters that our doctors would deem absurd. Yet each of them achieved a kind of success which, were it not so thoroughly supported by evidence, we should regard as impossible.[1]

This statement and other expressions of admiration for Lycurgos disturbed several commentators. They found it particularly strange that the great democrat, Rousseau, praised the military regime and discipline of classical Sparta. Lycurgos is praised, some claim, because he practiced a Machiavellian instrumentalism, according to which, doing what is best for society is a basic value synonymous with virtue. The basic assumption shared by these commentators is that Rousseau found the political education and system of Sparta virtuous *per se*.[2]

Many, then, have found a deep and disturbing gulf between Rousseau's radical proclamations and his practical proposals. When facing controversial political consequences of his beautiful words about justice, human rights, etc., he retreated. He turned out to be nothing more than "a simple déclamateur" whose utopian dreams were never intended for the real world.[3] Madeleine Ellis, for example, argued that when Rousseau asked the Poles to build "a republic in their hearts",[4] he never meant this proposition to be realised as a social policy. It was intended rather for a "city" to be established in the hearts of the citizens. He even says it himself: "that his city does not exist and never will, and that if it did, men would be like blocks of wood or, to use Socrates' word, like posts". If given the possibility to found "the republic of hearts" in real life he would have declined. "The republic of hearts" is purely utopian. And so Ellis outlines Rousseau's philosophy as a kind of therapy for rich and privileged members of society.

The city exists in ideas only. The city is no less and no more than a device for the personal perfection of the sage, Ellis claims. Rousseau's is a moral philosophy for the individual's inner life. It advises for the reader a *modus vivendi* whereby she "orders, preserves, and governs his own life after the manner of the ideal city, as God orders, preserves and governs the universe." This works in a world of injustices, with no corresponding societal change. In this way, the philosophy adopts a conservative political function. It is the privileged individual to whom Rousseau speaks, and the message is that "the main business of life" is to perfect oneself and wisely govern one's own inner life.[5]

Looking more closely at the text it seems, however, that the point is precisely the opposite of what these commentators claim. This becomes evident when one considers its context. The praise of Moses, Lycurgos, and Numa appears in the second chapter of the CONSIDÉRATIONS. This chapter is preceded by a chapter labeled "The issue posed"[6] which concludes with an assertion that people cannot be made to conform to laws unless laws conform to their passions; but that,

1. OC III, p. 956. [Rousseau 1985, p. 6] "Tous trois ont mis leurs principaux soins à des objets qui paroitroient à nos docteurs digne de risée. Tous trois ont eu des succés qu'on jugeroit impossibles s'ils étoient moins attestés.
2. Kendall 1985, p. XXXV. Paolo Cucchi has written an interesting essay claiming Rousseau's debt to Machiavelli (Cucchi 1969).
3. Chabert 1964, p. 355.
4. Kendall 1985, p. XIII.
5. Ellis 1977, pp. 377ff, 388f and 415.
6. "L'état de la question", OC III, p. 953.

nevertheless, implementing laws is one of the necessary tasks of government. This advice is tragic; to put laws over men is as difficult "as the squaring of a circle in geometry and the problem of longitudes in astronomy", the chapter claims.[1] The task then is to accomplish something which is necessary but as impossible as the squaring of the circle: to get laws to conform to the passions of the people.

This problem is central for Rousseau. It is a primary factor shaping his advice to Poland not to side with the modernists and open up the country to foreign political influence. The only available option for someone who wants the law to rule, is to try to make laws conform to men's "hearts". To accomplish this, either laws must be in the people's interest or their hearts must be moved.[2] Otherwise, the general will cannot rule, however much anyone claims to the contrary.

This point is also emphasised elsewhere. There is no possible substitute for social morale. No sanction system can compensate for its lack. No chains can bind a people to a certain behaviour as efficiently as conscience. Such chains would require such minute vigilance and still the chance to succeed would be minimal – with only five steps into the woods... Compared to the conscience, law is a "defied gnat".[3]

## *Squaring a circle*

The first chapter of the CONSIDÉRATIONS is followed by a chapter entitled "The spirit of ancient institutions"[4] which refers to the three classical constitutions created by Moses, Lykurgos, and Numa. But they are not brought in as examples of how societies should be organised in general. How could they be, dissimilar as they are? It is certainly never claimed that the government and morality of Sparta should be a model for the Poles to imitate. The point of holding forth Lycurgos' Sparta (or Moses and Numa) is not to communicate any general evaluation of the institutions of Sparta as such. There is another purpose at hand.

The introductory chapter may – especially considering the claim in its title, "on the issue posed" – present a clue on how to read the following one. Is it not thus reasonable to actually look therein for "the issue posed"? In fact, the first chapter closes with a formulation of the problem, which indicates that Rousseau does not try to define any general quality or virtue. The formulation reveals,

1. Ibid., p. 955. [Rousseau 1985, p. 3] "Il est impossible d'en [meilleurs loix] faire dont les passions des hommes n'abusent pas". The same metaphor was used earlier, in a letter of July 26, 1767 to Mirabeau, to point out the unrealistic anthropology in the theories of the mercantilists. OC III, p. 1744 (Fabre's comment): "Mettre la loi au-dessus de l'homme est un problème en politique, que je compare à celui de la quadrature du cercle en gèométrie." "...Mais jusques là soyez surs qu'où vous croiez faire régner les loix, ce seront les hommes qui régneront."

2. Ibid., "trouver un forme de gouvernement qui mette la loi au-dessus de l'homme". This task of government is also presented in the Discours sur l'économie politique as one of its most important concerns. OC III, p. 243.

3. OC III, p. 252. "He who has just defied the pains of conscience, will not be late to defy the torment; punishments less rigorous, less continuous, and from which he has at least the hope of escape; and despite which precautions are taken, those who only are kept from doing evil by the fear of being punished, hardly lack the means to elude the law or at least to escape from punishment." Here my translation is widely different from Cole's. [Rousseau 1983, p. 128]. "Celui qui vient à bout de braver les remords, ne tardera pas à braver les supplices; châtiment moins rigoureux, moins continuel, et auquel on a du moins l'espoir d'échapper; et quelques précautions qu'on prenne, ceux qui n'attendent que l'impunité pour mal faire, ne manque guere de moyens d'éluder la loi ou d'échapper à la peine."

4. "Esprit des anciennes institutions", OC III, p. 956.

rather, that Rousseau is theorising at a higher level of abstraction. He does not ask: what is virtue in society? Instead he asks, considering the dilemma of how to get laws to rule:

> by what means are we to move men's hearts?[1]

Consequently, his errand in Chapter 2, on ancient institutions, does not at all concern the essence of virtue, but the possibilities of instituting and nurturing an "ethos" – whatever its contents – that would make possible any government, regulated by law. At this point the reader certainly expects some potent suggestions, at least, about how to start this formidable task. But, anxious to hear Rousseau's answer, she cannot but be disappointed by what follows. All that is offered are two tiny, almost ridiculous examples: teach children through the games they play, and unite the people by good institutions that develop "habits that abide and attachments that nothing can dissolve!". Rousseau seems himself (in this very sentence) worried about the disappointment, fearing that a "superficial man would deem them pointless". He even predicts that he, himself, for this sake will be considered mad.

> If in saying this I am out of my wits, at least I am completely out of them. For I confess that I see in my folly all the hallmarks of reasonableness.[2]

This declaration closes the introductory chapter. In proposing his seemingly ridiculous means to move men's hearts, he had perhaps lost his mind, or at least might be presumed to have. From this statement he goes on, in the second chapter, to discuss the three "outstanding" ancient legislators about whose success there can be no doubt. But the remarkable issue is that (immediately after his characterisation of himself, in the beginning of chapter two) these leaders are ascribed epithets very similar to those Rousseau has used about himself. The three outstanding legislators did not propose ideas that "a superficial man would deem pointless", but something which "our doctors would deem absurd".

In this way, Rousseau completely transforms the context of his own proposals (found in the first chapter) and succeeds in having the reader associate his seemingly ridiculous proposals with those successful institutions (also ridiculed) created by the three great ancient legislators (discussed in the second chapter). The same theme that ended the first chapter with a reverberating chord in minor key, is now, so to speak, in the introduction to the second chapter, taken up again and exposed with the melody figure almost unchanged but modulated to a major key. Something which is considered foolish or absurd, but is perhaps necessary and even rational – Rousseau's proposals in the preceding chapter – is now

1. OC III, p. 955.
2. Rousseau 1985, p. 4. [OC III, pp. 955f]. "Par où donc émouvir les cœurs, et faire aimer la patrie et ses loix? L'oiserai-je dire? par des jeux d'enfants; par des institutions oiseueses aux yeux des hommes superficiels, mais qui forment des habitudes cheries et des attachemens invincibles. Si j'extravague ici, c'est du moins bien completement, car je vois ma folie sous tous les traits de la raison." Jean Fabre argues that the last sentence is an implicit reference to two of Rousseau's masters: Pascal and Montaigne. OC III, p. 1745

paralleled and associated with something else that appears foolish but is – according to thorough evidence – successful! Rousseau did not try to persuade his readers to attempt to copy Lycurgos' plans. This would truly have been absurd; not least in the eyes of that very author that in other texts. The DISCOURS SUR L'ORIGINE ET LES FONDEMENTS DE L'INÉGALITÉ in particular, showed him more deeply critical than perhaps any other contemporary political philosopher to the idea of deducing normative political principles from other times and situations. But Rousseau wanted, in the example of Lycurgos, to show precisely what his introductory words actually declare: that a project, deemed absurd, and that

> we would regard as impossible

actually was possible. These very legislators, however poor they were in other ways, however badly their government conformed to any democratic general will, still:

> achieved a kind of success . . . *thoroughly supported by evidence*[1]

The success of these three great legislators proved to Rousseau that it is not absurd to believe that it is possible to implement a "a republic of hearts", although most of his contemporaries "would regard it as impossible".

All the three ancient legislators "sought ties that would bind the citizens to the fatherland and to one another"[2] The Spartan tyrant made the people love their country, and be loyal to it, by means of a yoke of iron, by laws and customs and by educating the young, as Rousseau himself had proposed in chapter one.[3] Other references to Lycurgos in Rousseau's writings confirm this interpretation. In the CONTRAT SOCIAL, Lycurgos symbolises the regime of a vigorous people stimulated by laws generated by a true legislator and with a considerable homogeneity of interests.[4] But Sparta is no example to copy. In the DISCOURSE SUR LES SCIENCES ET LES ARTS it is described as, at the same time, both "excellent and *monstruous*".[5]

An early formulation in the second DISCOURSE, discloses why Lycurgos is so interesting to Rousseau. Most political systems are the result of a randomly process. They are arbitrarily repaired, completed or strengthened, he finds. But the peoples should have "swept their barns", removed all old material, and purposefully raised a new construction.[6] Lycurgos is, then, in a sense a representative of the enlightened dream of creating society, or at least of deliberately choosing the political system. He represents the dream of political empowerment.[7]

1. Cf., note 2 in this chapter. Italics addes.
2. Rousseau 1985, p. 8. [OC III, p. 958]. "Tous chercherent des liens qui attachassent les Citoyens à la patrie et les uns aux les autres."
3. OC III, p. 24, Rousseau's note. The DISCOURS SUR LES SCIENCES ET LES ARTS.
4. Ibid., p.324 and 372.
5. Ibid., p.24. Italics added.
6. Ibid., p.180.
7. The fact that Rousseau refers to Lycurgos' military success is no stranger than that Adam Smith discusses the consequences of the division of labour for the military capacity of society. Military capacity is a rather unambigous measure of one kind of strength in a society. Cf. Shklar 1985, pp. 14ff, and Smith 1976, ch. V.i.f., pp. 782ff.

Further evidence that the true aim of the enumeration in chapter two of the CONSIDÉRATIONS is to prove that it is realistic, in spite of the true nature of man, to try to create "institutions" for maintaining social solidarity, can be found in a remarkable unpublished fragment, "On the Jews". In this work, Moses is pronounced champion among the three ancient legislators. The laws instituted by Solon, Numa, and Lycurgos have long since been dead; but one legislative code lives on, the law of Moses, which is older than any of the others. Yet nevertheless its "spectacles" and institutions (only) still survive.

Although the Jewish people for almost 2000 years have been dispersed all over the world, and in spite of the endless persecutions they have suffered, they have been able to "conserve their customs, laws, traditions their patriotic love, and their original social union, although all liaisons seem to have been broken for them".[1]

> They have no more any rulers but remain a people; they have no longer any fatherland, but remain citizens.[2]

The only similarity between Jewish culture and Lycurgos' "iron yoke" is their mutual "success" with "the impossible". Far from being a utopian dream for an immaterial "republic", the very point of the example of Lycurgos is to show that the establishment of the "republic of hearts" is a realistic possibility.

## *Ancient institutions and modern society*

While the ancient legislators implemented institutions to stimulate a congruence of hearts by religious ceremonies, games, feasts, customs and traditions that brought the citizens together, contemporary European culture is more like children's innocent play: "If they have customs it is only because they must learn to brighten the idle hours of courtesans and to promenade their mistresses in a graceful manner."[3] This culture is monistic and even divisive.

Rousseau (in another context) even uses Shakespeare to show the absence of social morale in modern society. In the long note to the second DISCOURS. Rousseau exclaims that

> Thus it is that we find our advantage in the misfortunes of our fellow creatures... I have seen men wicked enough to weep for sorrow at the prospect of a plentiful season.[4]

1. OC III, p. 499. "conserver pourtant ses coutumes, ses loix, ses moeurs, son amour patriotique et sa prémiére union sociale quand tous les liens en paroissent rompus."
2. Ibid. "ils n'ont plus de chefs et sont toujours peuple, ils n'ont plus de patrie et sont toujours citoyens."
3. Rousseau 1985, p. 8. [OC III, p. 958]. "S'ils ont des usages, c'est pour savoir amuser l'oisivité des femmes galantes, et promener la leur avec grace.
4. Rousseau 1983, p. 107. [OC III, pp. 202f]. "C'est ainsi que nous trouvons notre avantage dans le préjudice de nos semblables"... ..."j'ai vue des hommes affreux pleurer de douleur aux apparances d'une anné fertile".

The last phrase resounds of a dramatic interlude in Macbeth. The interlude takes place the very moment when Macbeth has killed the king and returns to his wife, fearing discovery. He, as well as the audience, knows that at any second the guards will knock at the doors, the deed will be discovered and the whole castle put in terrified alarm. And, indeed, knocks are suddenly heard. But they originate from some gate other than the gate of the castle. Right at this very tense moment, Shakespeare disrupts the main story to tell about a moral perversion in his contemporary society, to tell about the perverted corn market. It is the gate to hell that is heard:

> [Porter]: Knock, knock, knock: Who's there in the name of Beelzebub? Here is a farmer that hanged himself on the expectation of plenty: Come in time; have napkins enough about you; here you'll sweat for it![1]

Rousseau demands something much more serious and reciprocal than the moral and cultural standard of his own time, and much of his policy is intended to stimulate its development. After having criticised religion, theatre and public celebrations in modern society, he closes with a characterisation of its residual customs, all those that he did not name: "the kinds of pleasures that are divisive, that most isolate people from one another, and that most deaden the spirit".[2] To develop community one must have cultural institutions and education.[3] It is possible to make people care as much for society as they care for their loved ones, perhaps even to a greater extent than in erotic love: the love of one's society can be "a hundred times more lively than the love of a mistress".[4] This teaching should not be moralistic, but rather practical – it should teach students that it is in their own interest to show a social morale. "It is not a matter of teaching me what is justice; it is a matter of showing me what interest I have in doing justice."[5] But the success of the teaching presupposes that the student is dependent on others. If not, he has no reason to find it in his interest to be loyal:

> 'I see well, I acknowledge the rule that I should consult. But I still don't see', our independent person will say, 'the reason why I should submit to that rule'.[6]

1. Shakespeare 1934, p. 519.
2. Rousseau 1985, p. 9. [OC III, p. 959]. "les plaisirs qui séparent, isolent le plus les hommes, et qui relâchent le plus les cœurs."
3. OC III, p. 258. "Ce n'est pas assez de dire aux citoyens, soyez bons; il faut leur apprendre à l'être;"
4. OC III, p. 255. [Rousseau 1983, p. 130]. "l'amour de la patrie [est] plus vif est plus délicieux cent fois que celui d'une maitresse".
5. OC III, p. 286. "Je vois bien là, je l'avoüe, la régle que je puis consulter; mais je ne vois pas encore", dira nôtre homme indépendant, "la raison qui doit m'asssujetir a cette régle."
"Il ne s'agit pas de m'apprendre ce que c'est que justice; il s'agit de me montrer quel intérest j'ai d'être juste."
6. Ibid.

## *The Theatre of Geneva*

In 1957 tôme VII of the Encyclopédie was published. It included an article on Geneva in which it was suggested that a theatre should be set up and a troupe of comediennes recruited to the city. Rousseau immediately opposed this proposal in a text that is usually abbreviated LETTRE À D'ALEMBERT.

Rousseau had a deep knowledge and a high regard for classical theatre; he knew well his Shakespeare, Racine or Molière.[1] So his opposition is not based on a criticism of theatre *per se*, but rather on its function in the creation of that social morale which is needed for the sake of good economy and true democracy. Contrary to other writers on economic policy of his time, he realised the need to tackle the conflict between individual and collective rationality. In the presence of the possibility to regard collective goods as "free", individuals could try free-riding and society would lose. While noneconomic conflicts between individual and collective rationality were being negotiated, individual agents could exploit the importance of their participation and demand huge compensation. Those "who can wait" could force the less privileged into bargaining process. He also realised, as shown above, other market imperfections. All of these dilemmas demanded a high social morale if they were to be overcome. Members of society must be concerned for one another, and must trust that others care for them, so that the "silent contract" would not be breached. If society failed to accomplish such a morale, it would face great economic losses.

With the examples of Lycurgos, Moses, and Numa Rousseau tried to show that it is a realistic option for society to implement a policy for concern and assurance. These three ancient legislators were, however, not useful for showing what needed to be done during Rousseau's own time. To that purpose he did not produce any particularly systematic program. Perhaps it was not even possible for him to do, since he always emphasised the importance of designing a policy well-accommodated to the particular culture and circumstances under consideration. Some rather fragmentary components of such a policy appear, however, here and there in his writings.

The purpose would be to direct the citizen's attention to the "self common to the whole", to make her realise her dependence on others, the very basis for the tacit contract. This calls for a moral *education* that makes each individual "believe himself no longer but part of the unity and no longer feel except within the whole."[2] To that purpose, the young should be taught to understand and respect the laws and "the general will" and be reminded of the "inestimable benefits" they receive from others and in common with them. Consequently, they would "learn to cherish one another mutually as brothers…".[3] The ultimate aim of moral education should be to influence the needs that individuals develop and to orient

1. See, e.g., Bernard Rousset's comment on this text. OC V, p. XXXVI.
2. Fralin 1988, p. 145 (Bloom's transl.). OC IV pp. 249 "Les bonnes institutions sociales sont celles qui savent le mieux dénaturer l'homme, lui ôter son existence absolue pour lui en donner un relative, et transporter le moi dans l'unité commune; en sorte que chaque particulier ne se croye plus un, mais partie de l'unité, et ne soit plus sensible que dans le tout."
3. Rousseau 1983, p. 136. [OC III, p. 260f]. " . . .s'ils sont environnés d'examples et d'objets qui leur parlent sans cesse de las tendre mere qui les nourrit, de l'amour qu'elle a pour eux, des bien inestimables qu'ils reçoivent d'elle, et du retour qu'ils lui doivent, ne doutons pas qu'ils n'aprennent ainsi à se chérir mutuellement comme des freres"

them in the direction of solidarity with the common cause. The citizens should learn to feel satisfaction in the happiness of others. "Enlighten his mind by new lights, warm his heart with new sentiments, that he will learn to multiply his being and happiness by sharing it with his likes".[1]

Such a policy, then, also implies that the individual really can trust that society will uphold the silent contract; for it requires a social security system guaranteeing everyone her certain subsistence. Moreover, everyone must be able to see that the affairs of the democratic institutions matter to her.[2] Everyone must participate actively in a democratic government. Tax in labour ("corvées") should be preferred before other kinds of taxes because it forces the tax payer to participate actively in the matters of society and makes it easier for her to control the use of her payments. And it should be demanded by anyone who is to develop a career that he started working with "the municipal hospital of the poor".[3] Finally, law must rule, not private interests.[4]

Rousseau even calls for women to help out with this plan. Because of their higher moral standards and their ability to manipulate men, women would, if they so wished, be able to force men into having high social morals. "Men are always such as pleases the women"; therefore, in Rousseau's calculus, women can control them.[5]

In his civilising project, Rousseau also gives important roles to music and theatre.

## *Music*

Rousseau loved music all of his life.[6] Music was also the battlefield for one of his great debates: that with the composer and theorist/philosopher of music, Jean Philipe Rameau. Rousseau knew and appreciated Rameau's music, theory and philosophy (which is evident from several articles on music in the Encyclopédie).[7] The problem for Rousseau was Rameau's claim to have constructed a scientific theory of the musical experience, a kind of theory of correspondences between the harmonics in the performed music and the sentiments perceived by the audience.

1. CONTRAT SOCIAL, the first version. OC III, p. 288. "Montrons lui toute la misére de l'état qu'il cryoit heureux, tout le faux du raissonement qu'il croyoit solide. Qu'il voye dans une meilleure constitution de choses le prix des bonnes actions, le chatiment des mauvaises et l'accord aimable de la justice et du bonheur. Eclairons sa raison de nouvelles lumiéres, échauffons son cœur de nouveaux sentimens, et qu'il apprenne à multiplier son être et sa félicité, en les partageant avec ses semblables."
2. OC III, p. 429. "Sitôt que quelqu'un dit des affaires de l'Etat, que m'importe? on doit compter que l'Etat est perdue."
3. OC III, p. 1010.
4. See, for example, part II of the DISCOURS SUR L'ÉCONOMIE POLITIQUE. [Rousseau 1983, p. 136] and The CONTRAT SOCIAL [ibid. 187]. OC III, p. 374. "Ainsi de même qu'une volonté particuliere ne peut réprésenter la volonté generale, la volonté générale à son tour change de nature ayant un objet particulier, et ne peut comme générale prononcer ni sur un homme ni sur un fait."
5. OC III, pp. 157f. For an example of the thought of using women to improve the virtues of men, see OC III, p. 965 and C III, p. 21, n. "Les hommes seront toujours ce qu'il plaira aux femmes: si vous voulez donc qu'ils deviennent grands et verteux, apprenez aux femmes ce que c'est que grandeur d'âme et vertu."
6. Wokler 1974 refers to CONFESSIONS, OCV I, p. 180f. "je sois né pour cet art, puisque j'ai commencé de l'aimer dés mon enfance"
7. Wokler 1974, pp. 186ff.

This causation was purely physical-mechanical and independent of cultural traditions.[1] Harmony, then, was the most crucial component of music. In this view, music had a kind of manipulative character and offered an excellent instrument to the modernist engineer.

Against this postulate Rousseau argues that there is no such direct physical correspondence between the musical expression and the perceived sentiment. Music is, on the contrary, always *culturally mediated* by the musical conventions in which the listener participates. Through taste, habit, and local culture the same chord sends different meanings to different audiences. Rousseau illustrates this point in his most voluminous work on music, the DICTIONNAIRE DE MUSIQUE, by giving some examples of diverging harmonic systems (from India, Persia, Greece and China).[2]

A second issue in Rousseau's criticism is that, not harmony, but melody (including rhythm) is the prime component of music. Harmony is (contrary to Rameau's view) merely an important embellishment of melody.[3] The "concours des vibrations" of a harmonic accord create nothing more than a purely physical effect, while melody, rhythm, beat, and accent are the features that could cause a moral resonance in the audience. These have a unique moral power somewhat like design in fine art.[4] The melody can touch the listener through:

> the cry of nature, the accent, the rhythm, the measure, the pathetic and passionate tone which the agitated soul gives to the human voice.[5]

Rousseau's third point is perhaps the clue to the fervor of his criticism in this argument. While harmony basically can be used as a means to manipulate the listener in a unilateral communication; melody, rhythm, measure and accent are efficient in a multilateral communication, wherein the audience participates actively, by dancing, singing, etc. Music and its "cry of nature" in the multilateral feasting has unique potentials for strengthening civility. There is consequently a moral aspect – related to our issue of preventing defective behaviour in the presence of bargaining possibilities and sub-optimal equilibria – behind Rousseau's special concern for melody and his critique of Rameau. The examples of Lycurgos (or better, the Jews)

1. Wokler 1974, pp. 189ff.
2. The article "Musique" and Planche N. OC V, pp. 924 and 1190f. The examples are brought from travel reports. At least one of them, the Chinese one lived a life of its own after Rousseau: in a piece by von Weber and later in the 2nd movement of Hindemith's Symphonic Metamorphoses, and Arthur Sullivan's "Mikado".
3. Wokler 1974, p. 195.
4. "Besides those cases that immediately concern our conservation, it is never purely physical causes that can move us at this point. You could beautifully modulate and combine the colours. Never did the most competent painter dispose them to excite either pity or wrath; but if he wanted to awaken our passions, he would take them in his service to represent by design moral effects to us." Wokler 1974, p. 218. (The principle of Melody) "Hors les cas que touchent immediatement à nôtre conservation, ce ne sont jamais les causes purement physiques que peuvent nous émouvir à ce point. Vous aurez beau nuancer et combiner des couleurs. Jamais le plus savant peintre ne les disposera de manière à exciter ni pitié ni colére; mais s'il veut éveiller nos passions, qu'il se serve de ces même couleurs à nous réprésenter par le dessein des effets moraux."
5. Wokler 1974, p. 218. "le cri de la nature, l'accent. le nombre, la mesure, et le ton pathethique et passioné que l'agitation de l'âme donne à la voix humain."

showed that true law-making was possible: implementing law that was alive with high social morale. Music was to be one of the roads to its modern realisation, imagination another.

## *Theatre and feasts*

Rousseau, as Philip Robinson has shown, treated theatre as a social *institution* and did in that way understand it as parallel with the development of society in general. In its contemporaneous institutional state it presented threats to the social morale, but it employed a competence that was urgent: the creation and maintenance of *imagination*.

Theatre, like music, had passed through history from being part of authentic, collective, and multilateral feasts to becoming an arena where people wanted to be considered by others, wanted to show themselves in a social parade. It became an entertainment for the leisure. The "outward sign receives progressively more attention than the inward joy of the activity".[1]

Nonetheless, there is a technique, mastered by actors, which moves the imagination of the spectators. This technique could potentially be useful to society, but in the context of the arena for social parades it does not allow appropriate responses and in that way becomes destructive. If the actors put imagination into action without causing an active response, but only "entertain" passive listeners or viewers, it is simply a waste of time, a tragically unhappy allocation of the badly-needed means to influence "imagination", and, in this process, the social conscience. It becomes a kind of "ethical masturbation, a 'dangereux supplément' which spills the seed of our positive moral impulses on the ground, and renders them sterile".[2] It breeds "false needs".

This means also that a great potential for strengthening the social conscience is misused. The imaginative capability of theatre has the potential to increase the ability of citizens to "see the self common to the whole". In Rousseau's work , pity, "pitié", is a natural sentiment, which is present regardless of civilisation or socialisation. Even non-humans, as for example horses, possess it. But in the state of society pity is taken into action by imagination; it is, perhaps, repaired from the paralysis of this state. It lets us be placed "outside of ourselves":

> Pity, although natural, would rest eternally inactive in the heart of a man, unless imagination put it into play. How could we let ourselves be moved to pity? By placing us outside of ourselves; by identifying ourselves with the suffering one. We only suffer as long as we judge that he suffers; it is not within ourselves, but within him that we suffer.[3]

Imagination extends the sentiment, extends the desire beyond the immediately perceptible – to serve the "social parade" or to follow in the service of true empathy.

1. Robinson 1984, pp. 83, 126.
2. Robinson 1984, pp. 140ff.
3. Robinson 1984, p. 133. "La pitié, bien que naturelle, au cœur de l'homme resterait éternellement inactive sans l'imagination qui le met en jeu. Comment nous laissons-nous émouvir à la pitié? En nous transportant hors de nous-mêmes; en nous identifiant avec l'être souffrant. Nous ne souffrons qu'autant que nous jugeons qu'il souffre; ce n'est pas dans nous, c'est dans lui que nous souffrons."

It even extends the physical desires (thus, in the former case, creating "false needs").

> It is imagination that extends for us the measure of possible things, of the good as well as of the bad, and as a consequence excites and nourishes desires by the hope of their satisfaction.[1]

To a reader of Aristotle, like Rousseau was, this statement has a specific flavour. When Aristotle in his NICHOMACHEAN ETHICS tries to delimit the field of political science he decides that it deliberates "about things that are in our control and are attainable by action." The Greek talks about "things possible". These things are contrasted to subjects irrelevant to political science, such as "the incommensurability of the diagonal and the side of the square", or for a Spartan to study "the government of Scythia" which he cannot influence. "By possible, I mean what can be performed by our agency – *things we do through the agency of our friends counting in a sense as done by ourselves,* since the origin of their action is in us," writes Aristotle.[2] It seems that Rousseau, in his claim that "imagination extends for us the measure of possible things", is also referring to its capacity to increase our circle of friends, whose actions are "in a sense counting as done by ourselves". It is not only a question of sympathy or pity for those in need, but is rather about a capacity to act in concert, a communicative competence. It is about empowering democracy and creating efficient solutions within that domain of the economy where individual rationality is not sufficient.

When Rousseau writes that imagination "extends for us the measure of possible things" he refers not only to the capacity to imagine a lot of potential objects of consumption. He also implies that through imagination and the extension of sympathy the circle of friends defining the potential agents of "the possible" might widen. It is one of the costs of corrupt theatre that it forsakes an opportunity to conserve or extend the "circle of friends".

* * *

Rousseau holds forth the feast as an alternative to theatre. But he never proposes how these feasts are to be. It has been suggested that they should be deeply founded in popular tradition.[3] Dances and festivals should allow everyone to be both watcher and participant; spectators and performers should be identical. In this way, there must be room for mutual recognition. The dance should be a pure expression of inner well-being, not a mirror of fashion or a "social parade".[4] In these feasts, people

1. Robinson 1984, p. 136. OC IV, p. 304. "Sitôt que les facultés [de l'homme] virtuelles se mettent en action l'imagination, la plus active de toutes, s'éveille et les devance. C'est l'imagination qui étend pour nous la mesure des possibles soit en bien soit en mal, et qui par conséquent excite et nourrit les désirs par l'espoir de les satisfaire."
2. Aristotle, pp. 135ff. (III.iii. 3-13.). Italics added.
3. Robinson 1984, pp. 254f
4. Robinson 1984, p. 256.

should be able to appear as they are, regardless of what is considered decent.[1] The feasts should strengthen the mores and influence the individual will.[2] By influencing the structure of ***individual preference,*** these true feasts – in sharp distinction to the gallant theatre according to the fashion of the Paris salons – could stimulate solidarity in society.

1. Fralin 1988, p. 135.
2. Robert Fralin questioned their interpretation, with due justification, as reducing the complexity in Rousseau's argument. But, nevertheless, this particular causal relation is not in question. Cf., Fralin 1988, p. 133.

## 10. NOTHING SOLID FOR THE HEART

# An Economy for the Quality of Life

ROUSSEAU WAS stubbornly preoccupied with problems of social morale. Why? It was not because he spoke for collectivist policies, in the way Morelly or Mably did. And neither was his concern merely the magnificent result of an unusually imaginative emotional fantasy. His pessimistic view on the implications of individual rationality and his unusual demands on the task of the economy forced him to search desparately for a way to credibility and trustworthiness in society. This view differed, certainly, from the doctrine and emphasis of other contemporaneous theorists. Adam Smith, of course, claimed that if each individual was rational, in the sense that she acted and chose so as to maximise her gain, then the totality of actions would make the consequent resource allocation optimal for society at large. Rousseau, on the other hand, could base his scepticism on a number of observations of different kinds of market imperfections that would make this kind of resource allocation suboptimal and thus unsatisfactory for a good political economy.

This difference in views is far from trivial. It is, for example, unfortunately not possible to reduce it to the straight moral question of whether private vices are, or can be, aggregated to a socially virtuous or nice totality. Individual rationality (even defined as rudely as in the former paragraph) is not synonymous with egoism, since there may be many reasons why the individual seeks to maximise her gain. She may urgently need to pay for hospital care for her sick child. Her family may be half starving and a single dime may make the difference between life and death for someone who depends on her. Or, truly, she may want to indulge in luxury. And similarly: whether or not society manages to allocate and use its resources optimally may make the difference between being able to finance a war operation or not, but also between famine and subsistence for the people. Thus, this rivalry in views concerns the choice of economic institutions and choice mechanisms and is only indirectly a question of egoism or altruism.

Rousseau in this sense represented a non-market alternative among some "rival views"[1] on the optimising capacity of market exchange prevailing at the time. His view focused on such imperfections of market exchange that we today would label collective good problems, external effects and information asymmetries, circumstances which may make the competitive market prices diverge from the social optimum, or make it non-existent. And the production of values by means of the market mechanism may involve transaction costs beyond the pure production costs, such as the buyer's costs for obtaining the necessary information about the quality of the good, or various costs for insuring that contracts are respected.

In a sense these pessimistic or optimistic "rival views" may be viewed as complementary domains, each relevant for the production of particular kinds of value. For quite some time now economists have seen the need for different domains of economics.[2] Paul Samuelson, for example, called attention to a non-market domain concerned with "collective consumption goods" which

> all enjoy in common in the sense that each individual's consumption of such a good leads to no subtraction from any other individual's consumption of that good.[3]

It is obvious that Samuelson's distinction has to do with the specific character of the various goods (or bads) which the production process creates. This connection between the specific character of the good striven for (or accidentally conceived), and the possibility of an optimum competitive market price was not exploited in Samuelson's very brief note and is apparently still not very frequently analysed in literature.

One of those scholars[4] who indeed has discussed this connection in an analytical way is Kenneth Arrow. In a well-known essay on the choice of "market versus nonmarket allocation" he tries to determine the implications (for the optimality of the competitive equilibrium) of different kinds of market failures. External effects (when someone's choice on the market effects someone else's utility) may cause market failures for *two* reasons, he observes. The first reason is that the consumption of a certain good is, by necessity, shared by several individuals and it is impossible to control who may use the good and who may not. Someone's use of the good cannot for that reason be dependent on whether or not she pays for the good (or if it is a bad, if she is compensated). There is no way to completely exclude people from utilising the good, why it is easy to free-ride or "throw one's waste in someone else's garden". The second reason is that external effects often involve very few sellers and also very few buyers. Transactions with external effects are in a sense often unique.

1. For a related comtemporaneous set of "rival views", see Hirschman, 1992.
2. Walras 1954.
3. Samuelson 1954, pp.387ff
4. See also, for example, Becker 1981 and others among his studies.

The conventional example of a negative external effect is that someone pollutes the water near his neighbours (like the tanner in Ibsen's famous play, An Enemy of the People). Arrow uses another classic example which is somewhat similar to Rousseau's stag hunt: the lighthouse. If a lighthouse is put up (perhaps because some seafarer pays for it) then this good would be available for all other seafarers too. No one can really be excluded from using it (if, for example, she does not pay). This circumstance tempts consumers to act like free-riders. But Arrow points out that there would still be a problem even if it had been possible to exclude people. Suppose, he says, that there was only one boat near the lighthouse (and only one lighthouse), then how could a competitive price be set?[1] It would rather be a case of bargaining where the price would be set by "the ability to wait". The seller would have no possibility to know how much the buyer really would be willing to pay and the buyer would not know what it really cost the producer to provide the lightbeams.

This is also the situation in the stag hunt. If it is figured in market terms, there is only one seller of labour craft (the hunter who is unique at his post) and one buyer (the hunting team). There are no other competing sellers or buyers. And for that reason it is not possible to determine in terms of a competitive price how much the hunter should be paid in order not to run for the hare.

Could it not be, then, that Rousseau's economic philosophy, which is sceptical to the traditional market domain (where individual rationality is supposed to produce the optimum choice), focuses on such economic values and qualities of life – like the lighthouse beams – which are not easily and efficiently provided within the market domain by means of a competitive equilibrium? May not Rousseau's concern correspond to a particular view on what qualities of life society should economise for? They may, for example, have to be collectively consumed or uniquely provided and thereby cause transaction costs and external effects. This last chapter is an attempt to show that this is indeed the case. Firstly, it proceeds to discuss how Rousseau conceptualises richness and abundance.

## *Abundance and Capability*

Richness and abundance are discussed by Rousseau in many contexts. But it is not all clear what they mean. In the DISCOURS SUR L'ÉCONOMIE POLITIQUE, abundance is described as a means to guarantee the safe physical subsistence of the citizens. Mostly, however, it is obvious that abundance signifies something beyond mere physical existence, something to which everyone is entitled. Sometimes it is used synonymously with survival (in a life of good quality). Everyone's right to live means in this case everyone's right to live *in abundance*. It includes an immaterial component that concerns the *capability* of the individual to create a good life with the endowments to which she is entitled, and refers to something beyond the bundle of goods she owns:

> One is rich from a ploughland land, the other poor in the middle of heaps of gold.[2]

1. Arrow 1983, pp. 146f.
2. OC II p. 530 (V:11) (FRAGMENTS POLITIQUES)

In one of the FRAGMENTS POLITIQUES[1] Rousseau observes that different individuals find happiness in different ways (according to their particular character and inclinations). Like Aristotle he finds that there is no universal standard medicine that works for everybody. Therefore, happiness must be created in different ways for each individual. Although the abundance of the people is a central concern of government, no government can produce those circumstances that may make a certain individual happy. Governments just have too little information to do that. On the other hand, family members may have more of the relevant information. This situation has consequences for Rousseau's political economy. While the members of the family should try to help provide one another with the qualities that make life worthwhile, government should not.

> To avoid further useless enumerations [in the discussion on the nature of the happiness of a people] one should distinguish the means used by the individual to make himself happy, everyone according to his character and inclinations, from those that the body of society can put into action with the same purpose. Because, as society can neither predict nor satisfy the different desires of those who compose it, it does not at all charge itself with that concern, but only with providing for the common protection and security, and when it comes to subsistence, to get the individuals *capable of providing for their needs themselves*.[2]

The last words in the quote implies that the economic policy advocated is far from the passive, liberal public policy of Adam Smith. Richness is individual but dependent on society and its policies. It is also culturally conditioned, like the pleasure in music and dance. If one has been accustomed to something for a long time, one's needs, interpretations and mentality are influenced. A town lady, writes Rousseau, who spends two hours in the fields during the summer and gets exposed to the sun for two hours will infallibly get sunstroke and "perhaps a mortal illness" while a peasant won't feel the least embarrassed. A "burgher" can only go the short distance to his country house by horse while his tenant walks it on foot all day. A courtesan, accustomed to riding in a postal chaise, is very uncomfortable when having to ride horseback. Everything, even poisons, may become physical needs through habit.[3] Similarly, then, what constitutes

1. In phrases almost word for word identical with those used in the DISCOURS SUR L'ÉCONOMIE POLITIQUE.

2.. OC III, p 523. "Pour écarter d'autres denombremens inutiles il faut distinguer les moyens que les particuliers employment à tâcher de se rendre heureux, chacun selon son charactère et sis inclinations, de ceux que le corps de la societé peut mettre en usage dans le même but. Car, comme la societé ne peut prévoir ni satisfaire les différens désirs de ceux qui la composent, elle ne se charge point de ce soin mais seulement de pourvoir à la défense et à la sureé commune, et, à l'egard de la subsistyance, de mettre les particuliers à portée de pourvoir par eux mêmes à leurs besoins, de sorte que tous les engagemens que la confederation peut prendre envers les confédérés se reduisent à ces deux points: la paix et l'abondance..."

3.. Ibid. "Ainsi une femme de la ville exposée pendant deux heures dans les grandes ardeurs de l'Eté en pleine campagne sans parasol y gagneroit presque infailliblement un coup de soleil et peut être une maladie mortelle, tandis qu'une Paysanne ne s'en trouveroit point incommodée, un bourgeois ne peut se passer d'un cheval pour aller à sa campagne dont son fermier fais tous les jouirs le trajet à pied..."

happiness for an individual is culturally conditioned. Happiness consists of a permanent and inner 'sentiment', strictly individual.

> None can therefore decide with certitude whether another person is happy. Consequently none can establish sure indications of someone else's happiness.[1]

Nevertheless, Rousseau concedes that it is the duty of government to make its people rich. Consequently the best government can do is to set up a policy well-suited to provide (materially and mentally) for the capability of each individual to make "a happy life" for himself. The best government, he writes in a FRAGMENT POLITIQUE:

> the best one is that which gives them the capability to do that.[2]

If the individuals are reasonable, Rousseau adds. Government must apply general principles and cannot base its policy on the "fantasies and inclinations" of each individual, although these are crucial for abundance.[3]

The need to define welfare in terms other than by the conventional bundle of goods is recognized in Amartya Sen's writings. In his "beginner's"[4] report, COMMODITIES AND CAPABILITIES,[5] he formulates a strong plea for a less simplified concept of welfare than is usual in most welfare economic literature. The traditional formulation has generally tried to reduce the complex and individual character of welfare to "one simple measure of a person's interest and its fulfillment. That measure is often called utility".[6] Like Rousseau, Sen searches for a richer concept of welfare that makes room for its strictly individual nature. His choice is precisely the concept of *capability*. Capability implies that one possess both the resources and the competence to use them well.

## *Growth*

If Rousseau is after a "richer" concept of abundance than that signifying a material bundle of goods, then what about growth? Several readers have denied that he recognised the possibility or desirability of growth in output and productivity. Among them are Fetscher, Talmon, Villers, Dahl, Colletti and Derathé.

These commentators find various reasons as to why Rousseau opposed economic growth. Fetscher claims that Rousseau thought that growth would generate ever-new needs which could "only be satisfied for the few". This would

1. (FRAGMENT VI:3) OC III, p. 510. "Nul ne peut donc decider avec certitude qu'un autre est heureux ni par consequent établir les signes certains du bonheur des individus."
2. OC III, p. 513. "le meilleur est celui qui les met en état se l'être s'ils sont raisonnables."
3. Ibid., "Car quoique les hommes se plaignent toujours, peut être dans quelque autre situation qu'on les mit se plaindroient ils encore davantage. Ce n'est donc pas par le sentiment que les Citoyens ont de leur bonheur ni par consequent par leur bonheur même qu'il faut juger de la prospérité de l'Etat."
4. Sen claims that his attempt "is, of course, no more than a beginning". Sen 1985, p. 71.
5. Sen 1985. Sen recognized, some years after publication of the book, that the welfare concept closest to his heart was close to the concept of happiness at the top of the ethical value hierarchy discussed in the Nichomachean Ethics [Sen 1993, note 2, p. 30]. See also Sen 1967.
6. Sen 1985, p. 2.

lead to inequality.[1] Talmon finds that Rousseau rejected economic growth because it would stimulate a flourishing acquisitive spirit and thus carry heavy moral costs.[2] Villers and Dahl argue that Rousseau looked at the economy basically as a cyclical mode of reproduction where growth was, at most, of secondary importance.[3] Colletti claims that Rousseau explicitly denounced the value of productivity growth.[4]

Most of the commentators at the same time argue that Rousseau did not really believe in the possibility of significantly increasing welfare or productivity. Fetscher states that Rousseau did not understand the potentiality of productivity growth and therefore regarded the distribution of income as exclusively a zero sum game.[5] According to him, Rousseau rejected labour-saving technology because he thought it would demand capital and for that reason exclude the "petit-bourgeoisie" from the possibility of gain.[6] Talmon writes that Rousseau did not realise the possibility of "expansion and increase of wealth and comfort". There was in his writings, as in those of his contemporaries, an "almost total lack of presentiment or understanding of the new forces about to be released by the Industrial Revolution".[7] Likewise, Derathé tries to show the uninformed nature of Rousseau's propositions on economic matters. He claims that Rousseau's economic "archaïsme" expresses a "hostility to all technical progress that increases production with diminished human effort".[8]

So, what is the evidence for these claims? The arguments of Fetscher, Colletti and Derathé are all dependent on a fragmentary text once intended for the CONTRAT SOCIAL. The fragment says:

> From this maxim, if true, follows, consequently, another: that in all that which depends on human industry one should prohibit with care every machine and every invention which could abbreviate the work, spare labour, and produce the same effect with less toil.[9]

Colletti quotes the fragment excluding the introductory condition "From this maxime, if true, follows" etc., and concludes, referring to his mutilated version that: "The backward and backward-looking character of Rousseau's economic views is beyond question".[10]

1. Fetscher 1960, pp. 214f and 242.
2. Talmon 1970, p. 59. See also Gossman 1964, pp. 336f., who thought that Rousseau disliked economic progress because it would cause inhuman working conditions in the new industry.
3. Villers 1964, p. 21f. Dahl 1980 note 43, p. 316. Like Fetscher (Fetscher 1960, p. 215) they found it pointless to accuse authors writing on the edge of the industrial revolution of lacking foresight.
4. Colletti 1974, p. 162 referring to Fetscher. Concerning the chronology and character of this text, as well as the scholarly controversy surrounding it, see Wokler 1987, note 95, pp. 79f.
5. Fetscher 1960, p. 215
6. Fetscher 1960, pp. 254f. Nor did Fetscher explain why Rousseau would have had reason to argue against something he wouldn't think possible.
7. Talmon 1970, p. 59.
8. OC III, p. 1532.
9. OC III, p. 525. "De cette maxime, si elle est vraie, se déduit consequemment celle-ci que dans tout ce qui dépend de l'industrie humaine on doit proscrire avec soin toute machine et toute invention qui peut abréger le travail, épargner la main d'œuvre, et produire le même effet avec moins de peine."
10. Colletti 1974, p. 162

There are several problems with this conclusion. Firstly, what can we really know by a text fragment that the author intended for a text, but later discarded, not including it in the finally published text? In a way he, by this act, declared that he did not accept the formulation, at least not in the intended context. Is it reasonable to let such lines testify to the position held by the author? Perhaps he held these ideas at one time, but later changed his mind (and for that reason excluded the fragment from the published version), changed again and changed back? Perhaps he simply tested the thought for fun? Perhaps he himself didn't know? There are many reasons to be careful with texts such as this. But the disadvantages of using it should be weighed against the advantages. Perhaps there may be some information in the paragraph which could, at least tentatively, enlighten the reading while other similar text fragments may not add anything at all to the problem to be investigated. Generally, in my attempt at a friendly reconstructive reading, I have tried to use as much information as possible, including the little information that may be available in such insecure text fragments – in the absence of better alternatives.

Secondly, the mutilated reasoning in this fragment at first seems hopelessly absurd if it is intended as anything but a sarcastic critique of some approach Rousseau wanted to combat. For that reason it is indeed a poor proof of Rousseau's indifference to economic growth. Even if we regard it as the expression of his true position, this fragment tells us very little about what Rousseau actually thought. The paragraph has an obviously conditional character: ("From this maxim, *if true,* follows…"). Rousseau's own attitude to the assumption is not truly revealed. Therefore, the argument may either be a statement in which Rousseau wants – sarcastically – to show the absurd consequences of some argument he rejects. Or, it may be an explanation starting with premises that he accepts. We simply do not know either the condition for the argument or Rousseau's evaluation of it.

Thirdly, there is reason to believe that the text is indeed intended to show the absurd consequences of a maxim Rousseau wanted to combat. It is difficult to identify any reasonable meaning in the following fragment in the Pleiade edition other than that it is a strong rejection of the "maxim", referred to in the previous fragment. Here is the full second fragment:

> Arguing in consequence, one should try hard to give little duration and solidity to the products of industry and make them as perishable as possible – and regard fires, shipwrecks and all other injuries that cause devastation for man as the true advantages.[1]

It is evident, to conclude, that in this statement a certain unknown maxim is discussed which could well be the maxim referred to in the previous fragment. The unknown maxime implies, for example, that "injuries that cause devastation" would

1. OC III, p. 525. "En raissonant bien conséquemment, on devrait s'appliquer à donner peu de durée et de solidité aux ouvrages de l'industrie et à les rendre le plus périssables possibles, et à regarder comme de vrais avantages les incendies, les naufrages et tous les autres dégats qui font la désolation des hommes."

be regarded as true advantages, something which Rousseau obviously regards as perfectly absurd. A tentative conclusion is that these two FRAGMENTS do not at all indicate that Rousseau rejects economic growth. Taken together the two fragments, with force, attack precisely such rejections by showing their absurd consequences.

A fairly safe conclusion is, then, that Rousseau finds it absurd to deny the possibility and desirability of economic growth. This conclusion is supported by other safer propositions in Rousseau's work wherein he quite unambiguously acknowledges that overall productivity may be increased by division of labour and by trade. Here is a passage from EMILE:

> though one man working alone can earn a man's living, one hundred men working together can earn the living of two hundred.[1]

But division of labour is not needed as long as production is merely to provide a limited population with bodily needs. Division of labour appears when all land is occupied; it appears when the precondition for society is established. The dynamic behind this productivity increase is explained to Emile:

> Given ten men, each will have ten different requirements. To get what he needs for himself each must work at ten different trades; but considering our different talents, one will do better at this trade, another at that. Each of them, fit for one thing, will work at all and will be badly served. Let us form these ten men into a society, and let each devote himself to the trade for which he is best adapted, and let him work at it for himself and for the rest. Each will reap the advantage of the others' talents, just as if they were his own; by practice each will perfect his own talent, and thus all ten, well provided for, will still have something to spare for others.[2]

All of this sounds somewhat like the INQUIRY INTO THE NATURE AND CAUSES OF WEALTH OF NATIONS, published 14 years later.[3] There is no ambiguity at all, in the statement, about the *potential* of productivity growth. The following lines

1. Book III. OC IV, p. 456. [Rousseau 1984, p. 148.] "La pratique des arts naturels auxquels peut suffire un seul homme mêne à la recherche des arts d'industrie et qui ont besoin de concours de plusieurs mains. Les prémiers peuvent s'éxercer par des solitaires, par des sauvages; mais les autres ne peuvent naitre que dans la societé et la rendent nécessaire. Tant qu'on ne connoit que le besoin physique, chaque homme se suffit à lui-même; l'introduction du superflu rend indespensable le partage et la distribution de travail; car bien qu'un homme travaillant seul ne gagne que la subsistance d'un homme, cent hommes travaillant de concert gagneront dequoi en faire subsister deux cens."

2. OC IV, pp. 466ff. [Rousseau 1984, p. 156] "Supposons dix hommes, dont chacun a dix sortes de besoins. Il faut que chacun, pour son nécessaire, s'applique à dix sortes de travaux; mais vu la difference de génie et talent, l'un réussira moions à quelqu'un de ces travaux, l'autre à un autre. Tous, propres à diverses choses, feront les mêmes et seront mal servis. Formons une société de ces dix hommes, et que chacun s'applique pour lui seul et pour les neuf autres, au genre d'occupation qui lui convient le mieux; chacun profitera des talens des autres comme si lui seul les avoit tous; chacun perfectionnera ler sien par un continuel exercise, et il arrivera que tous les di, parfaitement bien pourvus, auront encore du superabondant pour d'autres."

3. It may reflect their reading of Mandeville. See note 1, p. 13, and note 3 p. 15 in Smith 1976 which indicate the relation between Smith's argument and examples and earlier formulations, e.g., in French literature.

from the PROJET DE CONSTITUTION POUR LA CORSE show that neither can it be doubted that Rousseau found that regional specialisation (and exchange) would increase productivity,

> It is to an undeniable advantage to have each area produce that which it is best at producing; by that disposition one extracts more and more easily from a country than by any other disposition.[1]

Rousseau, then, clearly acknowledges the possibility of productivity growth and growth of the aggregated economic output. But what is its significance, its *value*? Rousseau is peculiarly silent about this question. Still, we know better than nothing. We know, for example, that the possibility of productivity growth certainly plays a very marginal role in his economic philosophy. He does indeed see the need for growth to support a growing population. But growth of the per capita consumption, of the living standard? It is not difficult to find examples where he condemns the growth in personal wealth as perverse and perversive. The drive among the privileged to accumulate more and more wealth in order to distinguish themselves in the eyes of others increases inequality and perverts prices. Monetisation and commercialisation facilitate such a growth and must, for precisely this reason, be prevented. As appeared above, division of labour would be necessary when people started demanding "superfluities". In the Emile paragraph about the potentials in the division of labour quoted above, Rousseau leaves this question open and only refers to the DISCOURS SUR L'ORIGINE ET LES FONDEMENTS DE L'INÉGALITÉ for the value of growth.

However, in his analysis of the household economy, in the DISCOURS SUR L'ECONOMIE POLITIQUE, the augmentation of wealth is given an important legitimate role. It is identified as a crucial task for the family economy. Such growth has a value of its own because the wealth one day has to be dissolved and divided among the children. It is therefore a legitimate aim of the household economy to conserve and increase the patrimony.[2]

> In a word, the little family is destined to expand, and to dissolve itself one day into several other similar families; but the big one [the government] is made always to remain in the same state; it is necessary that the first one accumulates in order to multiply itself, and it not only suffices that the other one conserves itself, but one can easily prove that all augmentation is more damaging than hurtful.[3]

Thus, augmentation in the domestic economy is legitimate, but not because of its potential to increase the standard of living for its members.

1. OC III, p. 924 (PROJET DE CONSTITUTION POUR LA CORSE). "C'est un avantage sans contredit de donner à chaque terrain ce qu'il est le plus propre à produire; par cette disposition l'on tire d'un pays plus et plus aisément que par aucune autre."
2. OC III, p. 242. "conserver et d'accroître le patrimoine du pere".
3. OC III, p. 242. "En un mot la petite famille est destinée à s'éteindre, et à se résoudre un jour en plusieurs autres familles semblables; mais la grand étant faite pour durer toûjours dans le même état, il faut que la premiere s'augmente, pour se multiplier: et non seulement il suffit que l'autre se conserve, mais on peut prouver aisément que toute augmentation lui est plus préjuduciable qu'utile." Italics added.

What about a policy for an augmentation not only to provide for the physical survival of an increasing number of people, but also to give room for an improved quality of life for the individual and her family? JULIE OU LA NOUVELLE HÉLOÏSE and EMILE contain plenty of indications of how Rousseau pictures the happy life. And there it seems that this question is not a political, but rather a literary or existential one. This is consistent with the maxime that popular political economy is designed to economise for the *capability* of the individual to create a good quality of life. And it certainly does not seem natural to Rousseau to quantify the aggregated amount of capability.

The key to Rousseau's ontological view on growth is available in his discussion of personal development. He certainly recognises that there is an expansive component in the inner needs of a human being.[1] In the intimate or autobiographical portrayals (as in JULIE OU LA NOUVELLE HÉLOÏSE) the men and women portrayed have an intense desire or need to reach outside of themselves, not in order to be considered, but to be encountered in common joy. Similarly, these portrayals show a deep need to improve things, the need to *perfect oneself*. In fact, this inner need to perfect oneself is presented as one of the most specifically human of all the characteristics of being human. It is a fundamental quality of life. It means growth in a certain sense (new insights, new techniques, increased efficiency, higher quality of sorts) but also, for example, moral improvement. So what is it, and what is its relation to growth?

## *Perfectibility*

The concept of perfectibility is introduced in the DISCOURS SUR L'ORIGINE ET LES FONDEMENTS DE L'INÉGALITÉ. Of all proposed characteristics of a human being, this is the least disputable. It is a capacity unique to man, whereby man, in contrast to animals, can acquire competences during life that vanish at death.[2] It is, however, a capacity that simultaneously has caused man happiness and (not only some, but) "all his mischiefs" throughout history. Perfectibility is intended to be a neutral concept. Its results are not necessarily desirable and it is for that reason probably difficult to describe them in terms of a growth figure. It is neither good nor bad in itself: it is in a sense pre-moral.

> It caused, over the centuries, his insights and his vices to flourish, as well as his virtues. In that way it finally made him the tyrant of himself and of nature.[3]

1. Grimsley 1974, p. 38.
2. OC III, p. 142. Italics in the original. ". . . l'homme reperdant par la vieillesse ou d'autres accidens, tout ce que sa *perfectibilié* lui avait fait acquerir . . ."
3. OC III, p. 142. "Il seroit triste pour nous d'être forcés de convenir, que cette faculté distinctive, et presque illimitée. est la source de tous les malheurs de l'homme; que c'est elle qui le tire, à force de tems, de cette condition originaire, dans laquelle il couleroit des jours tranquilles, et innocens; que c'est elle, qui faisant éclore avec les siécles ses lumiéres et ses erreurs, ses vices et vertus, le rend à longue le tiran de lui-même, et de la Nature."

Aristotle used the word "perfect" in a similarly neutral way to discuss the possibility that even evil deeds may be perfect.[1] Madame d'Epinay, Rousseau's patroness-persecutor, using the concept in a related sense, observed in a letter to Abbé Galiani that male imbeciles may, in spite of all their shortcomings, at least in one organ of their body achieve "une perfection monstrueuse".[2]

Rousseau is, however, the first known author to use the concept of "perfectibility". The concept is widely used in the history of ideas. It is usually understood as an expression of a positive concept of freedom in the sense of Isaiah Berlin. Berlin distinguishes two types of concepts of freedom: positively and negatively defined. In the latter, freedom is defined by the absence of certain restrictions, while in the former it is defined by the enumeration of certain predetermined properties that characterise "free" man.

Perfectibility as an expression of the positive concept of freedom has signified the unfolding of inherited talents to fulfill one's biological or moral (Kant, Hegel, Mill, Bosanquet etc.) or historical potentialities (Condorcet, Godwin, Comte, Marx etc.). To perfect oneself has been understood to mean to reach one's "allegedly most virtuous or rational essence", to reach a higher stage at a preset ladder of levels.[3]

In the historiography of political philosophy Rousseau's concept of perfectibility is usually closely associated with a positive concept of freedom since he apparently introduced the concept. This is, however, as Wokler has shown, not correct. In the passages just quoted, Rousseau describes perfectibility as a distinctive and almost infinite faculty, which ontologically is part of the very humanness of being human, but on the other hand has caused a great deal of harm. It is, from this and other passages, obvious that Rousseau, in fact does not operate with a positively determined concept at all, but rather the opposite: a negatively defined one.

Where does all this leave us on the question of Rousseau's lack of interest in the value of economic growth? My suggestion is that it has to do with the various roles of three different categories of values that could all be part of abundance in some sense. Firstly, there is abundance in the sense of means necessary for mere survival. Rousseau recognizes in all areas of his economic philosophy the urgent need for economic growth to supply a necessarily growing population with the necessary means for their physical survival. Growth in this segment of abundance plays an important dynamic role in Rousseau's economic philosophy. He advises the Corsicans to try a policy of autarchic self-subsistence *as long as the population is not too large*. The PROJET POUR LA CONSTITUTION DE CORSE clearly assumes that the growth of production implies an increased division of labour. But he seems, like so many others (Adam Smith being one of them), pessimistic about the prospects for productivity growth within agriculture.

1. Dahl 1980, Viroli 1988.
2. Wokler 1979, p. 238.
3. Wokler 1979, p. 233.

The second value category includes superfluities, chimeras, physical products of marginal significance to existential human happiness, but important on the social arena. These things of secondary importance to the welfare of adult women and men can be produced much more efficiently by an increased division of labour.

Thirdly, the capability to perfect oneself is given great importance for the wellbeing of the people, but Rousseau does not try to describe its potentials in quantitative terms. The task for government is rather to economise for a great freedom for people to perfect themselves in whatever ways they choose. But the right to perfectibility demands economic institutions and instruments beyond those of the rude market society, because the value of perfectibility appears, in his "text," either in individual seclusion or as a life in non-randomness requiring collective empowerment.

## *The unique: Julie's Elysium*

A concretely illustrative example of the individually unique character of abundance or perfectibility, in Rousseau's view, is the description of Julie's Elysium in JULIE OU LA NOUVELLE HÉLOÏSE. This wonderful garden is not open, not even visible to anyone other than Julie (and her husband and gardener).

Rousseau pictures in detail the rich life of Julie at the exemplary estate, Clarens. The background to this description in the immensely popular novel is the love story between Julie and St. Preux. The two, passionately in love with one another, were prevented from marriage by Julie's father, who insisted that his daughter marry another man – one of proper aristocratic birth – de Wolmar. After a long time, St. Preux visits the estate and discusses its rationale with de Wolmar and Julie.

Julie possesses a sizable endowment, including land. It is far from a puritanistic misery that is described. The meals served are "delicious", the dining room beautiful, although with no "golden porcelain" or "crystalline vases" or the like.[1] But the happiness and abundance of her life have as much to do with her capacity to use her endowment as with their pure size. The novel is full of ideas about how to get the best sensation from the pleasant wine or from the sensual dining room. The personal touch of Julie's concern and sensitivity increases the pleasure of the home, and not only in the eyes of the tragically passionate lover.[2] And while theatricality and conspicuous consumption (which are absent here) invite accumulation and greed, the physical accumulation of Clarens has a natural limitation.[3]

In his magnificent work LA CULTURE DES APPARANCES. UNE HISTOIRE DU VÊTEMENT XVIIE-XVIIIE SIÈCLE, Daniel Roche describes how the semantic function of appearance changes at Rousseau's time. While in earlier times the clothing expressed the social status of a person, e.g. the nobleman's, in this period

1. OC II, pp. 543f. (V:II). "...des surtout dorés autour desquels on meurt de faim, des cristaux pompeux chargés des fleurs pour tous dessert ne remplissent point la place des mets..."
2. OC II, p. 371. (III:XX).
3. OC II, p 544. (V:II)

it was to tell something about the qualities of the person. The customs of clothing became individualised.Appearance became part of public rhetorics and not only a means to confirm public status. Paraphrasing Roche: instead of the virtues of predictable monads there is an individualised culture of appearance. This development reflected itself everywhere in life, particularly in the big cities like Paris: in commerce, in literature, in the press, in art, in schooling in the crafts, and even in crime.[1]

The pleasure of Clarens is not for the sake of appearance; it is authentic. It is truly the individual sensing her being. There is no component of theatriciality, of trying to make oneself well considered by others. This nontheatrical authenticity is even physically manifested, in Julie's garden, her "elysium".[2] The elysium is a piece of land where Julie has carefully created a wonderful abundance by conserving wild nature according to ecological principles, but also by introducing and tending purchased plants and by actively cultivating other areas of the garden. So it is a built artefact, but one where nature is co-creator of its perfection.

The Elysium is nevertheless acquired; it is a piece of private property. Thus, it illustrates the double components of capability: the endowments themselves and one's capacity to use them. At times the latter is said to be the main source of richness.[3] There is definitely an expansive element in the garden: the increasing beauty, Julie's increased capacity and understanding. The value to the unique user is increased by good care, natural processes and, perhaps new acquisitions. The abundance of the Elysium does not convey a sense of stagnation but rather a constant innovative ingenuity and development. Julie describes a very intricate system of irrigation which she has constructed, a system with a combination of tubes and different kinds of soil beds.

> That order and that rule that multiply and perpetuate the usage of the goods can by itself transform pleasure into happiness. For if it is by our relation to things that real propriety is born, if it is our use of richness rather than its acquisition that gives it to us, what concerns are then more important than the household economy...?[4]

The garden is entirely secluded from the world. Not even *visible* for others, it *cannot,* then, be the object of theatrical (or conspicuous) consumption serving the consideration of others. Only Julie herself, her husband and her employed gardener have access to it:

1. Roche 1989.
2. The word "Elysium" refers to the Elysian fields, the place of the blessed in the Elysian mysteries.
3. There is certainly room for learning. Economic problems concerning the implications of learning processes for the utility of a good are discussed by authors such as Tibor Scitovski, George Stigler and Gary Becker, and Martin Hollis, are discussing such questions. Scitovski 1976; Stigler and Becker 1977, Hollis 1987.
4. OC II, p. 466. (IV:X). "L'ordre et la regle qui multiplient et perpétuent l'usage des biens peuvent seuls transformer le plaisir en bonheur. Que si c'est du raport des choses à nous que nait la véritable propriét'é; si c'est plutôt l'emploi des richesses que leur acquisition qui nous les donne, quels soins importent plus au pere de famille que l'économie domestique et le bon regime de sa maison . . ."

> Although the place is located very close to the house, one cannot see it even at close distance because it is hidden by the umbrageous alley separating it from the house. The tight foliage that surrounds it does not let the eye penetrate and the gate is always carefully locked.[1]

It is so carefully hidden because it is there only for Julie herself, only to satisfy her inner needs. And this seclusion, the absence of any potential for theatriciality, eliminates it from being a luxury. It is physically so constructed that the devouring ambition described in the DISCOURS SUR L'ORIGINE ET LES FONDEMENTS DE L'INÉGALITÉ "to increase one's relative fortune, less by a veritable need than in order to put oneself above the others"[2], cannot operate. Here, in contrast, Julie lives in true abundance, "sufficient to herself".

> An order of things in which nothing is conceded to opinion and in which everything has real utility defined by true natural needs constitutes a spectacle that not only can be approved by reason but also satisfies the eyes and the heart, in that man is seen only in an agreeable light, sufficient unto himself...[3]

Although created by humans it is impossible to see that it is human. It is an artificial wilderness where nature largely lives its own life, and where there is room for Rousseau's aesthetics as well as for berries to be consumed. Ecological processes are respected. Talking about a big bird cage without bars in the garden, St. Preux expresses that he likes to think that the birds "are guests, not prisoners". But Julie responds: "Whom do you call guests? ... We are the guests. They are masters here and we pay them our tribute for tolerating us now and then."[4]

Rousseau contrasts this kind of richness to the superfluities of rich people. Theirs is a kind of richness for those

> always in a hurry to enjoy.

For that reason:

1. Ib.id., "Ce lieu, quoique tout proche de la maison est tellement caché par l'allé couverte qui l'en sépare qu'on ne l'apperçoit de nulle part, L'épais feuillage qui l'environne ne permet point à l'œil d'y pénétrer, et il est toujours soigneusement fermé à la clé."
2. OC III, p. 175. "Enfin l'ambition dévorante, l'ardeur d'élever sa fortune relative, moins par un véritable besoin que pour se mettre au-dessus des autres, inspire à tous les hommes un noir penchant à se nuire mutuellement, une jalousie secréte d'autant plus dangereuse que , pour faire son coup plus en sûreté, elle prend souvent le masque de la bienveillance."
3. Starobinski 1988, p. 107. OC II, p. 547. "un ordre de chose où rien n'est donné à l'opinion, où tout a son utilité réelle et qui se borne aux vrais besoins de la nature n'offre pas seulement un spectacle approuvé par la raison, mais qui contente les yeux et le cÏur, en ce que l'homme ne s'y voit que sous des rapports agréables, comme se suffisant à lui-même . . ."
4. OC II, p. 476. "Cela est charmant ! m'´criai-je: Ce mot de voliere m'avoit surpris de votre part; mais je l'entens maintenant : je vois que vous voulez des hôtes, et non pas des prisonniers. Quáppelez-vous des hôtes, répondit Julie? C'est nous qui sommes les leurs. Ils sont ici les maitres, et nous leurs payons tribut pour en être soufferts quelquefois."

> power and money are the only means they know. They are like birds in a cage and like the friends of so and so much per month.[1]

An immediate, shortsighted, never-ending and ever-increasing consumption of new goods is typical of them. This kind of wealth is expansive and abusive, like:

> those scorching winds, which, covering the trees and plants with devouring insects, deprive useful animals of their subsistence and spread famine and death wherever they blow.[2]

The inner richness of Clarens, on the other hand, is available only for those who are able to lend their mind to whatever "objects strike their senses".[3] In contrast to the consumption of superfluities, this abundance is not threatening to the provision of others. It is an expression of the dream of a "non-abusive" richness. And it is undetermined and truly individual, like the play of children. When Julie's husband half-sarcastically praises Julie because her "child's games" (i.e., creating and tending the Elysium) never intrude on her "housewife's cares", St. Preux responds:

> 'I like children's games of this kind much more than men's work'.[4]

The non-intruding richness developed by women's capability for children's games, rather than candy-begging men's childish desire for an infinitely increasing amount of cash, creates true abundance.

### *Nonrandomness and empowerment*

The concepts of capability and perfectibility correspond to one another. Society is required to secure and tend the capability of the people to create a rich life, while the individual creates a rich life by trying to perfect herself. The intense individual happiness of Clarens may be an attractive portrayal of abundance in Rousseau's sense. It is the result of capable persons' striving for perfectibility. But there is something even more fundamental in Rousseau's concept of richness and freedom. It is not enough that the individual is granted the capacity to create what would make her happy as an individual. A crucial part of being happy is to be master of one's life. And, living in a society of interdependent persons, this can only be done with the help of others.

1. OC II, p. 476. "La patience et le temps, dit M. de Wolmar, ont fait ce miracle. Ce sont des expédiens dont les gens riches ne s'avisent gueres dans leurs plaisirs. Tousjours pressés de jouïr, la force et l'argent sont les seuls moyens qu'ils connoissent; ils ont des oisaux dans les cages, et des amis à tant par mois."
2. The first Discours. OC III, p. 206. [Rousseau 1983, p. 111] "Semblables à ces vents brulans du midi qui couvrant l'herbe et la verdure d'insectes dévourans, ôtent la subistance aux animaux utiles, et portent la disette et la mort dans tous les lieux où ils se font sentir."
3. OC I, p. 1063. [Rousseau 1984b, p. 109] "c'est dans les uns faute de sensibilité naturelle et dans la pluspart que leur esprit trop occupé d'autres idées ne se livre qu'à la dérobe aux objets qui frappent leurs sens."
4. OC II, p. 478. "Louez modestement des jeux d'enfant, et songez qu'ils n'ont jamais rien pris sur les soins de la mere de famille. Je le sais, repris-je, j'en suis très sur, et les jeux d'enfant me plaisent plus en ce genre que les travaux des hommes."

The importance of this component is evident from another description of idyllic individual happiness in LES RÊVERIES DU PROMENEUR SOLITAIRE, written during the last months of Rousseau's life. We read again about the wonderful happiness of a lonely, almost secluded existence as in the Elysium, in a kind of worldly paradise:

> I would make my escape and install myself all alone in a boat, which I would row out into the middle of the lake when it was calm; and there, stretching out full-length in the boat and turning my eyes skyward, I would let myself float and drift wherever the water took me...[1]

But this wonderful floating is an escape. It is unworthy of adult women and men. It is, for example, incompatible with the consistent striving for perfectibility. Living a happy life on one's own is described as a tragedy, as an escape from the possibilities and responsibilities of mature life. The reason for its tragic character is that it is a life *at random:*

> I reached the age of forty, oscillating between poverty and riches, wisdom and error, full of vices born of habit, but with a heart free of evil inclinations, living at random with no rational principles...[2]

This life is poor because the young man is not free to control his life, because he lives at random and does not attempt to perfect himself. This is not what Rousseau intended to idealise in his negative concept of perfectibility.

By subscribing to a negative concept of freedom, one avoids one threat to self-determinancy: that of predetermination. But on the other hand that means that one has to face randomness. Living at random is at least as intolerable as coercion. The need to live one's life non-randomly demands a feasibility to act and choose collectively without intrusion (or desertion), and on the basis of everybody's free will. Therefore, the pleasant lonely life drifting without direction or plan in a boat in the middle of Lake Bienne is merely an inferior substitute for the real life from which Rousseau found himself excluded:

> Ceasing therefore to seek among men the happiness which I felt I could never find there, my ardent imagination learned to leap over the boundaries of a life which was as yet hardly begun, as if it was flying over an alien land in search of a fixed and stable resting-place.[3]

1. Fifth walk. OC I, p. 1044. [Rousseau 1984b, p. 85] "... je m'esquivois et j'allois me jetter seul dans un batteu que je conduisois au milieu du lac quand l'eau étoit calme, et là, m'étendant tout de mon long dans le bateau les yeux tournés vers le ciel, je me lassois aller et dériver lentement au gré de l'eau..."
2. Third walk. OC I, p. 1014. [Rousseau 1984b, p. 50]. "Je parvins jusqu'à l'age de quarante ans flottant entre l'indigence et la fortune, entre la sagesse et l'égarement, plein de vices d'habitude sans aucun mauvais penchant dans le cÏur, vivant au hazard sans principes bien décidés par ma raison..."
3. Third walk. OC I, p. 1012. [Rousseau 1984b, p. 48]."Cessant donc de chercher parmi les hommes le bopnheur que je sentois n'y pouvoir trouver, mon ardente imagination sautoit déja par dessus l'espace de ma vie, à peine commencée, comme sur un terrain qui m'étoit étranger, pour se reposer sur une assiete tranquille où je pusse me fixer."

This pleasant lonely life, with its "desire for these sweet ecstasies", is merely a compensation for the absence of true human pleasures:[1]

> As long as others were my brothers, I invented plans of earthly happiness for myself; these plans were always universal in scope, I could be happy only in the happiness of all and my heart was never touched by the idea of private happiness.[2]

But later he searched in vain for brothers (and sisters?):

> when after vainly seeking a man I had finally to put out my lantern exclaiming: 'There is not a single one left,' then I began to see I was alone in the world, and I understood that my contemporaries acted towards me like automata, entirely governed by external impulses, and that I could only calculate their behaviour according to the laws of motion.[3]

True freedom, in the sense of non-randomness requires a sisterly or brotherly relation to others. When Rousseau found it lacking and only found predictable "behaviour according to the laws of motion", he resigned and tried the second best, the reveries of the solitary walker.

The tragedy of living-at-random is not, as some commentators have claimed, avoided by the existence of any purpose whatsoever, even that determined by a tyrant.[4] Life at random is, certainly, not only slavery but moreover a life as gelding or spayed because one is unfree and cannot fully strive for perfectibility. It is not possible for any other agent than oneself to do the perfecting – in Rousseau's sense – neither history, nor human nature, nor, of course, any dictator or mighty exchange partner. Not even an overwhelming majority of the citizens, dictating its will as if it were the general will. Perfectibility refers to executing one's freedom. The basic problem is how to avoid misusing the potentiality for perfectibility and how to avoid living at random *when living in a state of deep mutual dependence,* which is the unavoidable human predicament in the social state.[5]

In this way, an aspect of the dilemma about how to realise perfectibility and nonrandomness in a state of interdependence can be formulated as: the dilemma of producing a public good, or how to ensure that people conform to the general will, although they could gain by defecting or loose by staying if others defect (as

1. Rêveries, 5th walk, OC I, p.1047. [Rousseau 1984b, pp. 89].
2. 7th walk, OC I, p. 1066. [Rousseau 1984b, pp. 111f]. "Tant que les hommes furent mes fréres, je me faisois des projetys de f'rlicité terrestre; ces projets étant toujours relatifs au tout, je ne pouvois être heureux que de la félicité publique, et jamais l'idée d'un bonheur particulier n'a touché mon cour...
3. The lantern alludes to that of Diogenes. 8th walk, OC I, p. 1078. [Rousseau 1984b, p. 127]. "Quand aprés avoir vainement cherché dix ans un homme il fallut éteindre enfin ma lanterne et m'écrier, il n'y en a plus. Alors je commençai à me voir seul sur la terre et je compris que mes contemporains n'étoient par rapport à moi que des êtres méchaniques, qui n'aissoient que par impulsion et dont je ne pouvois calculer l'action que par les loix du mouvement."
4. Kendall 1985, p. XXXII., Fetscher 1960, p. 241.
5. Cohen 1986, pp. 287 and 294.

in the lesson of the stag hunt).[1] Rousseau's conception of freedom is strong and negative. But it is a concept that demands that the individual leaves her random life and becomes empowered to control her life using her freedom in common with others.[2] This requires a strong social morale. Otherwise, the collective, like the temporary "aggregation", as he describes it in the second DISCOURSE

> will be dissolved and without liaisons, just as an oak tree that falls and gets dissolved into a heap of ashes when it has been consumed by fire.[3]

In the RÊVERIES Rousseau concedes that it is a difficult lesson, often requiring a life of learning, to realise what makes one happy. It is a deeply individual matter, a matter of perfectibility but also a matter of empowerment. What is valuable is not universal over time and space. It is dependent on the inclination of the individual, her attempts to perfect herself, but also on the empowerment of society at large.

> Everything is in constant flux on this earth. Nothing keeps the same unchanging shape, and our affections, being attached to things outside us, necessarily change and pass away as they do … there is nothing solid there for the heart to attach itself to.[4]

## *Beyond Innocence*

Rousseau's economic philosophy is not a program for the maximisation of chimera. It is not a program for the maximal accumulation of whatever. It is rather an attempt at an economic philosophy that emphasises everybody's provisioning with the necessities of life; one's capability to perfect oneself with the most important qualities in life; and for the empowerment of the people. For that reason, it focuses on the need for social morale.

Further, his economic philosophy is not an attempt to describe a mental utopia of the individual, nor is it merely an uninformed projection of his own mental inclinations. Rousseau had a detailed knowledge of the discourse of his time and presented a strikingly consistent economic philosophy. His ideas on economics contain important messages, in spite of, or perhaps because of, the fact that he didn't ascribe to the premises which have so constrained present economic orthodoxy. Yet, therefore his ideas may appear awkward in the light of such theories.

1. Or how to secure an efficient choice in a strategic positive-sum game, i.e., one with a suboptimal equilibrium unique or not. See Cohen 1986, p. 278, note 7.
2. Cranston 1986, p. 83.
3. OC III, p. 359, ". . .son empire aprés lui reste épars et sans liason, comme un chêne se dissout et tombe en un tas de cendres, après que le feu l'a consumé."
4. OC V, p. 1191. [Rousseau 1984b, p. 88]. "Tout ets dans un flux continuel sur la terre: rien n'y garde une forme constante et arrêteé, et nos affections qui s'attacent aux choses extérieurs passent necessairement comme elles.
…il n'y a rien là de solide à quoi le cœur se puisse attacher." The reader familiar with Marshall Berman will recognise the essence of last line in the title of his fine book. Berman, of course, got the title from Karl Marx. Rousseau seems to have transformed a passage from a Persian song.

Rousseau, like Gary Becker and a few other present-day theorists, expands his economic analysis of consumption to such an extent that it transcends the revealed individual preferences of the market. He juxtaposes the market mode of provision with a subsistence mode, and analyses the options as cases of what (post-Rousseau) have been characterised as problems of information asymmetry and other market inefficiencies. Critical of the pale blackboard economics of his time, he felt obliged to base his analysis of economic matters on a realistic notion of human psychology. But he rejects the idea (so forcefully expressed by Mandeville and Smith) that egoistic individuals concerned only with their own gain would make an optimum economy. One reason for his stance is because he fears what in modern literature is labeled bargaining situations. He finds the – now, as well as then – conventional concept of richness in terms of one or another bundle of goods, to be an impoverished concept which fails to capture the manifoldedness of what most people regard as essential to a truly rich life. Instead, he prefers a more Aristotelian perspective on welfare, not unlike Amartya Sen's capability approach, whereby welfare is defined in terms of what people are capable of doing by means of their entitlements. As is indicated in Rousseau's writings, as well as in several recent texts by Sen, the consequences for economic policy of such an approach may, however, be far from trivial.

Rousseau emphasises two distinct properties of the most important qualities in life: everyone's need to perfect herself and everyone's need to live non-randomly, interdependent in society. Like Aristotle, he finds that real abundance is strictly individual. It is not possible to standardise or measure the happiness of the people. A crucial part of happiness is the individual's capability to perfect herself, to make something new, which no one has considered before, and which is not immediately comparable or substitutable. Perfectibility is the capability and willingness to diverge, to see and enjoy – not only those things one already knows how to reflect about, but to be willing to be surprised.[1]

The individualistic character of the most important qualities in life, in Rousseau's conceptualisation, as well as the importance of non-randomness, make it logical for him to focus on non-market domains of economics. The individualistic character of perfectibility makes one easily dependent on very few people (like Julie on her gardener). A person in such a monopolistic situation can, like the hunter who caught sight of a hare, engage in blackmail. She can demand a high compensation just because she knows that, at that particular place and time, no one else can do the job. One faces a bargaining situation rather than the supply of the competitive market. And since the job that needs to be done is unique (like that of the gardener's) there is also a situation of asymmetric information. The producer knows his capacity, and the true costs, but since the buyer cannot compare identical goods produced before, she has to trust the seller of the unique service or commodity. For such reasons it may be easier to provide these qualities by other allocation mechanisms than through the market.

1. Martha Nussbaum 1990.

Finally, Rousseau observes that full recognition of the complexity of the production-consumption process demands that the consumer be regarded as a co-producer of her own consumption, even when she acquires the good through market exchange. This way of looking at production-consumption opens up a more complete analysis of the whole production process, in Rousseau's sense, including the consumer's capacity to use, treat and maintain his or her endowments and artefacts , be they wild, bought or cultured.

* * *

If all of Rousseau's statements on the philosophy of political economy are summarised together, the result is a furiously stubborn and consistent attempt to seek out the fundamental requirements of a political economy. In Rousseau's emergent, conceptualised response what is required of a political economy is to affirm and protect the freedom of its citizens, to economise for the most important things in life. *Has anybody else, ever, more consistently and unconditionally demanded the freedom of the people as not only an absolute condition for economic policy but also a fundamental component of its goal?*

# *Bibliography*


## *Printed sources and abreviations*

*Correspondence Complète de J.-J. Rousseau:* ed. R. A. Leigh, vol. I-VIII, Genève, Les Délices, 1965-69. Abbr.: C.C.

*Correspondence Générale de J.-J. Rousseau:* ed. Dufour-Plan, vol. I-XX, Paris, Colin, 1924-34. Abbr.: C.G.

*Œvres complètes de J.-J. Rousseau I-V:* L'édition de la Bibliothèque de la Pleiade. Paris, Gallimard, 1959-95. Abbr.: O.C.

Rousseau, Jean-Jacques: *Lettre a M. d'Alembert sur son article* GENÈVE ed. Michel Launay, Paris, Garnier - Flammarion, 1967. Abbr.: L.A.

Aristotle: *Nichomachean Ethics:* transl. H. Rackham (1926), Cambridge, Mass, Harvard U. P., The Loeb classical library vol 73. Aristotle vol. XIX, 1982.

Cantillon, Richard: *Essai sur la Nature du Commerce en Géneral* (1755), Paris, Institut National d'études Démographiques, 1952.

Galiani, Ferdinando: *Dialogues sur le Commerce des Bleds,* (1770), Milano - Napoli, Richard Ricciardi Editore, 1959.

Mandeville, Bernard: *The Fable of the Bees; or Private Vices, Public Benefits* (1732), I-II, ed. F B Kaye, Oxford, Clarendon Press: 1924/29.

Mun, Thomas: *England's Treasure by Forraign Trade* (1664), Oxford 1949.

Pufendorf, Samuel: *On the Duty of Men and Citizen According to Natural Law:* ed. James Tully, transl. Michael Silverstone, Cambridge, Cambridge U. P. 1991.

*The Works of William Shakespeare,* vol. 4, London, William Cloves and Sons, 1934.

Smith, Adam: *An Inquiry into the Nature and Causes of the Wealth of Nations.* (1776), Oxford, Oxford U. P., 1976.

Steuart, sir James: *An Inquiry into the Principles of Political Economy.* (1767), London, 1967.

## *English translations of the printed sources used*

Rousseau, Jean-Jacques: *The Social Contract and Discourses:* transl. G. D. H. Cole, 1913, London, Everyman, 1983.

Rousseau, Jean-Jacques: *The Confessions:* transl. J. M. Cohen, 1953, Harmondsworth, Penguin 1984.

Rousseau, Jean-Jacques: *Emil:* transl. Barbara Foxley, 1911, London, Everyman, 1984a.

Rousseau, Jean-Jacques: *Reveries of the solitary walker:* transl. Peter France 1979, Harmondsworth, Penguin, 1984b.

Rousseau, Jean-Jacques: *The Government of Poland:* transl. Willmore Kendall 1966, Indianapolis, Hackett Publishing Company, 1985

## *Other literature*

Abel, Wilhelm: *Massenarmut und Hungerkrisen im vorindustrieller Europa; Versuch einer Synopsis,* Hamburg, Parcy, 1971.

Airiau, Jean: *L'opposition aux physiocrates a la fin de l'Ancien Régime,* Bibliothéque constitutionelle et de science politique; Tom XIX, Paris, R. Pichon et R. Durand-Auzias,1965.

Akerlof, George A.: "The Market for Lemons": Quality Uncertainty and the Market Mechanism", 1967, in his *An Economist's Book of Tales,* Cambridge, Cambridge U.P., 1984.

Arkhipoff, Oleg: "Le paradoxe de Condorcet est-il-un mythe?", in *Condorcet. Mathématicien, économiste, philosophe, homme politique.* Minerve, Colloque international, 1989.

Arrow, Kenneth: *Social Choice and Individual Values* (1951), 2nd ed., New Haven and London, Yale U. P., 1963.

Arrow, Kenneth: "The Organization of Economic Activity; Issues Pertinent to the Choice of Market versus Nonmarket Allocation" (1969), reprinted in Arrow, K.: *Collected Papers, Vol. 2; General Equilibrium,* Oxford, Basil Blackwell, 1983.

Baker, Keith Michael: *Condorcet. From Natural Philosophy to Social Mathematics* (1975), Chicago University of Chicago Press, 1982.

Becker, Gary: *A Treatise on the Family,* Cambridge, Mass., Harvard U. P. 1981.

Beretti, Francis: *Pascal Paoli et l'image de la Corse au dix-huitième siècle; le témoignage des voyageurs britanniques,* Studies on Voltaire and the eighteenth century, vol. 253, Oxford, The Voltaire Foundation at the Taylor Institution, 1988.

Bhaduri, Amit: *The economic structure of backward agriculture,* London, Academic Press, 1983.

Blanc, Hermann: *La chambre des blés de Genève 1628-1798,* Thèse No 57, Genève, Université de Genève; Faculté des Sciences Économiques et Sociales, 1939.

Bloch, Marc: "La lutte pour l'individualisme agraire dans la France du XVIIIe siècle", in *Annales d'histoire économique et sociale,* vol. 2, no 7-8 ,1930.

Chabert, Alexandre: "Rousseau économiste", *Revue d'histoire économique et sociale,* nr 3, p.345-356, 1964.

Coe, Richard N.: *Morelly. Ein Rationalist auf Wege zum Sozialismus,* Neue Beiträge zur Literaturwissenschaft, Band 13. Berlin, Rütten und Loening, 1961.

Cohen, Joshua: "Reflections on Rousseau; Autonomy and Democracy", in *Philosophy and Public Affairs.,* vol. 15, nr 3, 1986.

Cohen, Joshua: "Structure, Chice and Legitimacy; Locke's Theory of the State", in *Philosophy and Public Affairs,* vol. 15, nr 4, 1986a.

Colletti, Lucio: *From Rousseau to Lenin; Studies in Ideology and Society,* London, New Left Books, 1972.

Cranston, Maurice: *Philosophers and Pamphleteers. Political Theorists of the Enlightenment.,* Oxford, Oxford U. P., 1986.

Cucchi, Paolo M.: "Rousseau, lecteur de Machiavel", in Launay, M., (ed), 1969.

Dahl, Eva-Lena: *Överideologi och politiskt handlingsprogram. En studie i Lockes och Rousseaus tänkande, (Ideology and political program of action. A study in the Political Thought of Locke and Rousseau,* Göteborg, Gothenburg Studies in the History of Science and Ideas: 3, Acta Universitas Gothoburgiensis, 1980.

Denis, Henri: "Deux collaborateurs économiques de l'encyclopédie: Quesnay et Rousseau", *La pensée, Revue du rationalisme moderne,* Paris,1951.

Derathé, Robert: "Introduction; Discours sur l'économie politique", in *O.C. III.*

Derathé, Robert: *Jean-Jacques Rousseau et la science politique de son temps,* 2nd ed., Paris, Librairie Philosophique, J. Vrin,1977.

Drivier, C. H.: "Morelly and Mably", in Hearnshaw, F. J. C. (ed.): *The Social and Political Ideas of Some Great French Thinkers of the Age of Reason,* A series of lectures delivered at King's College University of London during the season 1928-29, London, Harrap & Co, 1930.

Duchez, Marie-Élisabeth: "Principe de la mélodie et Origines de langues", *Revue de musicologie,* 60, 1974.

Dufour, Alfred: "Pufendorfs Ausstrahlung im französischen und im angloamerikanischen Kulturraum", in *Samuel von Pufendorf 1632–1982. Ett rättshistoriskt symposium i Lund 15–16 januari 1982.* Lund, Skrifter utgivna av Institutet för rättshistorisk forskning. Rättshistoriska Studier Band 12, 1986.

Ellis, Madeleine B.: *Rousseau's Socratic Aemilian Myths; A Literary Collation of Emile and the Social Contract,* Columbus, Ohio State U. P., 1977.

Fabre, Jean: "Considérations sur le gouvernement de Pologne" and "annotations", in *OC III.*

Faure-Solet, Jean-François: *Economie politique et progrès au "siècle des lumières" (1750–1789),* Paris, Université de Dijon, Edition Gauthiers-Villars,1964.

Fedorowics, J. K.: ed., *A Republic of Nobles. Studies in Polish History to 1864,* Cambridge, Cambridge U. P., 1982.

Ferrero,Guglielmo: "Genève et le Contrat Social". *Annales de la Societé J.-J. Rousseau,* vol. XXIII, 1934

Fetscher, Iring: *Rousseau's Politische Philosophie; Zur geschichte des demokratischen Freiheitsbegriffs,* Politica; Abhandlungen und Texte zur politischen Wissenschaft, Band 1, Neuwied, Hermann Luchterhand, 1960.

Fogel, Robert William: *Second Thoughts on the European Esacape from Hunger; Famines, Price Elasticities, Entitlements, Chronic Malnutrition, and Mortality Rates,* Working paper series on Historical Fctors in Long-run Growth, No. 1, National Bureau of Economic Research (NBER), 1989.

Fox-Genovese, Elizabeth: *The Origins of Physiocracy; Economic Revolution and Social Order in Eighteenth-Century France,* Ithaca and London, Cornell U. P., 1976.

Fralin, Richard: "Rousseau and Community; The Role of Mœurs in Social Change", *History of Political Thought,* vol. VII, No. 1, 1966.

Fridén, Bertil: *På tröskeln till marknaden; Makt, institutionell kontext och ekonomisk effektivitet i Västsverige 1630–1800,* Göteborg, Meddelanden från ekonomisk-historiska institutionen vid Göteborgs Universitet, No. 62, 1991.

Gagnebin, Bernard and Marcel Raymond: "Confessions", in *OC I.*

Galliani, Renato: *Rousseau, le luxe et l'idéologie nobilaire – étude socio-historique;* Studies on Voltaire and the eighteenth century, vol. 268, Oxford, The Voltaire Foundation at the Taylor Institution, 1989.

Gearhardt, Suzanne: *The Open Boundary of History and Fiction. A Critical Approach to the French Enlightenment,* Princeton, Princeton U. P., 1984.

Gilje, Nils och Harald Grimen: *Samhällsvetenskapernas förutsättningar,* Göteborg, Daidalos, 1992.

Grange, Henri: *Les idées de Necker, Lille, Service de reproduction des theses,* Université de Lille III, 1973.

Gossman, Lionell: "Time and History in Rousseau", *Studies on Voltaire and the 18th century,* Vol. XXX, Geneva, 1964.

Grimsley, Ronald: *From Montesquieu to Laclos. Studies on the French Enlightenment,* Genève, Librairie Droz, 1974.

Grochulska, Barbara: "The Place of the Enlightenment in Polish Social History", in Fedorowics, J. K., 1982.

Grofman, Bernard and Scott L, Feld: "Rousseau's General Will; a Condorcetian Perspective", in *American Political Science Review,* vol. 82, No. 2, Junc 1988.

Hampton, Jean: *Hobbes and the social Contract Tradition,* Cambridge, Cambridge U. P., 1986.

Hardin, Garret: "The Tragedy of the Commons", *Science,* 162, 1968.

Hardin, Russel: *Collective Action,* Baltimore, The John Hopkins U.P., 1982.

Havens, George R.: "Rousseau, Melon, and Sir William Petty", in *Modern Language Notes,* November, 1940.

Hendel, Charles W.: *Jean-Jacques Rousseau; Moralist,* Indianapolis, The Bobbs-Merrilll Company, 1962.

Herlitz, Lars: "The Concept of Mercantilism", in *Scandinavian Economic History Review,* Vol XII, No. 2, 1964.

Herlitz, Lars: "Merchants and Jesuits : Thomas Mun's Balance of Trade", in his *Ideas of Capital and Development in Pre-Classical Economic Thought; Two Essays,* Göteborg, Institute of Economic History, University of Göteborg, Report 7, 1989.

Herlitz, Lars: "The Physiocrats", in his *Ideas of Capital and Development in Pre-Classical Economic Thought: Two Essays.* Göteborg, Institute of Economic History, University of Göteborg, Report 7, 1989a.

Herlitz, Lars: *Conceptions of History and Society in Mercantilism 1630–1730.* Göteborg University, Institute of Economic History, 1992.

Hermansson, Jörgen: *Rousseau on Justice; In search of an Argument,* Unpublished working paper presented at SCASS, fall, 1992.

Hill, Bridget: *The Republican Virago, The Life and Times of Catherine Macaulay, Historian,* Oxford, Clarendon Press, 1992.

Hirsch, Fred: *The Social Limits to Growth,* London, Routledge and Kegan Paul, 1977.

Hirschman, Albert O: *The Passions and the Interests; Political Arguments for Capitalism before Its Triumph,* (1977), Princeton, N. J., Princeton U. P., 1981.

Hirschman, Albert O: "Rival Views of Market Society" (1982), in Hirschman: *Rival Views of Market Society and Other Recent Essays,* Cambridge Mass., Harvard U.P., 1992.

Hollis, Martin: *The Cunning of Reason,* Cambridge, Cambridge U. P., 1987.

Hutchison, Terence: *Before Adam Smith; The Emergence of Political Economy 1662–1776,* Oxford, Basil Blackwell, 1988.

de Jasay, Anthony: *Social Contract, Free Ride; A Study of the Public Goods Problem,* Oxford, Clarendon Press, 1989.

Jedryka, Zygmunt: "Le contrat social économique: Jean-Jacques Rousseau fondateur de la démocratie économique", in *Revue internationale d'histoire politique et constitutionelle,* 1952.

Kaye, F. B.: "A commentary: critical, historical, and explanatory", in Mandeville, 1924.

Kendall, Willmoore: "Introduction. How to read Rousseau's Government of Poland" (1966), in *Rousseau* 1985.

Kula, Witold: *An Economic Theory of the Feudal System; Towards a Model of the Polish Economy 1500–1800,* London, New Left Books, 1976.

Lagercrantz, Olof: *August Strindberg* (1979), London, Faber & Faber 1984..

Langholm, Odd: *Wealth and Money in the Aristotelian Tradition; A study in Scholastic Economic Sources.* Bergen, Universitetsforlaget 1983.

Launay, Michel: *Le vocabulaire politique de Jean-Jacques Rousseau. Collection des index et concordances de J.-J. Rousseau,* Genève, Librairie Slatkine, 1977.

Launay, Michel: *Jean-Jacques Rousseau; Écrivain politique (1712–1762),* Deuxième edition revue et augmentée avec un préface de Jean Starobinski, Genève-Paris, Editions Slatkine, 1989.

Launay, Miche ed.: *Jean-Jacques Rousseau et son Temps; Poltitique et Littérature au XVIIIe siècle,* Paris, Librairie A-G Nizet, 1969.

Lewis, David: *Convention; A Philosophical Study,* Cambridge Mass., Harvard U. P., 1969.

MacAdam, James: "The Moral Dimensions of Property", in Cell, Howard and James MacAdam: *Rousseau's Response to Hobbes,* New York etc., Peter Lang, 1988.

Marshall, David: *The Surprising Effects of Sympathy; Marivaux, Diderot, Rousseau and Mary Shelley,* Chicago, Univ. of Chicago Press, 1988.

Mély, Benoît: *Jean-Jacques Rousseau; Un intellectuel en rupture, Voies de l'histoire.* Paris, Minerve, 1985.

Morishima, Michio: *Why Has Japan "Succeeded"? Western Technology and Japanese Ethos,* Cambridge, Cambridge U. P., 1982.

Namer, Gérard: "Mirabeau et Rousseau: Reflexions sur un texte inedit", in Launay, M. 1969.

Nussbaum Martha: *Love's Knowledge; Essays on Philosophy and Literature,* Oxford, Oxford, U.P., 1990.

Rapaport, Anatol and M. Guyer: "A Taxonomy of 2 x 2 Games." in *General Systems;* Yearbook of the Society for General Systems Research, Vol. XI, Ann Arbor, Mich., 1966.

Rapaport, Anatol: "Prisoner's dilemma", in *Game Theory, The new Palgrave:* Eds. Eatwell John, M. Milgate, P. Newman, London, The Macmillan Press, 1989.

Raphael, D. D. and A. L. Macfie: "Introduction", in Smith, Adam: *The Theory of Moral Sentiments:* Oxford, Oxford U. P., 1976.

Riley, Patrick: "Rousseau's General Will; Freedom of a Particular Kind", in *Political Studies,* Vol. XXXIX, 1991.

Robinson, Philip E J: *Jean-Jacques Rousseau's Doctrine of the Arts,* European University Studies, Série XIII, Vol. 90, Bern, Frankfurt am Main, New York, Peter Lang, 1984.

Roche Daniel: *La culture des apparences. Une histoire du vêtement XVII^e-XVIII^e siècle.* Fayard, 1989.

Roth, Alvin E: "Editor's introduction and overview", in his (ed.) *Game-theoretic Models of Bargaining*, Cambridge, Cambridge U. P., 1985.

Runciman, W. G. and Amartya K. Sen: "Games, Justice, and the General Will", in *Mind* 74, p. 554-562, 1965.

Samuelson Paul A,: "The Pure Theory of Public Expenditure", in *Review of Economics and Statistics*, Vol. 35, 1954.

Schmidt, Lars-Henrik: *Den sociale excorsisme – eller den tabte umiddelbarhed; Konstruktion af det sociale hos Rousseau og Nietzsche*, Århus, Modtryk, 1987.

Sen, Amartya: "The Nature and Classes of Prescriptive Judgments", in *Political Quarterly*, vol. 17, 1967.

Sen, Amartya: *Employment, Technology and Development*, Delhi, ILO, 1975.

Sen, Amartya: "The Impossibility of a Paretian Liberal" (originally published in *Journal of Political Economy*, 78, 1970), in Sen A 1982c; 1982a

Sen, Amartya: "Liberty, Unanimity and Rights" (originally published in *Economica*, 43, 1976), in Sen A 1982c; 1982b.

Sen, A: Choice, *Welfare and Measurement*, Oxford, Basil Blackwell, 1982c.

Sen, Amartya: *Poverty and Famines; An Essay on Entitlement and Deprivation*, Oxford, Clarendon Press, 1982d.

Sen, Amartya: "The Profit Motive", *Lloyds Bank Review*, 147, January 1983

Sen, Amartya: "Economics and the Family", in *Resources, Values and development*, Oxford, Basil Blackwell 1984a.

Sen, Amartya: "The New Economic Gospel", in *New Society*, July 26 1984b.

Sen, Amartya: *Commodities and Capabilities;* Professor Dr P. Henniman Lectures in Economics, Theory, Institutions, Policy; Volume 7, Oxford; North-Holland Amsterdam, 1985.

Sen, Amartya: "Social Choice Theory", in Arrow, K.J. and M.D. Intriligator: *Handbook of Mathematical Economics*, vol. III. Amsterdam 1986.

Sen, Amartya: "Capability and Well-Being", in Nussbaum, Martha and Amartya Sen. eds.: *The Quality of Life:* A study prepared for the World Institute for development Economics Research (WIDER), The United Nations University, Oxford, Clarendon Press, 1993.

Shklar, Judith N: *Men and Citizens. A Study of Rousseau's Social Theory.* (1969), Cambridge, Cambridge U. P., 1985.

Sraffa, Pierro: *Production of Commodities by Means of Commodities.*, Cambridge, Cambridge U. P. 1960.

Starobinsky, Jean: *jean-jacques rousseau: la transparence et l'obstacle, suivi de sept essais sur rousseau*, Paris, Editions Gallimard, 1971.

Starobinsky, Jean: *Jean-Jacques Rousseau; Transparency and Obstruction.* (Transl. of previous work), Chicago, The University of Chicago Press 1988.

Stigler, George J., and Gary S. Becker: "De Gustibus Non Est Disputandum", *Am. Econ Rev.*, 67 (1977), s.76-90.

Steffen, Gustaf F.: "Den demokratiska samhällsuppfattningen hos Platon, Rousseau och Quesnay", in *Ekonomisk Tidskrift*, Vol XV, Uppsala 1913.

Sugden, Robert: *The Economics of Rights, Co-operation & Welfare*, Oxford, Basil Blackwell

1986.

Talmon, J. L.: *The Origins of Totalitarian Democracy,* London, Sphere Books, (1954) 1970.

Thompson, E P: "The Moral Economy of the English Crowd in the 18th Century", in *Past and Present,* vol. 50, February 1971.

Villers, Robert: "Jean-Jacques Rousseau, la finance et les financiers", *Etudes sur le Contrat Social,* p. 329-342, Publications de l'Université de Dijon XXCX. Paris, Societé les Belles Lettres, 1964.

Viroli, Maurizio: *Jean-Jacques Rousseau and the 'Well-Ordered Society'.* Cambridge, Cambridge U. P., 1988.

von Wright, Georg Henrik: "Wittgenstein and the Twentieth Century", in Haaparanta, Leila and others (eds.): *Language, Knowledge and Intentionality,* Acta Philosophica Fennica 49, 1990.

Walras, Léon: *Elements of Pure Economics or the theory of Social Wealth,* London (1874), 1954.

Wokler, Robert : "Rameau, Rousseau and the Essai sur origine des langues", in *Studies on Voltaire and the 18th century,* 117, 1974.

Wokler, Robert: "Rousseau's Perfectibilian Libertarianism", in *The Idea of Freedom; Essays in Honour of Isaiah Berlin,* ed. by Alan Ryan, Oxford, Oxford U.P., 1979.

Wokler, Robert: *Rousseau on Society, Politics, Music and Language. An Historical Interpretation of His Early Writings,* New York and London, Garland Publ., 1987.

Zivkovic, Zagorka: "Kärlek, tillfällighet – och socialdemokrati", introduktion i Nussbaum Martha C: *Känslans skärpa – tankens inlevelse, Essäer om etik och politik,* Stockholm, Symposion, 1995.

# Index

abundance. . 18, 34, 59,72, 74, 77f, 97, 100, 139ff., 147ff., 155
Akerlof, George. . . . . . . . . . . . . . . . . . 42
appearance . . . . . . . 35, 40f., 74, 121, 148f.
Aristotle . 38, 73, 100, 122, 134, 140, 147, 155
Arrow, Kenneth. . . . . . . 102, 104, 123, 138
autarchy . 14, 33ff., 46, 55, 61, 77, 93, 107f., 120, 122
bargaining . . . . . . . . . . . . . 68, 71ff., 75ff., 88f., 95, 117, 130, 132, 139, 154f.
basic (judgment).22f., 28ff., 33, 60, 92f., 97
Becker, Gary . . . . . . . . . . . . . . . . . 30, 155
Bhaduri Amit. . . . . . . . . . . . . . . . . . . . 87
Buttafoco. . . . . . . . . . . . . . . . . 51, 55ff., 58
Cantillon . . . . . . . . . . . . . . . . . . . . 14, 74
capability. . . 16ff. , 59, 133, 139, 141, 146ff., 151, 153, 155f.
Cato . . . . . . . . . . . . . . . . . . . . . . . . 98f.
citizen. . . . . . . 16, 34, 58–9, 66, 68, 76, 91, 100ff., 115, 119–133, 139, 153, 156
Clarens . . . . . . . . . . . . . . . . . . . 45, 148ff.
collective good. . . . . . . . . . . . . . . 130, 138
Colletti Lucio . . . . . . . . . . . . . . . . . 141ff.
commerce. . . . . . . . 25, 64ff., 74ff., 85, 147
commodity. . . . . . . . . . . . . . . . 34, 93, 155
CONFESSIONS . . . 23, 35ff., 39f., 44, 51f., 54
CONSIDÉRATIONS SUR LE GOUVERNEMENT DE POLOGNE. .16, 24, 26, 29, 51, 55, 60, 65, 69ff., 125, 128
consumption . . . . . 33, 34, 37, 44ff., 48ff., 59, 66f., 77ff., 86ff., 112, 134, 138, 145, 148f., 151, 155f..
CONTRAT SOCIAL. . . . 23ff., 51, 53, 96, 100, 102, 111, 113, 127, 143
corn magazine . . . . . . . . . . . . . . . . 57, 119
corn market. . . . . . . . . 81, 85, 88f., 94, 129
corn prices . . . . . . . . . . . . . . . . 85, 93, 119
Corsica . . . . . . . . . . . . . . . 28, 51–8, 60ff., 75f., 105, 117, 147
Crusoe Robinson. . . . . . . . . . . . . . . . 108
Dahl, Eva-Lena. . . . . . . . . . . . . . 24, 141f.
de Mirabeau . . . . . . . . . . . 13, 74, 83f., 91
de Saint Pierre, abbé . . . . . . . . . . . 66, 118
democracy. . . . . . . . . 24, 26, 53, 57, 97ff., 104, 130, 134
Derathé, Robert. . . . . . . 72, 77f., 84, 141f.
Diderot . . . . . . . . . . . . . . . . . . . . 12, 66
DISCOURS SUR L'ÉCONOMIE POLITIQUE. . . . . . . 14, 53, 85, 87, 9ff., 102, 119, 121, 139
DISCOURS SUR L'ORIGINE ET LES FONDEMENTS DE L'INÉGALITÉ. . . 78, 108, 110, 114, 120, 127, 145f., 150
DISCOURS SUR LES SCIENCES ET LES ARTS . . . . . . . . . . . . . . . . . . 64ff.
domain . . . . . . . . . . . . 14ff., 19, 134ff., 155
domestic economy . . . . . 36, 40, 42ff., 97, 145
Ellis, Madeleine . . . . . . . . . . . . . . . . 124
Elysium . . . . . . . . . . . . . . . . . 16ff., 150ff.
EMILE. 22f, 28, 39, 43f40, 42, 44ff., 51, 60, 8240, 42, 44ff., 117, 14640, 42, 44ff.40, 42, 44ff.,
empowerment . . . . . . . . 130, 148, 151, 154

Encyclopédie . . . 12, 18, 22, 83, 96, 130, 131
equality . . 25, 26, 56, 63, 78, 80, 82, 91, 95, 108, 118, 142, 148
equilibrium. . 42, 47, 59, 75f., 92, 101, 115f., 138ff.
external effect . . . . . . . . . . . . . . . . . 138f.
family . . . 40, 43, 61, 97, 115, 137, 140, 145f.
Fetscher, Iring . . . . . . . . . 28, 60, 67, 90f., 105f., 141ff.
Fogel, Robert . . . . . . . . . . . . . . . 86, 88ff.
Forbonnais . . . . . . . . . . . . . . . . . . . . . 13
FRAGMENTS POLITIQUES . . . . . 65, 72, 79, 84, 140, 142, 144
freedom . . . . . . . 17, 23, 25f., 28, 53, 72, 96, 98f., 102, 109, 147f., 153ff.
Gagnebin, Bernard . . . . . . . . . . 39, 41, 50
Galiani, Ferdinando, abbé . . . 14, 91f., 147
Galliani, Renato . . . . . . . . . . . 2ff., 60, 69
general will . . 21, 69, 95f., 98-104, 106, 113, 118, 123, 125, 127, 129f., 153
growth . . . . . 17f., 59f., 76, 86, 95, 118, 121, 145ff.
Habsburg . . . . . . . . . . . . . . . . . . . 67, 73
Hardin Garret . . . . . . . . . . . . . . . . . 114
Harrod Roy . . . . . . . . . . . . . . . . . 49, 79
Hendel, Charles . . . . . . . . . . . . . . . . 23f.
Hobbes . . . . . . . . . . . . . . . . . . . . . 108f.
Holberg . . . . . . . . . . . . . . . . . . . . . . 68
Hume . . . . . . . . . . . . . . . . . . 14f., 23, 111
Ibsen Hendrik . . . . . . . . . . . . . . . . . 139
ideologie nobiliaire . . . . . . . . . . . . . 25ff.
independence . . . . . . 34, 36, 56f., 61, 70ff., 75, 77, 86, 108ff., 110, 114f., 118
information costs . . . . . . . . . . . . 44f., 95
innocence . . . . . . . . . . . . . . . . 16, 35, 128
Jews . . . . . . . . . . . . . . . . . . 124, 128, 132
JULIE OU LA NOUVELLE HÉLOÏSE . . 17, 22, 29, 36f., 40, 45, 47, 146, 148
Kendall, William . . . . . . . . . . . . . . 23f., 71
Kula, Witold . . . . . . . . . . . . . . . . 86, 93
Launay, Michel . . . . . . . . . . . . . . . . . 22
legislator . . . . . . . . . . . . . 125, 126ff., 130
LETTRE À D'ALEMBERT SUR LES SPECTACLES . . . . . . . . . . . . . . . . 22, 130
Lewis, David . . . . . . . . . . . . . . . . . 110ff.
Locke . . . . . . . . . . . . . . . . . . . . . 14, 103
luxury . . . . . . . . . . . . 25f., 44f., 48ff., 64, 67f., 85f., 116, 137, 150
Lycurgos . . . . . . . 23, 123ff., 127f., 130, 132
Machiavelli . . . . . . . . . . . . . . . . . . . . 124
Mandeville . . . . . . . . . . . . 14, 44, 67f., 154
market exchange . . 13, 18, 33, 36, 38ff., 50f., 82, 85, 91f., 94f., 138, 155
Marx Karl . . . . . . . . . . . . . . . . . . . . . 147
Melon . . . . . . . . . . . . . . . . . . . . . . . . 66
mercantilism 15, 46, 57, 67ff., 72f., 76, 78, 80, 90
mode of provision . . . . . . . . . 39, 106, 154
money . . . . . . . . . . . 25, 34f., 37ff., 45, 49, 56, 64, 69, 72ff., 76ff., 80, 82, 85, 89f., 94, 119, 122, 150
Moses . . . . . . . . . . . . . . . . 123ff., 128, 130
need . . . . . . . . 15f., 22, 29, 34f., 38, 40, 42, 46ff., 55ff., 74, 77f., 80, 82, 84f., 88, 91, 96, 103, 110f., 113ff., 116f., 119, 121f., 131, 133ff., 137f., 142f., 144f., 150, 152, 154f.
Netherlands . . . . . . . . . . . . . . . . . . . . 67
Numa . . . . . . . . . . . . . . . . . . . . 123ff., 130
opulence . . . . . . . . . . . . . . . . . . . 67f., 72
Paoli, general . . . . . . . . . . . . . . . 52, 55, 58
paretooptimum . . . . . . . . . . . 100, 113, 117
particular will . . . . . . . . . . . . . 68, 99f., 113
peasants 31, 43, 45, 55, 71, 77, 81, 85ff., 90ff., 95, 105f, 121f, 140
perfectibility . . . . . . . . 17, 146ff., 150, 152f.
Persia . . . . . . . . . . . . . . . . . . . . . . . 132
Petty . . . . . . . . . . . . . . . . . . . . . . . . . 66
physiocracy . . . . . . . . . . . 60, 81, 82, 89ff.
Poland . . . . . . . . 23f., 27ff., 61, 69f., 75, 125
political economy . . . . . . . . . . 12, 17f., 29, 38ff., 56, 59, 65, 69, 96ff., 100, 102, 137, 140, 146, 154
popular . . . . . . . . . . . 29, 51, 52, 54, 58, 83, 96f., 102, 134, 146, 148
positional reading . . . . . . . . . . . . . 20, 23
price . . . . . . . . 18, 42, 46ff., 56, 72f., 75ff., 83–90, 93f., 95, 105, 119, 138f., 145
prisoners' dilemma . . . . . . . . . . . . 101, 11f.
productivity . . . . . . . . 25, 84f., 90, 93, 116, 141f., 144f., 147

PROJET DE CONSTITUTION POUR LA CORSE....... 20, 27f., 51f., 65, 69, 85, 96, 119, 145
property .. 23, 25, 36, 57, 61, 64, 91, 93, 95, 102f., 107, 109, 115, 117f., 120ff., 149
Quesnay ............... 13f., 81, 90f.
Rameau ..................... 131f.
random man ........... 44, 127, 152ff.
Raymond, Marcel ........... 39, 41, 50
RÊVERIES DU PROMENEUR SOLITAIRE................ 23, 152, 154
Roche Daniel.................. 148f.
Saint-Preux ..................... 29
Schmidt, Lars-Henrik ............ 20f.
Scola, Ettore .................... 27
Sen, Amartya .... 30, 50, 101, 117, 141, 155
Shakespeare, William.......... 27, 128f.
simulated presence ................ 21
Smith, Adam . . 14f., 48, 69, 76, 136, 140, 147, 155
Socrates .................... 99, 124
Sparta ......17, 23, 66, 68, 82, 122, 125f, 127, 134
stag hunt.......... 110ff., 116ff., 139, 153
Starobinski, Jean. . 14, 18, 22, 33–43, 45, 50
state of nature..... 25, 97, 103, 108f., 115f.
Steuart .............. 14, 74, 106f., 118
Strauss, Leo ..................... 25
subsistence ........... 17, 31, 33, 35, 39, 41, 43f., 57, 60, 72, 77f.
Talmon, J L.......... 90, 96, 98f., 141f.
theatre ...... 17, 23, 27, 68, 123, 13f., 133ff.
transaction cost.............. 42, 138f.
transparency........... 34ff., 42, 47, 50
Turgot ......................... 13
Villers, Robert.................... 88
Voltaire .................... 24, 70
wealth ...... 15, 34, 37, 44, 48f., 68f., 72, 78f., 92, 95, 122, 142, 144f., 150
Wokler, Robert.................. 147

# ARCHIVES INTERNATIONALES D'HISTOIRE DES IDÉES
*
# INTERNATIONAL ARCHIVES OF THE HISTORY OF IDEAS

70. R. Simon (éd.): *Henry de Boulainviller.* Œuvres Philosophiques, Tome II. 1975
ISBN 90-247-1633-0
*For* Œuvres Philosophiques, Tome I *see under Volume 58.*
71. J.A.G. Tans et H. Schmitz du Moulin: *Pasquier Quesnel devant la Congrégation de l'Index.* Correspondance avec Francesco Barberini et mémoires sur la mise à l'Index de son édition des Œuvres de Saint Léon, publiés avec introduction et annotations. 1974 ISBN 90-247-1661-6
72. J.W. Carven: *Napoleon and the Lazarists (1804–1809).* 1974 ISBN 90-247-1667-5
73. G. Symcox: *The Crisis of French Sea Power (1688–1697).* From the *Guerre d'Escadre* to the *Guerre de Course.* 1974 ISBN 90-247-1645-4
74. R. MacGillivray: *Restoration Historians and the English Civil War.* 1974
ISBN 90-247-1678-0
75. A. Soman (ed.): *The Massacre of St. Bartholomew.* Reappraisals and Documents. 1974
ISBN 90-247-1652-7
76. R.E. Wanner: *Claude Fleury (1640–1723) as an Educational Historiographer and Thinker.* With an Introduction by W.W. Brickman. 1975 ISBN 90-247-1684-5
77. R.T. Carroll: *The Common-Sense Philosophy of Religion of Bishop Edward Stillingfleet (1635–1699).* 1975 ISBN 90-247-1647-0
78. J. Macary: *Masque et lumières au 18ᵉ [siècle].* André-François Deslandes, Citoyen et philosophe (1689–1757). 1975 ISBN 90-247-1698-5
79. S.M. Mason: *Montesquieu's Idea of Justice.* 1975 ISBN 90-247-1670-5
80. D.J.H. van Elden: *Esprits fins et esprits géométriques dans les portraits de Saint-Simon.* Contributions à l'étude du vocabulaire et du style. 1975 ISBN 90-247-1726-4
81. I. Primer (ed.): *Mandeville Studies.* New Explorations in the Art and Thought of Dr Bernard Mandeville (1670–1733). 1975 ISBN 90-247-1686-1
82. C.G. Noreña: *Studies in Spanish Renaissance Thought.* 1975 ISBN 90-247-1727-2
83. G. Wilson: *A Medievalist in the 18th Century.* Le Grand d'Aussy and the Fabliaux ou Contes. 1975 ISBN 90-247-1782-5
84. J.-R. Armogathe: *Theologia Cartesiana.* L'explication physique de l'Eucharistie chez Descartes et Dom Robert Desgabets. 1977 ISBN 90-247-1869-4
85. Bérault Stuart, Seigneur d'Aubigny: *Traité sur l'art de la guerre.* Introduction et édition par Élie de Comminges. 1976 ISBN 90-247-1871-6
86. S.L. Kaplan: *Bread, Politics and Political Economy in the Reign of Louis XV.* 2 vols., 1976
Set ISBN 90-247-1873-2
87. M. Lienhard (ed.): *The Origins and Characteristics of Anabaptism / Les débuts et les caractéristiques de l'Anabaptisme.* With an Extensive Bibliography / Avec une bibliographie détaillée. 1977 ISBN 90-247-1896-1
88. R. Descartes: *Règles utiles et claires pour la direction de l'esprit en la recherche de la vérité.* Traduction selon le lexique cartésien, et annotation conceptuelle par J.-L. Marion. Avec des notes mathématiques de P. Costabel. 1977 ISBN 90-247-1907-0
89. K. Hardesty: *The 'Supplément' to the 'Encyclopédie'.* [Diderot et d'Alembert]. 1977
ISBN 90-247-1965-8
90. H.B. White: *Antiquity Forgot.* Essays on Shakespeare, [Francis] Bacon, and Rembrandt. 1978
ISBN 90-247-1971-2
91. P.B.M. Blaas: *Continuity and Anachronism.* Parliamentary and Constitutional Development in Whig Historiography and in the Anti-Whig Reaction between 1890 and 1930. 1978
ISBN 90-247-2063-X

# ARCHIVES INTERNATIONALES D'HISTOIRE DES IDEES
*
# INTERNATIONAL ARCHIVES OF THE HISTORY OF IDEAS

92. S.L. Kaplan (ed.): *La Bagarre.* Ferdinando Galiani's (1728–1787) 'Lost' Parody. With an Introduction by the Editor. 1979 ISBN 90-247-2125-3
93. E. McNiven Hine: *A Critical Study of [Étienne Bonnot de] Condillac's* [1714–1780] *'Traité des Systèmes'.* 1979 ISBN 90-247-2120-2
94. M.R.G. Spiller: *Concerning Natural Experimental Philosphy.* Meric Casaubon [1599–1671] and the Royal Society. 1980 ISBN 90-247-2414-7
95. F. Duchesneau: *La physiologie des Lumières.* Empirisme, modèles et théories. 1982 ISBN 90-247-2500-3
96. M. Heyd: *Between Orthodoxy and the Enlightenment.* Jean-Robert Chouet [1642–1731] and the Introduction of Cartesian Science in the Academy of Geneva. 1982 ISBN 90-247-2508-9
97. James O'Higgins: *Yves de Vallone* [1666/7–1705]: *The Making of an Esprit Fort.* 1982 ISBN 90-247-2520-8
98. M.L. Kuntz: *Guillaume Postel* [1510–1581]. Prophet of the Restitution of All Things. His Life and Thought. 1981 ISBN 90-247-2523-2
99. A. Rosenberg: *Nicolas Gueudeville and His Work (1652–172?).* 1982 ISBN 90-247-2533-X
100. S.L. Jaki: *Uneasy Genius: The Life and Work of Pierre Duhem* [1861-1916]. 1984 ISBN 90-247-2897-5; Pb (1987) 90-247-3532-7
101. Anne Conway [1631–1679]: *The Principles of the Most Ancient Modern Philosophy.* Edited and with an Introduction by P. Loptson. 1982 ISBN 90-247-2671-9
102. E.C. Patterson: *[Mrs.] Mary [Fairfax Greig] Sommerville* [1780–1872] *and the Cultivation of Science (1815–1840).* 1983 ISBN 90-247-2823-1
103. C.J. Berry: *Hume, Hegel and Human Nature.* 1982 ISBN 90-247-2682-4
104. C.J. Betts: *Early Deism in France.* From the so-called 'déistes' of Lyon (1564) to Voltaire's 'Lettres philosophiques' (1734). 1984 ISBN 90-247-2923-8
105. R. Gascoigne: *Religion, Rationality and Community.* Sacred and Secular in the Thought of Hegel and His Critics. 1985 ISBN 90-247-2992-0
106. S. Tweyman: *Scepticism and Belief in Hume's 'Dialogues Concerning Natural Religion'.* 1986 ISBN 90-247-3090-2
107. G. Cerny: *Theology, Politics and Letters at the Crossroads of European Civilization.* Jacques Basnage [1653–1723] and the Baylean Huguenot Refugees in the Dutch Republic. 1987 ISBN 90-247-3150-X
108. Spinoza's *Algebraic Calculation of the Rainbow & Calculation of Changes.* Edited and Translated from Dutch, with an Introduction, Explanatory Notes and an Appendix by M.J. Petry. 1985 ISBN 90-247-3149-6
109. R.G. McRae: *Philosophy and the Absolute.* The Modes of Hegel's Speculation. 1985 ISBN 90-247-3151-8
110. J.D. North and J.J. Roche (eds.): *The Light of Nature.* Essays in the History and Philosophy of Science presented to A.C. Crombie. 1985 ISBN 90-247-3165-8
111. C. Walton and P.J. Johnson (eds.): *[Thomas] Hobbes's 'Science of Natural Justice'.* 1987 ISBN 90-247-3226-3
112. B.W. Head: *Ideology and Social Science.* Destutt de Tracy and French Liberalism. 1985 ISBN 90-247-3228-X
113. A.Th. Peperzak: *Philosophy and Politics.* A Commentary on the Preface to Hegel's *Philosophy of Right.* 1987 ISBN Hb 90-247-3337-5; Pb ISBN 90-247-3338-3

# ARCHIVES INTERNATIONALES D'HISTOIRE DES IDÉES
*
# INTERNATIONAL ARCHIVES OF THE HISTORY OF IDEAS

114. S. Pines and Y. Yovel (eds.): *Maimonides* [1135-1204] *and Philosophy.* Papers Presented at the 6th Jerusalem Philosophical Encounter (May 1985). 1986 ISBN 90-247-3439-8
115. T.J. Saxby: *The Quest for the New Jerusalem, Jean de Labadie* [1610–1674] *and the Labadists (1610–1744).* 1987 ISBN 90-247-3485-1
116. C.E. Harline: *Pamphlets, Printing, and Political Culture in the Early Dutch Republic.* 1987 ISBN 90-247-3511-4
117. R.A. Watson and J.E. Force (eds.): *The Sceptical Mode in Modern Philosophy.* Essays in Honor of Richard H. Popkin. 1988 ISBN 90-247-3584-X
118. R.T. Bienvenu and M. Feingold (eds.): *In the Presence of the Past.* Essays in Honor of Frank Manuel. 1991 ISBN 0-7923-1008-X
119. J. van den Berg and E.G.E. van der Wall (eds.): *Jewish-Christian Relations in the 17th Century.* Studies and Documents. 1988 ISBN 90-247-3617-X
120. N. Waszek: *The Scottish Enlightenment and Hegel's Account of 'Civil Society'.* 1988 ISBN 90-247-3596-3
121. J. Walker (ed.): *Thought and Faith in the Philosophy of Hegel.* 1991 ISBN 0-7923-1234-1
122. Henry More [1614–1687]: *The Immortality of the Soul.* Edited with Introduction and Notes by A. Jacob. 1987 ISBN 90-247-3512-2
123. P.B. Scheurer and G. Debrock (eds.): *Newton's Scientific and Philosophical Legacy.* 1988 ISBN 90-247-3723-0
124. D.R. Kelley and R.H. Popkin (eds.): *The Shapes of Knowledge from the Renaissance to the Enlightenment.* 1991 ISBN 0-7923-1259-7
125. R.M. Golden (ed.): *The Huguenot Connection.* The Edict of Nantes, Its Revocation, and Early French Migration to South Carolina. 1988 ISBN 90-247-3645-5
126. S. Lindroth: *Les chemins du savoir en Suède.* De la fondation de l'Université d'Upsal à Jacob Berzelius. Études et Portraits. Traduit du suédois, présenté et annoté par J.-F. Battail. Avec une introduction sur Sten Lindroth par G. Eriksson. 1988 ISBN 90-247-3579-3
127. S. Hutton (ed.): *Henry More (1614–1687). Tercentenary Studies.* With a Biography and Bibliography by R. Crocker. 1989 ISBN 0-7923-0095-5
128. Y. Yovel (ed.): *Kant's Practical Philosophy Reconsidered.* Papers Presented at the 7th Jerusalem Philosophical Encounter (December 1986). 1989 ISBN 0-7923-0405-5
129. J.E. Force and R.H. Popkin: *Essays on the Context, Nature, and Influence of Isaac Newton's Theology.* 1990 ISBN 0-7923-0583-3
130. N. Capaldi and D.W. Livingston (eds.): *Liberty in Hume's 'History of England'.* 1990 ISBN 0-7923-0650-3
131. W. Brand: *Hume's Theory of Moral Judgment.* A Study in the Unity of *A Treatise of Human Nature.* 1992 ISBN 0-7923-1415-8
132. C.E. Harline (ed.): *The Rhyme and Reason of Politics in Early Modern Europe.* Collected Essays of Herbert H. Rowen. 1992 ISBN 0-7923-1527-8
133. N. Malebranche: *Treatise on Ethics* (1684). Translated and edited by C. Walton. 1993 ISBN 0-7923-1763-7
134. B.C. Southgate: *'Covetous of Truth'.* The Life and Work of Thomas White (1593–1676). 1993 ISBN 0-7923-1926-5
135. G. Santinello, C.W.T. Blackwell and Ph. Weller (eds.): *Models of the History of Philosophy.* Vol. 1: From its Origins in the Renaissance to the 'Historia Philosphica'. 1993 ISBN 0-7923-2200-2
136. M.J. Petry (ed.): *Hegel and Newtonianism.* 1993 ISBN 0-7923-2202-9

## ARCHIVES INTERNATIONALES D'HISTOIRE DES IDEES
*
## INTERNATIONAL ARCHIVES OF THE HISTORY OF IDEAS

137. Otto von Guericke: *The New (so-called Magdeburg) Experiments* [Experimenta Nova, Amsterdam 1672]. Translated and edited by M.G. Foley Ames. 1994 ISBN 0-7923-2399-8
138. R.H. Popkin and G.M. Weiner (eds.): *Jewish Christians and Cristian Jews*. From the Renaissance to the Enlightenment. 1994 ISBN 0-7923-2452-8
139. J.E. Force and R.H. Popkin (eds.): *The Books of Nature and Scripture*. Recent Essays on Natural Philosophy, Theology, and Biblical Criticism in the Netherlands of Spinoza's Time and the British Isles of Newton's Time. 1994 ISBN 0-7923-2467-6
140. P. Rattansi and A. Clericuzio (eds.): *Alchemy and Chemistry in the 16th and 17th Centuries*. 1994 ISBN 0-7923-2573-7
141. S. Jayne: *Plato in Renaissance England*. 1995 ISBN 0-7923-3060-9
142. A.P. Coudert: *Leibniz and the Kabbalah*. 1995 ISBN 0-7923-3114-1
143. M.H. Hoffheimer: *Eduard Gans and the Hegelian Philosophy of Law*. 1995 ISBN 0-7923-3114-1
144. J.R.M. Neto: *The Christianization of Pyrrhonism*. Scepticism and Faith in Pascal, Kierkegaard, and Shestov. 1995 ISBN 0-7923-3381-0
145. R.H. Popkin (ed.): *Scepticism in the History of Philosophy*. A Pan-American Dialogue. 1996 ISBN 0-7923-3769-7
146. M. de Baar, M. Löwensteyn, M. Monteiro and A.A. Sneller (eds.): *Choosing the Better Part*. Anna Maria van Schurman (1607–1678). 1995 ISBN 0-7923-3799-9
147. M. Degenaar: *Molyneux's Problem*. Three Centuries of Discussion on the Perception of Forms. 1996 ISBN 0-7923-3934-7
148. S. Berti, F. Charles-Daubert and R.H. Popkin (eds.): *Heterodoxy, Spinozism, and Free Thought in Early-Eighteenth-Century Europe*. Studies on the *Traité des trois imposteurs*. 1996 ISBN 0-7923-4192-9
149. G.K. Browning (ed.): *Hegel's* Phenomenology of Spirit: *A Reappraisal*. 1997 ISBN 0-7923-4480-4
150. G.A.J. Rogers, J.M. Vienne and Y.C. Zarka (eds.): *The Cambridge Platonists in Philosophical Context*. Politics, Metaphysics and Religion. 1997 ISBN 0-7923-4530-4
151. R.L. Williams: *The Letters of Dominique Chaix, Botanist-Curé*. 1997 ISBN 0-7923-4615-7
152. R.H. Popkin, E. de Olaso and G. Tonelli (eds.): *Scepticism in the Enlightenment*. 1997 ISBN 0-7923-4643-2
153. L. de la Forge. Translated and edited by D.M. Clarke: *Treatise on the Human Mind (1664)*. 1997 ISBN 0-7923-4778-1
154. S.P. Foster: *Melancholy Duty*. The Hume-Gibbon Attack on Christianity. 1997 ISBN 0-7923-4785-4
155. J. van der Zande and R.H. Popkin (eds.): *The Skeptical Tradition Around 1800*. Skepticism in Philosophy, Science, and Society. 1997 ISBN 0-7923-4846-X
156. P. Ferretti: *A Russian Advocate of Peace: Vasilii Malinovskii (1765–1814)*. 1997 ISBN 0-7923-4846-6
157. M. Goldish: *Judaism in the Theology of Sir Isaac Newton*. 1998 ISBN 0-7923-4996-2
158. A.P. Coudert, R.H. Popkin and G.M. Weiner (eds.): *Leibniz, Mysticism and Religion*. 1998 ISBN 0-7923-5223-8
159. B. Fridén: *Rousseau's Economic Philosophy*. Beyond the Market of Innocents. 1998 ISBN 0-7923-5270-X

KLUWER ACADEMIC PUBLISHERS – DORDRECHT / BOSTON / LONDON

MIX
Papier aus verantwortungsvollen Quellen
Paper from responsible sources
FSC® C105338

If you have any concerns about our products,
you can contact us on
**ProductSafety@springernature.com**

In case Publisher is established outside the EU,
the EU authorized representative is:
**Springer Nature Customer Service Center GmbH**
**Europaplatz 3, 69115 Heidelberg, Germany**

Printed by Libri Plureos GmbH
in Hamburg, Germany